Your Defensive Rifle Training Program

Michael R. Seeklander

Shooting-Performance LLC

Owasso, OK

Copyright © 2014 by Michael R. Seeklander.

All rights reserved. No part of this publication may be reproduced, distributed or transmitted in any form or by any means, including photocopying, recording, or other electronic or mechanical methods, without the prior written permission of the publisher, except in the case of brief quotations embodied in critical reviews and certain other noncommercial uses permitted by copyright law. For permission requests, write to the publisher, addressed "Attention: Permissions Coordinator," at the address below.

Michael Seeklander/Shooting-Performance LLC
P.O. Box 2016
Owasso, OK/74055
www.shooting-performance.com

Book Layout ©2013 BookDesignTemplates.com

Ordering Information:
Quantity sales. Special discounts are available on quantity purchases by corporations, associations, and others. For details, contact the support@shooting-performance.com or via mail at the address above.

Your Defensive Rifle Training Program/ Michael Seeklander. —1st ed..
ISBN (10) 1482537680
ISBN (13) 978-1482537680

Contents

Introduction and Background 5

Defining and Understanding Training 15

Selecting and Accessorizing Your Rifle and Gear 23

Mental Preparation For The Fight 59

Physical Preparation For The Fight 81

High Performance Rifle Manipulation and Marksmanship Techniques 97

Rifle Skill Development Training Program and Drills 149

Alternate Methods Of Training 205

Documenting Your Training Sessions 211

Testing Your Skills With The Rifle Skills Test (RST) 223

Manually Operated Rifles 229

Dedicated to the defenders of our freedom and safety. The elite U.S. Military, highly trained Law Enforcement community, and all others that bear arms to protect the innocent.

"The rifle itself has no moral stature, since it has no will of its own. Naturally, it may be used by evil men for evil purposes, but there are more good men than evil, and while the latter cannot be persuaded to the path of righteousness by propaganda, they can certainly be corrected by good men with rifles."

— *Jeff Cooper, Art of the Rifle*

CHAPTER 1

Introduction and Background

You have committed your money, and soon your time in the contents of this book and the results you will get from your effort. I thank you for taking that step, and applaud you for joining the ranks of those that favor preparation versus luck. There have been more AR style rifles sold in the last five years than the previous twenty and yet a large majority of those purchasers failed to take the rifle out of the box and actually address the issue of preparing the firearm and themselves for the possibility that they might need to use it for something other than shooting at soda cans on a country range. You are different, welcome to the world of the prepared!

Covered in this chapter:

1. *Background and Sources*
2. *Discuss Action Vs. Intent*
3. *Stuff vs. Fluff*
4. *Technique Discussion*
5. *Definitions*
6. *Chapter format and my writing style*
7. *An overview of the training program*

Background and Sources

Congratulations on your purchase of this book. It is my third book written for the specific purpose of giving you a full training program that you can follow to develop your shooting skill to a very high level. This book is written for those of you that own, or have recently purchased a rifle and intend to use it for defensive (or in some cases "tactical" purposes). That said, I have utilized several sections of this book as written in my other book "Your Defensive Handgun Training Program." The purpose is to keep your training as consistent as possible and the overlap/reprinting of material is by design. I hope to keep both your defensive handgun and rifle training programs as consistent as possible. One last thing, as you read this and plan to use a rifle as a self-defense platform, I believe if you have armed yourself with a rifle, then you have made the wisest choice possible as the weapon is truly a superior tool to the handgun. That said, I also believe the situation to be very serious and the threat level to be elevated when compared to the spontaneous use of a handgun.

A bit more about me (as taken from Your Defensive Handgun Training Program): My passion is shooting and my specific interest is in performance at the top end of the competitive shooting spectrum. This passion led me to shoot in almost every type of practical shooting match that exists, as well as attend dozens of firearms courses. I also sought every opportunity to train with the best shooters I could find with the intent to prepare myself to the highest level possible. On the other side of the coin, as a member of the U.S. Military and law enforcement community, my initial interest in performing well came from a need to protect others and myself if I ended up in a shooting situation.

This experience led me into the training business where for many years I have spent most of my adult life training professionals to use their firearms for combative purposes. Hopefully you are beginning to see the whole picture now and understand that why I am inclined to focus on concepts that apply in both arenas. The common denominator that I am really passionate about is performance. Performance, "on demand" (without warning), is the common goal of both the professional warrior and competitive athlete. Each seeks the same thing and will only find it one way, by training correctly. When you hear the term "professional warrior", you may not find this term directly applicable to you, but I disagree. While you may not make a living as a "warrior" (military or law enforcement), you still have the same level of responsibility when it comes to deploying a rifle. My personal desire would be for each and every one of you to accept this level of commitment and train to it. Remove all excuses and realize that you might be the person that is in the spot to defend innocent lives from a lethal threat. Once you accept that, you can train to that level.

Figure 1 You might not make your living assaulting houses like this SWAT team does, but if you choose to protect yourself and others, you are a warrior. Accept that and act like one.

I can't remember how many times I have heard, "I don't know how to train." This book will show you how. It is written with a stuff and "no fluff" style and it is broken down into multiple chapters that you can easily follow. Each chapter concept is thoroughly explained, summarized and most have action steps at the end. Read the material, learn from it, and use it in an actionable manner.

In addition, this book is largely drawn from a compilation of my experiences as a trainer, but beyond that I have drawn from about every reference you can think of. There are also several sections that were partially written by recognized rifle shooters **Steve Aryan** and **Erik Lund**. **John Paul** of JP Rifles also helped with the book, including a great section on the pitfalls' of using SBR's (Short Barrel Rifles) with barrel lengths that compromise the ballistics of the round. It's a *very* informative section! Both guest authors are instructors that represent the cutting edge of the material they teach and are great additions to this book. For more information about Steve and Erik, please visit my website to read their biography's (http://shooting-performance.com/instructors.html).

Otherwise, I want to credit the many instructors, shooters, and various materials I have absorbed along the way and cannot credit due to lack of specific sources where I got it. The truth is, I have been training and teaching and absorbing material for well over twenty years now and I simply can not remember where I may have learned some of it. Please consider looking at my reference materials for this book, as well as the recommended reading list and purchasing some of those works, they will be well worth your money.

Additionally I did not want to re-invent the wheel when writing this book. I was tempted to skip some of the sections contained within simply because the material occurs in several other books and is very well done. In the end, I included the material in the case what I had to say impacted and taught you something that the other books did not. Please understand though that you are missing some great material and references if you do not own the other books mentioned. This book also uses some of that material as referenced material, in hopes that I could provide to an extent, a "one stop shopping" experience.

Introduction to the Program

This is a comprehensive training program that will show you how to train and develop the skills necessary to survive a lethal encounter (A gunfight). I own and have read dozens of books that focus on principles, tactics, and techniques. One thing that I have found is that finding a book that offers a training program that can be followed is difficult to find. In addition, I now that most people really desire the knowledge to be able to perform a task, yet are often times best served with a system that they can simply follow. My *Defensive* and *Competitive* handgun training books were written exactly for that purpose. This book is an extension of those programs that specializes on training with a rifle.

As in the other programs, I wanted to lay a path that you could follow and guarantee success in your training efforts. I know this means that you will have to work at it and put the time in. If you are the person who will only touch your gun once per month no matter what, I doubt my program will help you much. If however, you are willing to put the practice time in to save your own life, then this book will guide you through the process. I tried to stay away from useless knowledge and information that would bog you down in the learning process. I guarantee that if you follow my program you will indeed train yourself to a high level of preparation. At the time I write this, my intent is to leave most of the specific defensive rifle technique to be learned in a class, or from a DVD. Having said this, I will address the technique that I emphasize during the drills. The defensive rifle technique section in this book will do two things for you. It will help you find, analyze, and select good techniques from other sources, and secondly it will give you enough material so you can effectively use the drills in the development section. Once again, I recommend the DVD that compliments this book or a class if you learn better visually. The chapters in this book each serve a different purpose:

Chapter 1, Introduction and Background – This chapter introduces you to the program, and my thought processes. It will help you understand where the material you are about to read came from.

Chapter 2, Defining and Understanding "Training" – This chapter introduces you to the concepts and theories of training, and how they work. The chapter will teach you more about how you learn, and give you some principles that a good training program should follow.

Chapter 3, Selecting and Accessorizing Your Rifle and Gear – This chapter will cover the details of actually selecting a rifle for use as a defensive tool and accessorizing to maximize your effectiveness. There are key features that a good rifle should have, and while this chapter focuses on the AR-15 type systems it also includes some rifle selections that you might not have thought about. In addition, caliber and ballistics are discussed in this chapter.

Chapter 5, Mental Preparation for the Fight – This chapter will guide you through the process of mentally preparing yourself for a fight. Not many of us were born with the desire to harm others. Therefore, this chapter will help you prepare your mind by breaking down the process of developing skills programs, teaching you the importance of visualization, and giving you some tools to control your stress levels during a lethal encounter. Additionally this chapter will also help you *mentally connect* better to your training, and increase the value of each training repetition you execute.

Chapter 6, Physical Preparation for the Fight – This chapter addresses the much-overlooked physical fitness aspect of winning a fight. I often hear how a gun toting individual will simply shoot someone if they are attacked, but often that response is difficult if not impossible to pull off in certain situations. Being physically fit is a huge part of succeeding in any venue, from high level competitive shooting to a gunfight. This chapter will teach you how to prepare.

Chapter 7, High Performance Rifle Manipulation and Marksmanship Techniques – Since this book is not just about technique, this chapter will give you some thoughts on how you should go about finding good sources of technique, and how to evaluate and weed out those information sources that will be a waste of your time and money. This chapter also contains the material you will need to understand and utilize the dry and live fire training drills. I strongly recommend you get your technique from a better source than a book, either real instruction or a video format like the DVD that will be produced to compliment this book. There simply is no other way to learn something with the same level of effectiveness. Even though this book is not about technique, I felt it important that I cover enough so that you could read through and understand the technique and terminology referenced in the drills. This section is what I know to be the best technique to date and comes from a wide variety of sources. I give credit to instructors who taught me the technique where applicable, but understand that I have been around many different instructors over the years, so if I missed someone who should be thanked or credited, thank you.

Chapter 8, Rifle Skills Development Training Program (Training Drills and Schedule) – This chapter is largely the "meat and potatoes" of the book, and it addresses how to develop your shooting skills to the highest levels through dry fire and live fire drills in preparation for that lethal day when you have to use them. I drew largely from my experience in the high performance competitive rifle and multi-gun world in writing this chapter, as competitive shooters have taken high performance shooting to the next level. It should be clearly understood that there is a difference in combative use of the rifle and competitive use of it, but there are also many parallels. This chapter will explore those similarities. In addition, this chapter will provide your full training program and a schedule to follow in your training.

Chapter 9, Alternate Methods of Training – Ammunition is expensive! This chapter discusse s the use of airsoft and .22 caliber conversion kits for training purposes.

Chapter 10, Documentation and Modification of the Training Program – This chapter is taken directly from Your Defensive Handgun Training Program and is included because of the importance of documenting your training and modifying your training program for continued evolution.

Chapter 11 Testing Your Skills with The Rifle Skills Test (RST) – This chapter contains a simple, yet effective and objective live fire test to measure your skill level.

Chapter 12 Manually Operated Rifles (for Self Defense) – If you are limited to a manually operated rifle, you are certainly not alone! This chapter quickly discusses key concepts of selection and use.

Think of each chapter you go through as a step in the process you need to go through to develop your skill and truly prepare yourself for a lethal encounter.

Action Vs. Intent

Spend your time doing things that are all of good use and do nothing that wastes your time. This book exists because I have spent countless hours wasting my time with a technique, or training method that failed to produce results. I hope to greatly reduce your own exploration process, and also teach you how to think analytically about a new technique or training method. Spend every available moment working toward your goals, even if it is something small, *do something*. Action rules. This book will "take you by the horns" and guide you through each step in the process. At the end of most chapters, you will find an action plan with exercises, assignments, and the material paraphrased so you can do a "quick reference" anytime you like. I also suggest you start a "to do" list of sorts and add things you want to accomplish at the end of each chapter. <u>Your next move will be to take action on those things</u>.   I will close by saying that there is a *big* difference between "action" and "intent." Everyone has intent, and if you are reading this book you likely have great "intentions" but great intentions never got anyone anywhere.   Follow this program and do the work.

Stuff vs. Fluff

The "stuff vs. fluff" term is one I coined, along with my good friend Rich, many years ago. We had a common saying when we read a book, watched a video, or took class that the material was either "fluff" or "stuff." Fluff is the material that authors use to fill chapters and increase the price of their books. Or tactics and techniques instructors may use to add an extra day and charge more for a class. The "stuff," is the material of real value. These are the things that will take you to the next level. Most often this information is the stuff that will stick with you without a note taken. If I were to ask you what you remembered from any training manual, video, or program you participated in, the things you could write down from memory would more than likely be the "stuff." I worked ensure what you read in this book is the stuff, so if you hit a chapter that does not apply to you, simple skim over it and focus on one that does.

Technique

Initially I did not want to include a detailed technique section in any of my books. Although this book does contain a section on technique, I promised myself when I started this or my other project that this would not be another "Here is how to do XX technique" book. Rather, it is a manual on understanding the concepts of high performance training methods and a complete program to facilitate that goal. For that reason, rather than just tell you what technique I use, I also show you how to analyze different techniques using objective analysis. I want you to pick the right ones based on *your* dynamics. This allows you to select techniques that work for you and build your individual style.

Please understand that technique by itself is very important, yet not the only ingredient for success. Think about it for a minute. If you were to interview the ten best shooters (on the planet) and ask them all the exact same questions about how they perform certain techniques, it is likely that you would get ten different answers. Since the ten best shooters achieved similar results with different variations of the techniques, then the common denominator can't be technique, can it? Don't get me wrong, I pay attention to how I train and the techniques I use, but I don't treat any one thing as the gospel. Students I worked with five years ago, or even a year ago may have received a slightly different version of what I teach today. Technique is (and always should be) evolutionary.

Definitions

In order for you to understand what is contained in this book, it is important that you understand some of the terms I use. Here they are:

- *Combative* - I use this term in the book to differentiate training purposes. Combative means to use in combat, and not necessarily military combat. This word refers to training for offensive or defensive use of a firearm against a person or animal. This ranges from a legal concealed carry holder using a gun in self-defense to an elite military operator using the gun in an offensive attack.
- *Defensive* – I use this term much like the word combative, and it means the use of the firearm in self-defense.
- *Competitive* - This term refers to training for competition in a scored event. This type of reference is directed toward the sporting purpose of the gun.
- *Operator* - This term is used to describe professional military or law enforcement personnel who carry and use firearms in the performance of their missions.
- *Athlete/Shooting Athlete* - I use this term for competitive individuals who engage in a firearm sport of any type.
- *Lethal encounter* – This phrase refers to any situation where there is an immediate or impending threat of death or serious bodily harm due to an attack from a human or animal.

Chapter Format and My Writing Style

I admit I am a professional trainer and shooter. I spent my entire life training and teaching what I write about in this book. I address you, the reader, in the first person. Hopefully this will feel as though I were speaking directly to you. This is less formal, works best for me and hopefully allows you to easily understand what I am guiding you to do. Please focus on the information and intent to get the material across as bluntly and efficiently as possible without grammatical flare. My only goal is to clearly relay information as efficiently as possible.

Program Overview

This training program is not a "XX week" program like my competition-training program that you find in my book: "Your Competition Handgun Training Program." It is a life-long program. While training cycles can be broken down in length, there is no end to a self-defense program unless you want to lose the skills you have worked for. In a later section, I give you a thorough understanding of how you actually learn, and one of the learning factors for any skill is that it must be trained repetitively and regularly. The following table will list the elements of the program that you will go through during your training year. It is the minimum I recommend if you are serious and want to really increase your skill. The program can/should be repeated multiple times, and one of the last chapters of this book discusses the process of reviewing your notes and modifying your program. All training drills are in my program simple, yet effective. *One last thing, I strongly suggest you read this entire book before beginning the program. This will give you an overview of the entire system (I call this a systematic approach to training) that includes the mental, physical, technical and legal aspects of training for the defensive use of a firearm.*

An overview of the program (you may modify this slightly under my guidance, I am available for consultation).

Training Module	Description	Time (per week)
Live Fire	A minimum of one live-fire training sessions per week. The program is also designed to allow you to do more or less depending on your individual circumstances.	1-3 hours
Dry Fire	2-3 dry-fire training sessions per week. This 15-minute session will focus on your manipulation skills.	1+ hour
Mental Preparation	Weekly mental toughness routines. Mental training will help you connect better with what you are doing and perform on demand.	1+ hour
Physical Preparation	3+ physical fitness training sessions per week is strongly recommended.	3 hours
Total Time		6-8 hours

Table 1: Weekly Training Program

Safety Rules

Without Safety, my goal in writing this book will never be met! Here is your warning: <u>Firearms training is a risky business even for an experienced person.</u> We must always be very aware of the fact that we are using extremely dangerous tools that could harm others or ourselves at any time. For these reasons, I require that you follow these safety rules anytime you are around firearms. If you do not understand, or if you are new to shooting, then I <u>strongly</u> recommend that you find a competent instructor or training academy to assist you in your initial training. **If you do not agree, then drop the book in the mail to me for a refund. This is non-negotiable!** Please read each of the following rules in detail:

1. **Always** treat every firearm as if it were loaded all the time.
2. **Always** keep the firearm pointed in a safe direction – a direction where a negligent discharge would cause minimal property damage and zero physical injury.
3. **Always** keep your trigger finger off the trigger and outside of the trigger guard until you have made a conscious decision to shoot.

4. **Always** be sure of your target, backstop, and beyond, as well as items in the foreground that may deflect bullets causing injury.
5. **Always** have an emergency plan, communication device, and first aid kit available in case of a range accident.

Chapter Summary and Action Steps

1. Review and ensure you understand the safety rules, and general firearm safety.
2. Make a decision to choose action versus intent. This book was written to give you a training program that will help you save your life, or the lives of others.
3. Consider reading this entire book before planning and beginning your training sessions (the range part of this book).
4. Get your mind prepared to think. The next STEP gets a bit technical, but don't worry, it's worth the brain strain.

CHAPTER 2

Defining and Understanding Training

It's almost unbelievable to me, but the large majority of those who own a gun for defensive purposes never train with it. Concealed carry permit holders who own a handgun are much more likely to train sporadically with their handgun, but even those individuals who do are a very small percentage of the total group. Defensive rifle owners unfortunately train even less. Before I give you training drills and the details behind them, I first want you to understand the principles that will make those drills work.

Covered in this chapter:

1. *Purpose of Training*
2. *The Learning Process*
3. *Principles of Effective Training*
4. *Parts of a Training Program*
5. *An Overview of the Training Program*

Purpose of Training

What is training? If you asked five different people, you may get five different answers. The definition that I like best is: "acquiring of skill." While the definition is only three words, the key word is "skill." Skill could also be defined in simple terms, but for most shooting-related goals there is much more to that word than meets the eye. Simply developing or improving physical skill is a goal in most training programs. Yet in order to succeed at a complex goal, much more is needed than physical skill. Decision-making skills (tactics), visual skills, marksmanship skills, manipulation skills, movement skills, all tied together with mental preparation are needed to meet the goal of successfully using a rifle to defend yourself.

In order to develop all of those skills, you need to train. If you want to be effective in finding and putting all of the pieces together, you will need a comprehensive and effective training program. A "program" consists of all of the elements or parts that make the whole preparation process work. If you attempt it one piece at a time you will rarely get the desired results. Thus, it is the synergistic effect of all the elements working together that produces the desired outcome.

Key Note: I use the term "train" and "practice" interchangeably throughout this book. While the definition of train somewhat means that the session is instructor led, the words are synonyms.

How We Learn

What happens when you do something repetitively that causes you to "learn" a skill? The answer is a bit long, but well worth the education. When we repeat a physical movement, we learn it by improving our neurological and cognitive ability to process information and fire our muscles (by nerve impulses). We can break down learning into two areas: subconscious and conscious processing.

Subconscious Processing / Mylenation (nerve impulse transmission improvement)

This is the ability to become more efficient in a movement at a purely physical level by increasing the efficiency of the nerve/muscle connection. This happens by a process called mylenation, which is defined as: "the change or maturation of certain nerve cells whereby a layer of myelin forms around the axons which allows the nerve impulses to travel faster." In simpler terms, when we practice something we cause a group of nerve cells to fire muscles to do something, all beginning at our control center (the brain). When we repeat this process, certain cells secrete a substance called myelin, which increases the speed that those nerves can transmit a signal, and thus fire a muscle causing them to do something. The more we repeat the movement, the more we coat that particular pathway with myelin, and the more efficient the action becomes because the signal travels faster. Our subconscious has been named by some as our "skills factory."[1] The subconscious learning process is simple to understand, yet difficult to explain. In scientific circles, the subconscious is known as an extremely powerful storage area of the brain that will run what I call a "skill program" when prompted. This is because when we learn a skill through repetition, our subconscious stores these skills we have programmed for future use. The subconscious learns without filtering the information and does not analyze input as right or wrong. In other words, if you practice a move incorrectly, you may consciously know you are doing it wrong, but the subconscious is still recording the move as a learning experience even though it is wrong. I will get into more detail about this in the mental section of this book.

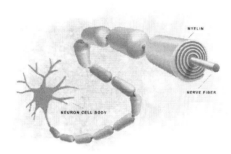

Figure 2 A depiction of the myelin sheath that layers and covers nerve fibers with repeated electrical signals. The more the circuit is myelinated, the more efficient the signal travels.

---

[1] Lanny Bassham, <u>With Winning in Mind</u> (Wilsonville: BookPartners, Inc., 1995).

[2] 3-gun is a common term used in today's practical shooting competitive community that denotes a competition using three

Conscious Processing

At the conscious level, we learn through our senses and memorize information. Conscious learning is based on increasing the decision-making ability and reacting quicker to something we perceive through our senses. We see, hear, smell, and feel things that relay information to our brain. We learn by filtering the input that comes in through our senses and store the information in an analytical manner. While this is great, it does not mean that we can rely on the conscious and its logic to help us operate under stress. That is the role of the subconscious, as it is much more powerful and useful when we need to process information and react extremely fast.

Where firearms skills are developed

If you asked all shooters this question, 95% of them would probably say, "On the range while you are shooting." The 5% of the shooters who said something different are probably the professionals (professional shooters and warriors) who know the real answer. They would tell you that skill is developed in *multiple* areas such as dry fire practice, live fire practice, mental (focus) practice, and supplemental training such as physical fitness training, visual training, and proper planning. This skill would obviously be accompanied during its development by learning correct "tactics" for the individual's environment. In terms of shooting, I personally think the majority of skill needed to manipulate and fire a handgun, rifle, or shotgun with a high level of skill can be developed with proper instruction and then a relentless amount of dry fire practice, with very little live fire. Even so, reaching a high level of skill is much easier if the end user takes a systematic approach to training rather than a linear approach and just focusing on one area at a time. If I had to chart what was important to skill development I would draw it like this:

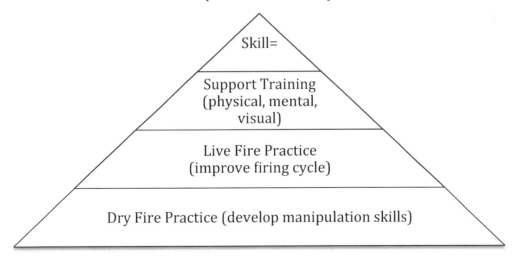

Figure 3: Skill Development

Notice that dry fire practice is the biggest area. Just dry firing and manipulating your firearm with the proper training drills will dramatically increase your ability because manipulation of the weapon is one of the most important areas of skill you will need to develop. The great news is that dry fire manipulation training can be done almost anywhere, and without spending a dime on ammunition. As long as you recognize its limitations, dry fire training will be a big key to your future success. I know of at least one top shooter who has built world level skill without firing more than about two thousand rounds per year (and most times much less) while other professional shooters often shoot more like thirty thousand rounds per year or more. Live fire training sessions should ultimately be reserved for the improvement of the firing cycle, which is the process of controlling recoil, manipulating the trigger, and monitoring the alignment of the gun (through the sights if necessary) while doing the first two.

I design almost all of my training drills to improve different elements of the firing cycle while still supporting the manipulation skills built during dry fire. The better you are at doing these things, the better you will be at hitting your target. The cycle may be slightly different for different guns. I expand on the technique and mechanics behind this cycle in the technique section. A visual example of what the firing cycle consist of can be seen in this flow chart on the next page:

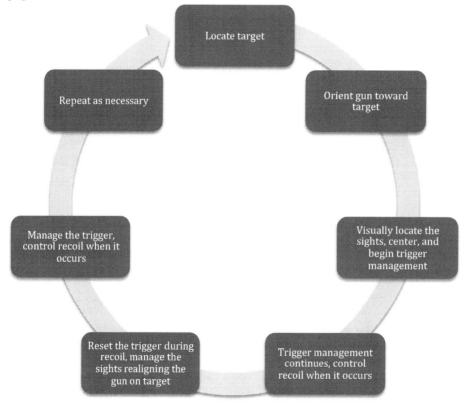

Figure 2: Firing Cycle for a Semi-Automatic Handgun or Rifle

The cycle looks simple, but the actual act of "shooting" and hitting one's intended target happens during this cycle. The skills we really need to learn to shoot well can be found in the firing cycle and must be developed with live fire training. Other skills, such as manipulating the firearm can be developed elsewhere (dry fire, etc.).

The Six Principles of Effective Training

In order for a training program to be effective, it must follow certain principles. Failure to contain or follow even one of these principles will render a program ineffective. Although I have provided a program for you in this book, by the end of it you should thoroughly understand how to develop your own program. Validate your program by comparing it against these principles on a regular basis.

1. *Training drills must be designed correctly.* This is the first validation of your program. It could not be simpler, but this is often the area that is wrong with most programs and/or drills that I have come across during my career. The learning goals must be thought out and clearly defined and then applied throughout the drills. Even programs developed with the best intent will be problematic if you don't pay attention to design. I will expand on this in the "Training Design Cycle" section. The two key areas you should validate in the design of your program are:
   a. Skills developed must be compatible with the key factors involved: environment, gear, and dynamics. This means that you must ensure that you are developing skills that correlate with the circumstances you might need them. For example, if you lived in an extremely cold climate, and spent your training time in an indoor range, you may never learn what it is like to shoot with gloves on, yet you likely wear them every day.
   b. Skills developed must replicate the actual key skills needed. Although I freely admit that this is an area that some really good shooters/operators argue about, because everyone has a *slightly* different idea about techniques and tactics.
2. *Training repetitions must be executed perfectly.* This principle is simple, and is a key component to success. Repetitions must be done as correctly as possible or the skills developed will be wrong. Under duress the skill developed (the "program") will not give the desired result.
3. *Training sessions must be done at regular intervals.* In order to develop skill (purpose of training), the brain and neuromuscular system must be exposed to developmental sessions on a regular basis. How often is very much debated. It will generally depend on one's goal. But across the board, almost all of the experts agree that development must take place a minimum of two times or more every week during the initial learning phase. In order to maintain a skill only one time per week may be necessary.
4. *Training sessions must be documented.* In order to monitor the program's success, training programs must be documented. Key metrics should be written down for future reference, and you will use this data to modify the program as you go.

5. *Skills and abilities developed must be measured.* Simply "feeling" that you are improving is unproductive. Take the time to record and measure your skills on a regular basis. Dr. H. James Harrington once said: "Measurement is the first step that leads to control and eventually to improvement. If you can't measure something, you can't understand it. If you can't understand it, you can't control it. If you can't control it, you can't improve it." Measure your skills regularly to guide you through the program modification phase. Measurement may consist of time factors or accuracy factors or a combination of both with a keen awareness that tactical procedures are followed.
6. *The Program must be modified based on results (game day).* A good training program MUST be modified. If not, results will stagnate and skills will remain in one place. You will need to reflect on your training logs and modify your program to continue your evolution.

Parts of a Training Program

A full training program has multiple parts. Each has a purpose in keeping your training organized and executable. In this book I have provided some parts of your program, such as the dry and live fire drills, schedule, etc. You should do the others. Your yearly plan and monthly training matrix must be planned and built by you, as only you know your schedule. Let me introduce you to the parts of a full program:

Yearly Plan

This document (you could build a written document or use a calendar) gives one the big picture. It includes the entire yearly training sessions and events you plan to attend. It doesn't really matter if you are working toward a competitive goal or a combative goal; it is good to have a document so you can view the entire year. Normally, I recommend that you do training in cycles, specializing on one skill area or weapon type at a time, with support training done for the other skills or weapon systems. Your goals will dictate how your year is broken down. Since you are interested in honing your defensive rifle skills, that will probably be your focus, but an example of honing that skill through a training cycle (8-12 weeks), and maintaining another might be found in someone who is in the military and needs to keep their skills sharp with a rifle or other weapon systems at the same time.

Monthly Training Matrix

This document is built to give you an overview of the training sessions you will do weekly. It gives a generic look at what type of training you will execute. Additionally, your matrix documents the frequency and duration of each training session. We all have busy lives and many of us have multiple training priorities. A monthly training matrix will help those who have numerous skills to maintain or develop stay organized and ensure they address all of their skill needs through the use of dedicated planning and scheduling. If you are in a line of work that requires you keep multiple skills honed, then laying out your monthly training blocks in some sort of matrix like this is a must.

Daily Training Plan

For this program I will provide your daily plan through the training program. After you complete the program, ensure you continue to have some sort of daily training plan for your sessions. A daily training plan is just as simple as it sounds. It is a written plan that guides you through your training session. It should contain all details about what you plan to do in that particular session, except the intimate details of each drill. That specific material is found on the drill sheets. If you plan your training in advance, you can type your training plans up and take notes, modifying them as necessary. There is also nothing wrong with handwriting what you plan to do in a given session. Just make sure you have a plan before you hit the range.

Training Drills Sheets

Drill sheets include everything you would need to know about the drill, including purpose, target setup, round count, recommended repetitions, measurement metrics, visual cues, key points and drill details (what to do when performing). The drill sheets for the program in this book are in chapter 9 and are both live fire and dry fire drills. The main thing to remember about the training drills is that they are each designed to allow you to work on key areas of skill, sort of like developing pieces of a puzzle. Then when you need to finally put any given puzzle together (lethal encounter), you can simple plug them in where necessary.

Documenting Paperwork

The name is self-explanatory. You need to track your training performance so you know if you are improving, how fast, and what you need to do to shift course (I will discuss the training design cycle in the next chapter). I use a training logbook to document my sessions with pre-formatted sheets. Each one is designed so I can easily document the session and how I performed. The sheets are also carefully designed to make sure that I document the things that I need to analyze my training and judge my results. I did not document the numbers in the past like I do now, and I regret that deeply. The data I did not write down and overlooked may very well have taken me to new levels along the way.

Chapter Summary and Action Steps

1. *The purpose of a training program is to develop skill, and the skill developed will reflect the training repetitions done in the program.*
2. *Myelination is a biological process that supports how we learn. A "myelinated" nerve pathway becomes a habit, or subconscious routine that the body will use to execute a skill. If the routine is written incorrectly, that will be the result when the skill is used.*
3. *Firearms skills are developed in a variety of ways, including live fire, dry fire, and support training.*
4. *The six principles of effective training are:*
    a. *Training sessions must be designed correctly.*
    b. *Training repetitions must be executed perfectly.*
    c. *Training sessions must be done at regular intervals.*
    d. *Training sessions must be documented.*
    e. *Skills and abilities developed must be measured.*
    f. *The Program (training) must be modified based on results*
5. *A training program consist of a yearly plan, monthly training matrix, daily training plan, and training drills sheets.*
6. *Your training program will require a logbook so now is the time to purchase something you can use to document your future training sessions.*

CHAPTER 3

Selecting and Accessorizing Your Rifle and Gear

This chapter is all about getting the right tool for the right job. It is critical that instead of looking at making the gun and gear you have work (unless that is your only option) you should select the gun and gear that will guarantee your success. Remember, failure in this case is not an option, so if you can affect the outcome by choosing the right tools, then it would be foolish not to. As a reminder before you dig into this chapter, the material is subjective to an extent, based on what I like and have found works for me. As I write this, I am no longer in the military or law enforcement, and the purpose I focus on is the civilian defensive context. I feel that what I have to offer is applicable to multiple arenas as well, but keep in mind that the information provided is simply a guide that will hopefully educate you on the principles behind selecting the right gun and gear and that ultimately you need to make the final decision on what will work best for you.

The things I will cover in this chapter:

1. *Rifle Selection*
2. *Rifle Modification*
3. *Gear Selection*

Rifle Selection

The key to selecting the right rifle is to find one that will meet your needs. Even before selecting a specific model there are the question of operating system, manufacturer, caliber, and length/weight. Each choice should be thought out and validated by looking at your specific context and needs. Getting the right rifle for the right situation is the key. If we narrow our field to just the AR platform, there are a mind-boggling number of choices. It seems like every company in the firearm industry is making a AR/M4 variant of some sort or another. And that is just one model of rifle, now add the dozen or so other possibilities and you have your hands full selecting a rifle. To keep this simple, I am going to try to break down each of the above selection criteria and focus on the objective principles I think you should stick to and hope that gives you enough guidance to make a wise choice if you do not already own a rifle.

Figure 4 So many rifle choices and so little time! Get one of each. The reality is that there are many good manufacturers out there. These are JP's made by JP Tactical in Minnesota.

Operating System

The operating system you choose will make a big difference in the effectiveness of the rifle. This book was written from the intent to focus on the AR platforms and any similar semi- or fully-automatic rifle that would be suitable for defensive purposes. Mechanically operated rifles such as pump, lever, and bolt action rifles have been used effectively for many years to take lives and I want to make sure you don't think that I feel like these rifle types are ineffective if trained with and set up properly. I do however want you to understand that there is probably a reason why a significantly large percentage of the current military and law enforcement agencies use a modern self-feeding (semi-/fully-automatic) rifle as their choice versus a manually-operated rifle. My strong suggestion is to select a reliable semi-automatic rifle unless you have a definitive reason not to. This book does however have an appendix that is devoted to manually-operated rifles that give you tips on operation and using the drills in this book for those systems. See page 205 for more.

Selecting your operating system, if you choose a AR style rifle, is a choice that you will have to make wisely. In writing this section, I asked my good friend and Shooting-Performance instructor Erik Lund to help me out. His discussion of the AR operating systems is what follows.

Direct Impingement vs. Piston Driven

In the search for your AR-15 defensive rifle, you will eventually discover that AR rifles are offered with two types of operating systems; The Direct Impingement (DI) system and the Piston Driven (PD) system. Both systems have their merits and their disadvantages, the real challenge is understanding how each of these systems works and how these systems can work to your favor or detriment based upon your personal situation and intended applications. Be forewarned, just as in any debate as to which caliber is better such as the 9mm vs. 45acp or the 5.56 vs. 7.62 debates, discussions about operating systems tend to get just as heated with all kinds of misinformation slung about like snowballs during the first snowstorm of winter. The path through all the lies, misinformation, and downright slander is simple – education. Take the time to understand what each system brings to the fight and make an informed decision as to which system will better meet your needs.

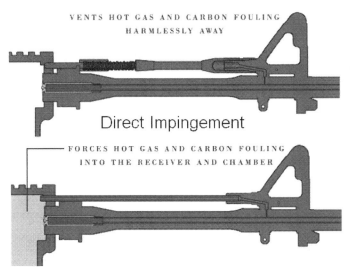

Figure 5 This diagram shows the difference between the Piston and DI systems.

The operating system of any rifle is usually a pretty long and complex story involving many iterations and improvement over the life of the design. Many of what we consider "modern" designs are really nothing more than improved versions of ideas and concepts first introduced in the early 1900's on through WWII. Tracing the evolution of each design from initial concept through current design is really beyond the scope of what we're trying to accomplish here. Our goal is to provide a brief understanding of how each system operates and how those differences affect the AR's performance. So without going too far down the rabbit hole, let's take a look at the basics of each system.

Before we can discuss the merits of each system, we need to have a fundamental understanding of how each system works. While each operating system is unique, both systems function by siphoning off a portion of the rapidly expanding gasses that are generated after the firing pin strikes the primer, causing the primer to detonate, igniting the powder contained inside the rifle cartridge. Those rapidly expanding gases push and accelerate the bullet down the barrel. As the bullet is propelled down the barrel, it will pass a small hole or port drilled into the barrel. While most of the gasses will continue to push the bullet down the rest of the barrel until the bullet exits the muzzle, a portion of those gases will escape through the port in the barrel. The gas that travels through the port is used to operate each system. Imagine a water hose with a small hole poked into the hose about 6" from the spout. As long as there is water pressure available, water will continue to flow out of the hose, with a little bit of that water shooting out the hole poked into the side of the hose. That little bit of water coming out of the side of the hose is similar to the little bit of gas the exits the gas port in the barrel and it's that little bit of gas that is used to operate each system.

The Direct Impingement (DI) System

The DI system is the original operating system of the AR-15 and is the foundation for what has become the longest serving rifle in the history of the United States Military. After some very well documented initial issues, the system has now been successfully operated in every environment around the globe. It has developed a reputation for reliability and durability when properly maintained. The "properly maintained" part we'll explore a bit later, but first, let's look at how the DI system revolutionized arms development.

The DI system functions by using gas flowing out of the gas port in the barrel and redirecting it into the operating system to function the rifle. Attached to the barrel over the gas port opening is a gas block. Attached to the gas block is a gas tube that runs back down the length of the barrel, back towards and into the action. The function of the gas block is to provide a place for the gas tube to attach. The expanding gasses flow from the gas port into the gas block which houses the gas tube. Think of the gas tube as a one-way tunnel. The gas flows into the gas block, then into the gas tube and then flows down the tunnel back into the upper receiver. The gas tube extends into the upper receiver about one inch. It's at this point that the bolt and bolt carrier enters the equation. The bolt carrier is essentially a steel tube that has a gas key on the top and an AR bolt that fits inside of the bolt carrier. The gas key on top of the bolt carrier is nothing more than a slightly larger steel tube that interfaces with the gas tube to provide a way for the expanding gasses in the tube to enter the bolt carrier. The diameter of the gas key tube is barely larger than the gas tube.

As the bolt carrier comes forward the gas key slips over the gas tube to provide a nice seal for the gas to continue travelling from the gas tube into the bolt carrier. Think of this interface as taking two drinking straws and squeezing one end of the straw into the end of the second straw to combine two strays into one, making a longer straw. This is essentially how the gas key slips over the gas tube in the upper receiver. Once the gas goes into the gas key, it's funneled down into the bolt carrier. Think of the gas key as an exit ramp off the one-way tunnel the gas uses to get from the gas block to the upper receiver. As the gas flows into the bolt carrier, it enters a small gas chamber formed by the tail of the AR bolt and the inside rear portion of the bolt carrier. As the gas flows into the gas chamber, it starts to fill and build pressure. As pressure builds in this chamber, the buffer spring located in the stock of the rifle pushes on the back of the bolt carrier keeping it pushed forward or in the closed position during the firing cycle. When the pressure in the gas chamber reaches a high enough level it will overcome the buffer spring tension and force the bolt carrier to the rear. As the bolt carrier now accelerates to the rear, a cam slot in the bolt carrier essentially acts on a cam pin attached to the bolt and pulls the bolt out of the barrel extension allowing the bolt carrier and bolt to travel to the rear inside the upper receiver.

It's at this point that the fired cartridge is extracted from the chamber and ejected out of the ejection port in upper receiver. Once the momentum energy of the bolt carrier dissipates, the buffer spring overcomes the dwindling energy and pushes the bolt carrier back forward. As the carrier comes forward, it strips a fresh round of the top of the magazine and feeds it into the chamber. (Side note: this action of the bolt carrier cycling to the rear and returning forward also re-cocks the hammer.) As the bolt carrier comes fully forward to its closed position, the cam pin slot acts upon the cam pin attached to the bolt, causing it to rotate in the barrel extension, locking it into place. Once fully locked into position, the rifle is now ready to fire another round. Clearly, there is a lot going on during the firing cycle of an AR rifle, but the amazing part is that all of this occurs during a fraction of a second. Now that we understand the basic mechanics of DI operating system, let's take a look at the Piston Driven system.

The Piston Driven (PD) System

PD operating systems are a fairly new innovation to the AR-15. Although they have been around for several decades, it's only recently that commercially successful PD systems have become available. While there are several "different" types of PD systems available for the consumer, all of the PD systems operate off the same concept with minor variations on how they accomplish this operation. Essentially, a PD system replaces the gas tube of the DI system with a steel operating rod and a small piston. Inside of the gas block is a small gas chamber with a small piston that moves back and forth within the gas block. The gas tube is replaced with a steel operating rod that extends into the back of the gas block and contacts the back face of the piston. The operating rod extends along the length of the barrel into the upper receiver where the other end of the rod contacts the bolt carrier gas key.

In a PD system, since gas is no longer needed to operate the system, the gas key of the DI bolt carrier is replaced with a solid steel strike face that is integrally machined into the bolt carrier. The other end of the operating rod contacts the strike face of the bolt carrier. When the buffer spring pushes forward on the bolt carrier, forcing it forward into its closed position (fully forward), the strike face of the bolt carrier key pushes on the back of the operating rod, pushing it slightly forward. This causes the other end of the operating rod to make contact with the piston inside of the gas block, pushing it slightly forward within the gas chamber in the gas block.

When the expanding gasses flow through the gas port into the gas block, instead of travelling down the gas tube into the upper receiver, the gas pressurizes the gas chamber inside of the gas block. When the pressure is sufficient, the gas forces the piston inside of the gas block to quickly move rearward about one inch. The front of the operating rod is in contact with the back of the gas piston and when the piston moves rearward, it pushes the operating rod rearward also. The back of the operating rod is in contact with the strike face of the gas key on the bolt carrier. As the operating rod moves rearward, it in turn pushes the bolt carrier to the rear, which initiates the same extraction, ejection, and feeding process previously discussed in the DI operating section. When the buffer spring pushes the bolt carrier back into its fully closed and locked position, the bolt carrier strike face pushes on the back of the operating rod, which in turn causes the front part of the operating rod to push on the backside of the piston inside the gas block, returning it to its original position within the gas block. Now the PD system has fully cycled and is ready for the next firing process.

Direct Impingement Vs. Piston Driven Systems…What's the Real Deal?

Now that we have a basic understanding of the differences between the systems and how they both operate, we can now move into discussing the merits of each system. The DI system is revolutionary for its compactness and simplicity. There are very few moving parts and those parts that do move are contained within the upper receiver. This means that all of those components that are critical to the reliability of the operating systems are ingeniously protected from environmental hazards such as dirt, mud, and other debris by encasing them inside of the rifle itself.

The fewer moving parts an operating systems uses, the fewer parts that can break or malfunction. Fewer parts also translate to lighter weight. AR-15 rifles with DI operating systems are some of the lightest rifles available on the commercial market. The DI system also had the unanticipated benefit of proving to be a very inherently accurate design. When a bullet is accelerated through the barrel, the barrel will actually flex and whip around; this is known as barrel harmonics. Consistency is a critical component of accuracy. Enhancing consistency in a barrels harmonics increases the accuracy of the rifle. The more consistently your rifle performs, the more accurate it will be. The nature of the AR design has only the gas tube and the handguards being attached to the barrel; very little affects the barrel harmonics during the firing process. Once free-float handguards were developed to remove all contact with the barrel, allowing even more consistency in the barrel harmonics, an already accurate system became truly exceptional. AR-15's with DI operating systems set the standard for accuracy among all semi-automatic rifles. It is not uncommon for AR's with high quality components to achieve five shot groups at 100 yards that measure an inch or less. Well-tuned AR's are capable of even better accuracy when using match grade components and ammunition.

So to recap, the DI operating system is simple, lightweight, and requires very few moving parts. It's a time-proven system with over 40 years of service that has been battle tested in every environment on earth, so what's not to like? Remember earlier when we set aside the "Properly maintained" caveat?

Well, now comes the AR-15's biggest weakness – it internally fouls itself. The same revolutionary DI operating system that is a model of simplicity and elegance also craps itself every time it fires. Remember how the DI system operates by using a portion of those expanding gasses to circle back into the bolt carrier via the gas tube to cycle the action? Well those gases are hot, filthy, and full of carbon fouling. If you have ever cleaned a rifle, any rifle, after firing a number of rounds through gun, what does that first cleaning patch that you push through the barrel look like? No surprise here, they all look the same. The patch is totally covered in black, sooty, gunk. This gunk is the leftover debris from the process of pushing the bullet down the barrel with those extremely hot, expanding gasses generated from the burning powder in the cartridge case. When a portion of those gasses are funneled back into the bolt carrier to operate the action (the DI operating process), a similar portion of that gunk is carried back and deposited inside of the bolt carrier and onto the tail section of the bolt. Being that all of this travelling gas is still under very high pressure, it escapes the confines of the bolt carrier's gas chamber and finds its way into every nook and cranny in the upper receiver. This combination of carbon, soot, and gunk eventually collects on every surface inside of the upper receiver and if not addressed, will eventually induce a malfunction.

It's an extremely rare occurrence to have an AR malfunction as a result of outside environmental contamination (dirt, mud, etc.) It's an all too common occurrence to have AR's malfunction as a result of internal fouling, which is a result of the DI operating system. This was not an entirely unanticipated problem. To some degree, the AR basic design allows for a certain amount of dirt to accumulate in the upper receiver without compromising the reliability of the system. The key to maintaining this reliability is keeping the AR well lubricated. Over the decades of service, the AR has earned its reputation for reliability from being properly maintained and operated as a "wet" system (this holds true except for desert type environments). This means keeping the moving parts well lubricated, as in "too much is probably enough." To err on the side of caution, a little more is better than a little less. When properly maintained, cleaned on a regular basis, and well lubricated, the DI operating system can be extremely reliable over many thousands of rounds. There are plenty of torture test videos showing DI operating systems firing several thousands of rounds with nothing but copious amounts of lubrication needed to keep them operating without fail. As impressive as these videos can be, remember that not all AR's are of equal quality and these types of tests tend to be the exception and not the rule. Still, the DI operating system can be a very reliable system and is an outstanding choice for a Defensive Rifle.

If the DI operating system has developed such an outstanding reputation for reliability, then why is there even a need for a PD operating system? The answer lies in man's innate desire to build a better mousetrap – his desire to improve a design regardless of how effective the original design operates. Such is the case with the PD operating system. The PD operating system was designed to overcome the perceived flaw of the self-fouling DI system by simply moving the gas chamber from the inside of the bolt carrier back out to the gas block. This design change now allows all of the fouling to accumulate at the gas block and not in the upper receiver. None of the hot gasses or dirty carbon fouling ever travels back into the bolt carrier and upper receiver area. This improvement allows for virtually no fouling accumulation in the upper receiver area except for the slight amount that occurs from the chamber area during the firing process. The PD operating system is an extremely clean system that runs reliably without copious amounts of lubrication. From a mechanical point of view, it is truly a cleaner operating system.

It *is* a better mousetrap; but nothing in life is free and the cost for this improvement is complication. The PD operating system is a more complicated system. It takes the simple elegance of the DI operating system and adds a few more moving parts to accomplish its mission. As we discussed previously, both systems use the expanding gasses to operate the action during the firing process. The DI system directs that gas into the bolt carrier to function, the PD system collects its gas inside the gas block attached to the barrel, but something additional is required to transfer this energy developed by the expanding gasses back to the bolt carrier to function the action. This necessitates the addition of a piston, operating rod, and bolt strike face. Not only does this complication increase the number of moving parts, it also increases weight. More moving parts also increases the opportunities for parts to malfunction or break. The PD system is a cleaner system, but it's also a more complicated system. So which system is better?

And the Winner is…..

From a theoretical design perspective, the PD operating system is a better design. It improves the AR rifle by eliminating the major design flaw of the DI operating system. The system runs cooler, cleaner, and more reliably with the addition of a few parts. Those parts are essentially steel tubes and rods, with very remote chances of breaking. The trade-off of a slight increase in complication is well worth the increase in operational reliability. Anyway you frame the theoretical discussion; an AR with a PD operating system will outperform a DI system and is the clear winner.

Theory is just that though, theory. Reality is what matters and the reality of the discussion is that a DI operating system, when properly maintained and lubricated will provide the user with all the reliability one could need. It's hard to envision any reality-based scenario where a defensive rifle user would fire thousands of rounds without the opportunity to perform the most basic maintenance. A quick pass of a bore snake down the barrel, a quick wipe down of the bolt carrier, and a few squirts of lube and in less than a minute, the DI operating system is ready to go for many more rounds. The AR rifle with a DI operating system has been serving our country's warriors faithfully for decades; it will serve you just as well.

The real winner is you, the consumer. Regardless of which system you choose, both will give you long-term reliability, durability, and performance. Choose a system based upon your needs and your requirements. If you're the type of person who regularly maintains firearms and likes to keep your firearms clean and ready for use, then the DI operating will meet all your needs. If you're the type of person who only performs the most basic maintenance or only when absolutely needed, then the PD operating system is probably a better choice for you. Either way, the AR rifle is an excellent choice for your defensive rifle.

Manufacturer

This one is a tough one to be specific about because there are so many companies making good rifles these days. My personal rifles are JP Tactical Rifles (as well as my 3-gun rifle), and full disclosure here (as always); JP has provided me rifles for several years now. I am biased only by the fact that they are incredible rifles, and in my opinion the best on the market. Having said that JP products are incredible rifles, I do want to clearly acknowledge there are several other brands on the market that I have owned and I would highly recommend them. I have owned and shot JP's (JP-15 and SCR-11), a Larue Tactical, and several Smith and Wesson (M&P 15T's) with great success. I have put more rounds by far through my 14 and 16 inch JP-15's, but can say the other rifles performed very well too.

Figure 6 A S&W M&P 15 T (my first non-competition rifle) on the top and the S&W .22 caliber rifle on the bottom. A great training combination!

My goal with this book is to give you a training platform that will make you a much better shooter, not to try to sway you in the direction of shooting the rifle I shoot. My suggestion is to look at the companies I have mentioned, along with the other major manufacturers, and select a rifle that offers the features and benefits you want and need. Keep in mind that almost every major manufacturer now makes a AR type system, and if they are one of the big companies you can bet the product probably solid. There even companies that make left handed AR systems for those shoot "wrong handed" (STAG Arms). Pick a company with a good reputation, that has a rifle platform that meets your needs, and offers a solid warranty and you will be on your way.

Calibers by Steve Aryan (www.greyfoxinc.com)

Over the years we have seen a huge growth in the selection of calibers for the AR15 platform. From close range heavy hitters to long range wind dodging projectiles. This chapter will discuss the pros, cons and application of these cartridges. The import thing to remember is all these calibers will allow you to utilize your standard AR15 lower receiver. Sometimes you will need to have a dedicated bolt, buffer, buffer spring, or a mag adapter but no permanent modifications are necessary. I asked long-range expert and one of my Shooting-Performance senior instructors his thoughts on calibers suitable for AR/Defensive rifle platforms and got some great information, as follows.

6.5 Grendel and 6.5 Les Baer:

6.5 Grendel: When this cartridge was first released I was very intrigued. Who wouldn't want a 6.5mm bullet in a AR15 platform? Based off the 7.62x39 case with a 6.5 projectile it's a low-recoil round, it has great long range ballistics and it's shooting anything from a 90gr varmint round to a 140gr bullet that packs enough energy to take most game in North America. From the competition side you have a flat shooting round that allows you to get back on target and the 6.5mm minimizes the winds effect on the bullet. Although I think this round shines with the 22"-18" barrel its certainly not limited to that. A 16" or 14.5" would be still be a great selection for someone wanting a heavier projectile for hunting but not needing the extra feet per second gained by a longer barrel.

6.5 Les Baer: This round is very similar to the 6.5 Grendel and so much so that it takes the same 6.5 Grendel ammunition. There are slight differences in the chamber that warrant a different name but the same ammunition can be used.

Pros:

- High ballistic coefficient bullet that stays above the speed of sound out to 1,000 yards (using the right barrel and load of course) in a smaller lighter weight platform than the AR10 series.
- Larger grain bullets packs a good amount of energy for soft targets.
- Fits in a standard AR15 upper and lower, uses same carrier (different bolt though). One could have a 6.5 Grendel dedicated upper and use it on his or her AR15 lower.
- Hornady and Wolf are producing commercially available ammunition, now available at most retail locations.
- Low Recoil. This allows you to get back on target quickly whether it's at a match, on a prairie dog town, or in a Law Enforcement application.
- Great brass available for reloader's. Lapua and Hornady both produce brass for the 6.5 Grendel using Small Rifle primers so your existing 223 or 5.56 Primers stash can be put to use with this as well. Not having to change primer sizes is one of the little things that makes reloading much easier.

Cons:

- Cost per round. It's not as bad as some, but it is more expensive and that will limit your shooting.
- Availability of ammo. Although it's been at several of my local sporting good stores it's not, and probably won't ever be as common as 223/5.56. When it is available, quantities may be limited.
- Dedicated magazines/followers. You can't just load it in your existing 223 magazines. You must have dedicated followers, which means more than likely dedicated magazines. This isn't a deal breaker, but it is a factor. Also, note that because of the additional size of the cartridge,

your magazine capacity is lowered. A standard 30-round magazine is now a 25 using the 6.5 Grendel.
- Dedicated bolt. Since it is based on the 7.62x39 cartridge, this will not work with your 223 bolt. I recommend having a dedicated bolt to each upper anyways even if they were all 223 so, again, this is not a deal breaker. Also, being an uncommon bolt means replacement parts will not be as readily available as the 223 version.

6.8 Remington SPC

Released around the same time as the 6.5 Grendel, these cartridges are often compared although they are really apples and oranges. The 6.8 SPC was built to run in short-barreled rifles and provide better energy than the 223. It was developed in collaboration with the Army's Marksmanship Unit to possibly replace the 5.56 in short barrel rifle configurations. It was shown as being ideal for Personal Security Detail environments. The ideal ranges for the cartridge being between 100-300 meters. The bullet grain weight varies from 90gr to 120gr with the 110-115gr bullets being the most popular.

Pros:
- More energy than a 5.56/223 with heaver grain projectiles available.
- Very little increased recoil, considering the terminal performance gains.
- Ammo is available at most retail stores and by most major manufactures such as Remington, Hornady and Federal.

Cons:
- Cost of ammo. Your cost of FMJ plinking ammo is close to 3x that of 5.56.
- Slightly reduced magazine capacity and proprietary magazines and followers.
- Not a large improvement in longer distance shots past 500 meters. The round was designed for, and is best suited for engagements between 0-300 yards.

300 AAC Blackout

AAC Corporation, in collaboration with Remington Defense, designed the round to provide 7.62x39 supersonic performance, the ability to cycle the action with subsonic ammunition, and utilize standard AR15 magazines. They achieved this by using the 5.56/223 cartridge and a .30 caliber projectile. This means the magazines and bolt of the AR15 can remain the same which is a huge plus when considering availability of replacement parts. Reloaders will also enjoy the fact that being based off the 5.56 cartridge you can simply trim you old brass and resize it into 300 BLK brass. If you are not a reloader, ammunition is available from most of the major manufacturers.

Pro's:
- More energy than standard 5.56/223 making it great for game hunting.
- The round will cycle the action of a AR15 even when shooting subsonic.

- Utilizes standard AR15 bolt carrier group and lower.
- Same magazines.
- Brass can be made from old 223/5.56 brass.

Cons:

- Ammunition availability and cost
- A round can be chambered and fired in a 223, which will result in blowing up the rifle.
- The round is unproven and can be finicky, based on barrel length and buffer combination.
- Slow round has lots of vertical drop over distance.

223 / 5.56

By far the most common round used in the AR15 system. The round has proven itself in the U.S. military for almost 50 years and with proper bullet selection can be used very effectively on most game animals. Ammunition is affordable and widespread. You can choose from 40r varmint rounds to 77gr boat tail hollow points to shoot out to 1,000 yards. The 223 has recorded kills in combat out to 820 yards using the 77gr ammunition and a 18" barreled AR15 variant. If you own an AR15, this is a very versatile round for most of your needs. It is what I suggest to get for everyone purchasing an AR15 for the first time. The low recoil is a great plus for taking friends out to shoot, or for younger shooters.

Pros:

- Ammunition is widespread and relatively cheap.
- Can be shot out to distance with proper bullet selection.
- Low recoil makes this great for newer shooters and younger ones.
- Magazines are cheap and available at most places that sell firearms.

Cons:

- Bullet diameter is .22 which is means proper bullet selection is a must for self-defense purposes

5.45x39

This round came from the AK74 and was utilized in the AR15 primarily because the ammo was about half the cost of 223 and has similar ballistics to it. Recoil is similar to 223 but it does require its own magazines and its own bolt carrier group. The ammunition that was normally available was corrosive and the rifle had to be cleaned quickly after shooting to prevent any problems. There are also not many options out there for ammunition.

Pros:

- Cheap to shoot and very similar ballistics to 223
- Ammo typically comes in "spam cans" and can be stored for a long time

Cons:

- Requires its own magazines
- Requires its own bolt
- Ammo is typically corrosive
- Small selection of ammo type

Length and Weight

The length of your rifle will be a consideration that will directly relate to the environment you operate and shoot it in. For example, a long barreled 20-inch AR system is a very effective longer-range gun with the ability to maximize the rifle's ballistics. The AR system was designed around a longer barrel, and the short-barreled rifle (SBR) craze these days has caused some reliability issues and other concerns. I had a conversation with John Paul owner of JP rifles (www.jprifles.com) one day about the tendency of rifles getting shorter and shorter, and he relayed to me he that did not believe that a sub 14-inch gun was worth the return in compactness. He graciously accepted my request to expand on his opinion for this book and the information is excellent.

Figure 7 Shorter is not always better. Although this is technically a pistol, the barrel length is very short. Beware of extremely short-barreled rifles!

John Paul on Short Barreled Rifles (SBR's)

The short barreled rifle (SBR) has become steadily more prevalent and recently exploded in popularity due to the BATF ruling on the SIG arm brace allowing a designated "pistol" AR-type weapon that may be legally shot from the shoulder. I own several myself. They're fun to shoot, more accurate than you'd expect and pretty handy for some applications. However, would I bet my life on an AR-type weapon that has a barrel much less than thirteen inches? Definitely not. Here's the why of it and a bit of the applied physics to back it up.

First, remember that the AR-15/M-16 was originally designed as a 20" rifle with what we now call a "rifle" length gas system. This created an ideal port position resulting in optimal timing of the actuation of the operating system and also optimized dwell time of the gas impinging on the bolt/carrier system. The simple fact is that the further we diverge from this original format, the smaller what I like to call the "operational window" of the system becomes.

There is a reason the M-4 configuration has a 14.5" barrel. It is about as far as we can stretch the concept [short-barreled] and still have duty reliability. (*Duty reliability*: someone's life depends on it going bang every time.) I know what you're saying. "But I have a 7.5" shorty that works all the time." Sure you do. As long as everything is perfect, as in you always use the same type of ammo and the stars are in alignment.

Here's the real truth of it. The SBR by its very nature requires the gas port to be moved to some compromised position that still allows the rifle to cycle (most of the time). This is a lot more complicated than it sounds.

The closer the port is to the chamber, the sooner the operating system actuates, unlocking and attempting to extract the fired round from the chamber. The fired round needs time to de-pressurize and "release" the chamber. Remember that the purpose of the brass case is to seal the pressure in the chamber during the ignition cycle and it does that by forcing itself against the walls of the chamber with near perfection. Proper metallurgy in the case allows it to form itself to the chamber with virtually no gas leakage under the tremendous pressure of ignition. It also allows it to assume the shape of any minor irregularities in the chamber such as pits, dings, scratches, reamer marks, fouling and even microscopic anomalies in the chamber. Trust me; there is no "perfect" chamber.

The more imperfections that are present in the chamber, the more difficult it is for the case to release the chamber prior to extraction. The closer the port is to the chamber, the more perfect the chamber must be to allow the case to extract when you're trying to pry it loose before it's ready to come loose! That is the essence of the SBR, trying to extract a case that is not ready to be extracted. Even 16" rifles with carbine port positions are prone to extraction failures due to fouled or bad chambers.

Second, the less barrel you have AFTER the port, the less dwell time you have on the operating system. The operating system functions best if it is pressurized gradually, not with a sudden spike. Remember that the 20" barrel with its port position offers the ideal combination of timing and dwell time to reliably cycle the weapon under a wide variety of environmental conditions. It has plenty of barrel ahead of and behind the port.

The shorter the barrel becomes, the further back towards the chamber the port must be moved and the closer it gets to the muzzle. It is the worst of all worlds for a gas-operated system. Now in order to get enough gas into the bolt/carrier group, the port must be enlarged as there is no longer enough dwell time on the operating system due to the lack of barrel between the port and the muzzle. This has the effect of over pressurizing the Bolt Carrier Group (BCG) and is very inefficient at the transfer of kinetic energy to the BCG and may even blow a gas ring seal eventually. Not to mention that it is very abusive to the cam pin and cam pin hole in the bolt itself. This is a common failure mode on SBRs – bolt failure in the cam pin hole. It is common with these short-barreled configurations to see a stuck case with the rim ripped off by the extractor. All the above-mentioned conditions lead to this eventuality.

The SBR operating system actuates before the case has had time to relax and release the chamber. The case has formed itself to a less than perfect chamber. The BCG has started moving to the rear with such force due to the fact that it must be over-pressurized to work at all that it now just rips the rim off the case that has decided NOT to be extracted just yet.

Oh, did I mention about all the people that have injured or blown off fingers with shorty SBRs? This is another dirty little secret of the ultra-short SBR. If you can get a finger in front of a muzzle, sooner or later you will. I let one of my highly experienced team shooters use my 7.5" SBR one time and if he wasn't wearing a glove, he would have taken most of his left index finger clean off as he had it up next to the muzzle device. His personal shooting style was to point his support hand index finger at the target while gripping the hand guard. I know from my law enforcement contacts that this is not an uncommon occurrence.

OK, now you're saying that "But I've got a piston gun and it solves all of that stuff." Not so fast, buddy. Piston systems have their own set of issues and I will not even go into that here, but suffice it to say that extreme SBRs based on the AR platform in 5.56 are nice toys and great novelty items, but I'm not betting my life on one if I have a choice.

Does this apply to 9mm or blow back pistol cartridge ARs? No, that is one of the exceptions. A blow back system is not subject to any of the aforementioned issues; you can have pistol cartridge chambered ARs with barrels as short as your pistol and they still work. The 300 BLK is also a departure as it operates at near pistol chamber pressures with a precipitous drop in the pressure curve as the bullets pass the port. This allows for configurations with pistol port positions that will function quite reliably with both super- and subsonic rounds, interchangeably.

The other consideration here is ammunition. Not all ammunition is created equal. and the ultra-short SBR by its very nature will be ammunition sensitive. By that I mean, if they work they will require a round that delivers a pressure curve that is compatible with the compromised port position. I've seen some that will literally only function with one particular round.

Over the past few years, we (JP Rifles Inc.) have walked away from sizable orders from law enforcement agencies that think they *have* to have a 10.5" (or shorter) SBR. This is probably a result of watching too many action shows with movie weapons. Unlike other companies that must take every order no matter if it makes sense or not, we are sufficiently financially secure that we don't have to. That's why our credibility is so high. I don't want to hear that some officer had a rifle go down at a critical moment because it was a poor compromise in configuration.

What we do offer is a 13.5" SBR with our 12.5" modular hand guard system. For the departments that are a little more open-minded, once they test this configuration against the ultra-short SBRs, they see the light. It is still very easy to manage in and out of vehicles and tight confines, but has the full real estate on the hand guard tube for any realistic compliment of accessories. And you will not accidentally get a finger up by the muzzle. They are sub-minute accurate with high grade ammunition and deliver external ballistics very close to an 18" carbine, not to mention a recoil impulse (sight recovery) that is right in there with our race guns. In fact, Hornady 53 grain Vmax SuperPerformance ammunition clocks about 3000 feet per second maximum velocity out of this configuration. Now that's rifle performance, and isn't that the idea?

This year, just to prove a point, I shot one of our off-the-rack 13.5" SBR LE patrol rifles at the JP Rocky Mountain 3 Gun World Championship. I had no problem with engagement out to 600 yards and finished high super senior. Sorry for the sales pitch but that's the price of this little dissertation.

John Paul,
JPE

Mike's Note: Please take the information above serious before investing in a defensive rifle that is shorter than 14 inches, and for me, I mirror what John says – "I'm not betting my life on one!" My current guns are in 14, 16, and 18-inch configurations. I find the 18-inch gun perfect for 3-gun competitions that require longer ranges, and the 14 and 16-inch guns are my "tactical" teaching guns. I prefer the 14-inch gun for defensive purposes, as it is perfect length when getting into and out of cars, and serves the home defense purpose well. I can also reliably hit out to 300 yards and beyond with that gun with a one power Aimpoint micro (T-1) scope, which is farther that any engagement I can imagine myself getting into unless the zombies really do attack.

R.E.A.P Test

One of the first questions people will ask during class when we are gearing up and see my rifles is what gun I like the most. While I clearly love the JP Rifles I own and shoot, the answer usually surprises them when I tell them that it really does not matter as long as the gun scores high in my R.E.A.P. test.

When selecting a gun for defensive purposes, I use what I call the R.E.A.P. test. This acronym stands for: *reliability, ergonomics, accuracy* and *power*. For me, reliability is number one, because in a gunfight, as well as my secondary use for most of my guns (competitions), reliability is very, very important. One other note before I break down R.E.A.P. into more details, I strongly recommend picking one model of rifle that will meet all of your priorities and needs, and spend your time and money (for ammunition) on that one gun. If you are a very experienced shooter, then you can make the decision to switch back and forth between different guns, but the new shooter should stick to one model if possible. This will allow you to focus on developing skills to advanced levels rather than chasing equipment and the newest gun or gimmick. Remember the saying: "beware of the man with only one gun, because he probably knows how to shoot it."

Figure 8 With high quality ammunition, good magazines, and a clean rifle you should be able to open a case of ammunition and shoot it all without a problem. Anything less is NOT reliable.

Here is what you need to look at when selecting a firearm for combative purposes, <u>listed in order of priority</u>:

- *Reliability*: The number one thing a firearm must do is work. Nothing else matters if you have a malfunction during a fight. What is reliable? I think that you should be able to open a case (1000 rounds) of high-quality ammunition, and, if using reliable magazines in a gun that is lightly lubricated, run through that case without a single problem. That is reliable.
- *Ergonomics*: The second thing I look for in a firearm is its physical design and ability to be manipulated and shot well. My personal opinion is that it is hard to beat the controls and ergonomics on an AR system. There is a reason a huge number of top 3-gun competitors as well as real-world military and law enforcement operators use an AR, or that type of system. They are simply hard to beat. If you choose or own a different rifle, that is fine, just be sure you have the ability to operate it without fighting it. Don't use a gun you can't operate well! You are already in one fight against the person; there's no reason to fight your rifle.
- *Accuracy*: Accuracy is third on my list because while it is important, it is relevant and specifically based on your particular context. If you own a 1000 acre ranch and want a rifle that will serve as a good home defense rifle *and* ranch rifle for predators, then accuracy will be more important for you than someone that lives in a built-up area. I do prefer a very accurate rifle *if* I can get the first two requirements (reliability and ergonomics) met. Any reasonably high-quality rifle you purchase should exceed the accuracy requirements most of you have for your rifle.
- *Power*: Power is an interesting discussion when looking at rifle calibers. Read the caliber selection section for detailed information. I prefer the .223/ 5.56 caliber rifle for my defensive rifle, but some of you might have a need for a larger, heavier bullet. It is commonly know that a .30 caliber round and bigger will offer more stopping power than a .223, but there is a trade off in recoil and capacity if you choose it. In addition, if you have concerns with penetration of the walls or your environment, then be cautious of using bigger, heavier bullets. Do the research and pick the best caliber you can, so you can spend your time training for better shot placement at faster speeds while others argue about stopping power.

Rifle Setup

The simplest way to break down the rifle setup would be to work from the front of the gun back and cover everything in between the muzzle and the stock. Keep in mind that there are almost limitless variations of parts and pieces you can add to the popular rifles made these days, and each of them have the potential to effect how the rifle handles and shoots. I believe that keeping the "add on" parts to a minimum will serve you well. In addition, most current rifles are designed to be functional and reliable out of the box, so the more you change the more you increase your risk of potentially causing a problem. Internal modifications such as switching out springs, or modifying or changing internal parts will almost certainly cause a shift in reliability. It's your job to make sure you affect it in the right direction!

First of all, the base rifle you pick needs to be one that is a reliable, well-built gun with a decent trigger. Remember, you get what you pay for and spending a bit more money on a brand that is reliable is an absolute must for a defensive rifle. All mechanical devices fail at times, but given good ammunition and good magazines, a quality rifle should not fail if it is relatively clean, even if it is shot hundreds if not thousands of rounds.

Ok, so lets assume you have a great base rifle that came with the basics including a good set of iron sights and a good trigger (we'll talk about replacing that too). The goal now is to figure out what else you need on the rifle, and what you don't. In the context of this section, lets assume this rifle is going to be set up for defensive purposes for a civilian defending his home, law enforcement officer, or military operator operating in an environment where the shooting would occur from close range to a maximum of a few hundred yards. That means to me that the ability to shoot and hit a threat at 300 yards is probably not likely unless your description of "defensive" is defending your perimeter in Afghanistan. My thought on civilian rifles is that you will almost never have the ability to articulate a reason to shoot someone much more than fifty yards away, but I completely understand that most "ranch" rifles found in the hands of someone who owns a large piece of land might be used to engage animal targets at a couple hundred yards. Your goal should be set the gun up for the context in which it is going to be used.

Consistency is the Key

First, I want you to know that everyone's personal preference that will dictate some of the accessories on a rifle. That said, I firmly believing in keeping things simple, functional, light, and most importantly consistent. The word consistent might stand out to you, and what I mean is that if I have four different rifles, I try to keep them set up as consistently as possible. If you looked at my 14- and 16-inch JP Rifles, you would find them set up the same, keeping aftermarket accessories in the same location if possible.

For example, if I mount a light on each with a pressure switch, I will mount the light and pressure switch on each in the same location. Or maybe if I have a Magpul BAD level on one gun, if possible I want one on all of them. The point is that I want to be able to operate each of them in the same manner under stress.

In the next section I asked Erik Lund, one of my Shooting-Performance senior instructors to give me his thoughts on setting up an AR type system for defensive use. Keep in mind we are referring to an AR system, but the basics of setting up a defensive rifle could be applied across the board, no matter what model rifle you select.

Erik Lund on Accessories for the Defensive Rifle

Now that you've chosen to acquire an AR-15 for use as a defensive rifle, serious due diligence on your part must be given to selecting the proper accessories to enhance the capabilities and performance of both you and the rifle. One of the main reasons for the immense popularity of the AR-15 rifle is the massive aftermarket parts and accessories market. The modular design of the AR rifle really allows the end-user to configure and customize the rifle for a myriad of roles and missions. The danger in this ability to widely configure the AR is having too many options; attempting to configure your defensive rifle to deal with every contingency, at any possible range, and under every possible condition. There's a saying that works in this situation, "If you try to see everything, you'll see nothing. If you try to see a little, you'll see a lot." With this in mind, let's try to see a little and define exactly what the purpose of a defensive rifle is and how we can best configure it for success. To properly configure a defensive rifle, we need to examine the environment it will need to effectively operate within. The primary purpose of a defensive rifle is to protect our home and immediate vicinity and the two elements we must consider in its employment are distance and time.

Distance is our primary element when configuring a defensive rifle. The distance at which we expect to use the rifle will drive the element of time. Developing a realistic expectation of our engagement distances is critical to maximizing the performance of our defensive rifle. Although each homeowner's situation is unique, a performance range of less than 50 yards (150 feet) with a more realistic range being less than 15 yards (45 feet) is probably a safe starting point. These distances are based upon the sizes of most homes, not from any statistic. An examination of your home will show most distances where you might have to engage a threat entering your home will tend to be 45 feet or closer.

Time is our second element and it refers to how much advance warning or time can we expect to have once a threat breaches our home to prepare for the assault. Time will be dependent upon two factors: the configuration of our homes and the security measures in place to alert us to an intrusion. The layout of the home is vitally important to our overall home defense plan. Consider two homes, one with the master bedroom on the main floor next to the home's entrance and a two-story home with the master bedroom on the second floor at the rear of the home. When a threat breaches the front door, which homeowner will have more time to react to the intrusion and properly prepare to deal with the threat? That reaction time is reduced even more if the intruder is not detected until after they have entered the home. The second factor of time is our security measures. Things such as home alarms, strong steel security doors with deadbolts, and motion sensor security lights with audible alarms are a few options to improve our security measures. The sooner we can detect an intruder and the more we can delay their entry into our home, the more time we'll have to initiate our family defensive plan and prepare for the intrusion. This additional time gives us more opportunity to get our defensive rifle into the fight.

Upon examination of our two elements, a few things become apparent. The distances will be close which means threat engagement times will be fast. Our advance notice of a threat, based upon the layout of our homes and our security measures, could be very short. The short notice of an imminent threat, translates to very little time to prepare for the engagement. Put simply, the engagement will happen fast. Based upon this examination, one thing is clear. A defensive rifle needs to be optimized for speed, both in its employment and its performance. A standard

AR-15 in a carbine configuration with a 16" or 14.5" barrel is optimum for this requirement. Accordingly, accessories to the Defensive Rifle should be selected to enhance those qualities. When it comes to selecting accessories for the defensive rifle, they should be divided into two categories, essentials and luxuries. Let's examine the essentials.

There are three accessories we consider essential on a properly configured defensive rifle, but before we examine these items, let's establish a baseline stipulation of our starting point. We have already acquired a high-quality AR rifle, magazines, and ammunition from manufacturers with a proven history of performance, reliability, and durability. We are now at the point of improving the performance of our defensive rifle. Our four essential accessories, in their order of importance are a *sling, weapon-mounted light*, a *red dot sight*, and a quality *drop-in trigger pack*.

Slings

A sling on a rifle is an incredibly important and inexpensive piece of gear that is a must. The rifles issued to me years ago in the Marine Corps all had a sling issued as part of the essential gear, but the sling was a 2-point system meant primarily as a method of carrying the weapon. We did use the sling for better long range marksmanship by wrapping our lead arms around the sling and using it to steady the rifle (a technique I will not cover), but those sling systems and methods have been much improved upon. Currently you will find predominantly single and multi-point slings on most modern AR systems. The difference between a single or multi-point attachment slings simply means that a single point sling attaches at one point. A two-point sling attaches at two points. The most common slings are single and two point attachment slings, and you should select one or the other.

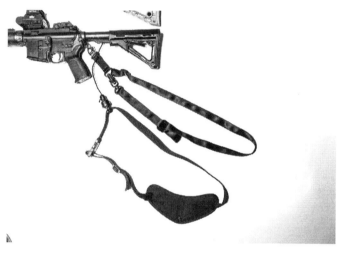

Figure 9 The Safariland and Magpul single point slings I prefer. Notice how each has a single attachment point.

I personally use both the Magpul MS2 and Safariland Sling Model 4016 single point slings on my rifles, and much prefer the single point models because to me they are easy to transition to either shoulder, and work smoother when I am transitioning to a handgun. That said, I have many operational friends that love single point slings, and probably just as many that strongly prefer two point slings.

Figure 10 Kyle Lamb and his VTAC sling system, the two-point I recommend if you choose a two-point sling.

Kyle Lamb of Viking Tactics (http://www.vikingtactics.com) sells one of the most popular slings on the market called the VTAC sling and if you go with a two point, I recommend his. In either case, a sling is a must on a rifle for various reasons.

One will allow you to sling the rifle and do numerous things you could not do with it in your hand. A sling will also help you retain your rifle in a fight or a fall. Lastly, when transitioning to a secondary weapon (handgun), a sling is a must.

WEAPON-MOUNTED LIGHTS

Figure 11 A weapon mounted light/laser combination is a great choice for a defensive rifle. The laser is a great back up sighting system and also allows you to shoot from positions where you can not look through your optic yet still see where you will hit.

Our first essential item is a dedicated rifle-mounted light. It's no secret evil likes to hunt at night or in dark places. Half of our world is dark at any point in time. It would be wise to have the capability to operate the rifle during the day or night. Before you can engage any perceived threat, you must positively identify it as a threat. Society demands this, but more importantly, your moral code should demand it. Society has provided a mechanism for you to legally protect yourself from danger. That mechanism allows you to take the life of another person if certain conditions are present. If you are willing to accept that awesome responsibility, then you also need to accept the conditions upon which that responsibility is based. You MUST positively identify any potential threat PRIOR to engaging it and that requires a light. Understanding that time is not necessarily on our side during an encounter in our home, it only makes sense to have a light permanently attached to our Defensive Rifle. This way, the light is always with the rifle and is always available for use. A weapon light should have the brightest possible light in the smallest lightweight package available, within reason. The "reason" I write it like that is because there are actually lights made today that are too bright for certain uses. Some of the lights on the market that could be mounted to a rifle today might have more than 300 lumens (and some double that!). A light this bright will almost instantly blind you in confined spaces with light colored walls. A light that that much intensity is best served on a hunting platform (if legal) or possibly on a rifle that will be exclusively used outside. The Streamlight TLR-2 HL light/laser combination I have on my rifle is probably the upper end of intensity I would want to use. Streamlight advertises this light as 630 lumens and 12,000 candelas. Streamlight also makes a TLR-1 HPL (High Lumen, Long-Range Rail-Mounted tactical Light) that is advertised with 775 lumens, and an incredibly focused beam. A light this would be overkill and a detriment if your defensive solution was your house and yard. The light is so bright and focused that it creates a blindingly bright spot when it hits a wall and this "hot spot" stays imbedded in your vision after illuminating it. I would not suggest a light this powerful. It should have a provision for momentary and permanent activation through the use of a remote pressure pad or through direct hand activation. Batteries should be of a standard size that is easily acquired at any store without special order. Care must be given as to the placement of the light on the Defensive Rifle. Ensure placement of the light or the activation pressure pad is consistent with your hand placement during the shooting process. Placement should be at our near your support hand position. Switching hand positions to activate the light is inefficient. Proper placement brings efficiency

Figure 12 The top light is the Streamlight TLR-2 HL light/laser combination I like. The bottom is the TLR-1 HPL, and great light but made for a specific purpose. Make sure you select the right light!

to our technique and speed is a byproduct of efficiency. If you have a vertical or angled foregrip on your rifle, then make sure you find a mounting solution for your light activation switch that will be consistent with either hand. I have had many students in my classes realize that their mounting solution was poor when I had them switch to the other hand and they had the light pressure switch mounted and accessible only on one side of the gun.

> *Mike's Note:* The light position on the rifle is of critical importance. I have tried the three, nine, six and twelve o'clock positions and one thing to consider is the fact that when a light is mounted anywhere other than six o'clock, you will have problems. In the past I experimented extensively with light positions. One position I tried was the twelve o'clock position, mainly because I figured mounting a Surefire or similar light at twelve o'clock and using my thumb to activate the toggle switch was a simple solution that would allow me to skip mounting a pressure pad on the rifle. In past testing with this position, I had observed problems with the smoke from the rifle muzzle obscuring the target. While I knew that the twelve o'clock mounting position of the light was not the best option, I had convinced myself that at the ranges I would likely operate my rifle, the smoke obscuring my vision would not be an issue. I was wrong! Even at closer ranges of ten yards, the smoke became an issue with multiple rounds fired, and with the light mounted at twelve o'clock; the smoke issue was huge, especially when using an optic (an Aimpoint C3 in this case).
>
> At more than fifty yards, the smoke completely covered the targets and kept me from shooting for a second or so until it cleared enough for me to see the next target. After I mounted the light at the six o'clock position, the smoke problems became almost none existent due to the fact that the light was no longer illuminating the smoke in front of my scope. As stated before, the three and nine o'clock positions are not recommended because of the increase in splash back that the shooter will get from those positions while working around cover. See the photo below for exactly how and where I mounted my light.

Notice the following four pictures that depict the light position on the gun. One works, the others not so much. I strongly recommend sticking to a six o'clock position.

Figure 14 Light mounted on the left side of the rifle will illuminate and wash back into the operators eyes when working the edge of a wall to the right.

Figure 13 Light mounted on the right side of the rifle will illuminate and wash back into the operators eyes when working the edge of a wall to the left.

Figure 15 Light mounted at the 12 O'clock position will illuminate the smoke from the muzzle and make it very difficult to see the red dot.

Figure 14 Light mounted at the 6 O'clock position with the pressure activation switch on top of the handguard. This is the superior position to mount a light on a rifle if possible.

RED DOT SIGHTS

When selecting an optical accessory for the defensive rifle there are two classes of options to consider: Magnified Optics and Red Dot Sights (RDS.) Magnified Optics is any style of optical scope that uses some level of magnification to enhance the image quality. They usually have a range of power settings such as a 3-9x (power) or a 4-16x. There are optics with very high magnification ranges that are primarily used for long-range precision shooting. Optics with mid-power magnification ranges provide good performance at a variety of distances, but even low-powered magnification range scopes work well from very close distances to several hundred yards. Magnified optics offer the end user a lot of capability but at the cost of a larger, heavier, and more complex operating design. This is not to say that magnified scopes are not reliable or durable, just that their performance comes at a price. RDS designs use an electronic image projected onto a glass or plexiglass style lens. The image is usually a dot, but several manufacturers offer reticles of various designs.

Note: For those that might not know the term, a reticle is a net of fine lines or fibers in the eyepiece of a sighting device (scope). Originally called and sometimes referred to as crosshairs because early designs used small pieces of hair to make the reticle.

Figure 16 Variable scopes like this are great options if you want to build a multi-purpose rifle. Make sure to select one you can dial down to true 1X and that has an illuminated dot.

Several different sizes of dots are also available depending upon the preference of the end user. RDS designs offer no magnification options unless coupled with a separate magnifier specifically designed to be used in conjunction with the RDS. Think of an RDS as a small section of PVC tube with a red dot projected into the center of the tube. There is no magnification so the image the user sees "inside" the tube is on the same visual plane as any images outside of the tube. Essentially, the user looks through the tube and superimposes the red dot onto target (Note- not all RDS designs incorporate a tube. There is a new class of RDS known as Mini Red Dot Sights that still use projected dot technology, but they accomplish this using only one lens in a flat screen type housing instead to a tube with two lenses.) RDS designs are superior for close range shooting as there is no change of focus or shifting visual planes to manage. When the optic is properly zeroed, place the dot on the target and shoot. RDS designs are usually smaller, lighter, and less complex when compared to magnified optics and their zero magnification designs are faster to operate at very close distances.

Figure 17 Two excellent red dot optics, the Aimpint Micro and Eotech. I prefer the Aimpoint, but both are excellent. Don't buy a cheap optic; you get what you pay for.

The weak link in RDS design had always been the dual combination of poor battery life and minimal durability. Most RDS designs would burn through a battery in only a few hours of operational use and if battery life managed to hold up, rough use would cause the unit to fail. In recent years, technology has improved both issues to the point where RDS are standard issue for militaries around the world. They have earned a reputation for durability in every environment in the world and technological improvements in certain models have stretched battery life to an amazing five years of constant operation. There can be no doubt that the RDS's combination of speed, reliability, durability, and extremely long battery life; all in a lightweight and compact package that minimizes threat engagement times and maximizes personal performance is an essential accessory for any defensive rifle. Simply put, it's a must-have piece of gear when configuring your defensive rifle.

Mike's note: I have used both Aimpionts (Micro and Comp C3) and Eotech red dot sights over the years and have not had an issue with either. I personally prefer the Aimpoint due to simple reason like the fact that the Eotech's have an auto shut off feature and has to be turned on to use. Comparably, the newer Aimpoints have excellent battery life and can literally be turned on and left on full time if desired. The key is to switch the battery out every so often. This makes a rifle ready to use when grabbed. That said, the U.S. Special Operations Command (USSOCOM) chose the Eotech as their primary 1X optic, so as you can see it is a solid choice as well. The below chart compares popular 1X scopes so you can quickly view some of their features.

Optic	Aimpoint T-1	Eotech EXPS3	Vortex SPARC II	Trijicon Reflex
Battery Life	50,000 hours	600 (at nominal setting	300-5000 hours (Max/Min Brightness)	Unlimited (Battery free illuminated reticle)
Dot Size (MOA)	2 or 4	1 with outer ring and various reticle options	1	4.5 (dot) – 12.9 (Triangle)
Auto Off?	No	Yes (4-8 hours)	Yes (12 hour)	No
Battery	3V CR2032	123 Lithium	3V CR 2032	None
Price	$650-700	$679	$289	$560-700

If you are considering a RDS for your Defensive Rifle, then you must also consider the acquisition of Back-Up Iron Sights (BUIS.) Regardless of what RDS you select, you must accept the reality that anything mechanical or electrical can fail. While the modern RDS is a durable and rugged piece of kit, all systems should have built-in redundancy. If you choose a RDS as your primary sighting system, then you need BUIS's to satisfy the required redundancy of a secondary sighting system. BUIS are available in both fixed position models and folding flat models where the front and rear sights lay flat along the upper receiver of the rifle and are flipped up into position when needed. Fixed BUIS's have the advantage of being instantly available if needed, but they also are visible through the RDS all the time and can give the appearance of cluttering up the optic. Folding BUIS's have the

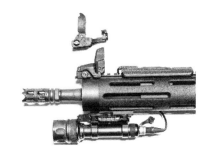

Figure 18 No matter what optic you choose, it's a wise move to have iron sights on your rifle as well. This photo shows a couple options including the Magpul flip up sights, which I have on my rifle. Whichever you choose, make sure you can deploy them quickly.

advantage of being stored flat along the upper receiver until needed, thereby not obscuring the optics field of view, but they are slower to deploy should they be needed. Some users prefer to use a combination of the two by have a fixed front BUIS and a folding rear BUIS. The front sight appears inside the optics field of view and can act as a reference point for use in close quarters shooting should the RDS fail. If no immediate threat is present the operator can then deploy the rear BUIS to complete the sighting system for use until the RDS can be returned to service.

DROP-IN TRIGGER KITS

The last item we consider essential to a properly configured defensive rifle is a quality non-adjustable, drop-in trigger kit. The concept of considering an aftermarket trigger pack as an essential item on a defensive rifle is not without controversy. There will always be those who choose to err on the side of caution and recommend that unmodified factory triggers should be the standard on any firearm being considered for personal protection. Any modification to improve the quality of the trigger pull creates a situation known as a "hair trigger" and such decisions show the evil intent of the end-user to create a more deadly weapon; therefore, you were building a weapon in anticipation of a confrontation and that shows you had prior intent to murder your victim.

Figure 19 JP Drop in trigger kit. There are several good manufacturers out there, but beware of compromising reliability.

As contorted as that logic is, there are those that actually believe this makes sense and recommend this course of action. We do not subscribe to that philosophy. Regardless of its application or caliber, a rifle is a very powerful weapon that can inflict great damage over very long distances. Accurately controlling that power is the responsibility of the user. When using a rifle that can intentionally kill people at ranges of over 1,000 yards, great care and responsibility must be taken to ensure that if the rifle is used during a hostile encounter, it's used with the utmost precision. Any round that is discharged without due care and misses its mark has the real potential to travel long distances, unintentionally striking an innocent person. It's no secret that a key aspect of accuracy with any type of firearm is trigger control. All other factors being equal, a firearm possessing a trigger pull that is crisp, predictable, repeatable, and free from excessive trigger pull weight will allow the end-user to personally perform at a higher level when compared to a firearm with a trigger lacking these qualities. The choice to equip your defensive rifle with a quality trigger demonstrates that you understand the capabilities of your firearm and that the morally responsible course of action you have chosen is to ensure that you can accurately fire your rifle, thereby reducing the possibility of any unintentional collateral damage. The sole reason that rifles, most notably AR-15 style rifles, are manufactured with horrendously heavy trigger pulls is to prevent lawsuits related to unintentional or accidental discharges with their products. Factory rifle trigger pull weights are designed to prevent accidental firings, not to promote accuracy.

When researching trigger options for your defensive rifle, you will certainly encounter trigger units being described as having a single-stage or a two-stage trigger. Understanding the differences between to two types of triggers will assist you in determining which type of trigger you prefer. A single-stage trigger performs exactly as it is described. There is very minimal or no perceived movement of the trigger prior to releasing the sear, initiating the firing process. The entire pull weight of the trigger is felt during that one trigger activation.

A two-stage trigger also performs as described. A two-stage trigger is essentially two distinct, partial trigger pulls combined into one longer pull. Two-stage triggers allow for a portion of the total trigger pull weight to be manipulated during the first stage, prior to reaching the distinct second stage of the trigger pull where the rest of the total trigger pull weight is manipulated. Two-stage triggers allow for a splitting of the trigger pull weight between the first and second stage. The advantage of a two-stage trigger is that the unit can still possess a relatively heavy trigger pull weight, but being distributed between two separate stages allows for a moderate initial pull weight and a very light second stage pull weight. This design allows the unit to operate with a very light final trigger pull without being considered unsafe or possessing a "hair trigger." For example, if you have a trigger with a 5 lb. trigger pull weight, the first stage of the trigger can be adjusted to require 3.5 lbs. of trigger pull to manipulate trigger while the second stage of the trigger pull weight would only require 1.5 lbs. to manipulate. This system allows the operator to "prep" the trigger by negotiating the first stage of the trigger and holding the trigger at the second stage until final corrective adjustments are made to the sight alignment on the target. When the operator is satisfied with the corrective adjustments, the second stage of the trigger pulls requires only the minimal 1.5 lb. trigger manipulation to release the sear and initiate the firing process, but the overall trigger pull weight is still 5 lbs.

We find that single-stage triggers are better for speed applications due to their short movement and quick resets. Two-stage triggers are best suited for longer-range precision work where the end-user has the time to properly use the two different stages of the design to maximize their trigger control. While that is our preference, there are plenty of two-stage triggers being used in defensive rifles. Take the opportunity to examine both styles of triggers and make an informed decision as to which design compliments your individual shooting style.

Aftermarket drop-in trigger kits are available in both single and two-stage trigger designs and are available in two configurations, adjustable and non-adjustable. Adjustable trigger kits allow the end-user to fully adjust the features of the trigger. Features such as pre-travel, over-travel, spring tension, pull-weight, and others are manipulated through all manner of setscrew adjustments and spring kits. These types of triggers are fully tunable and are able to provide the end-user with a truly incredible and lightweight trigger pull that is measured in ounces and not pounds. While these types of triggers offer incredible performance, they also demand high maintenance and attention to detail. Fully adjustable triggers can be precisely manipulated to provide outstanding performance but they can also fall out of adjustment just as easily. An out-of-adjustment trigger can cause all manner of failures to include slam-fires, doubling, or just outright failure to work. Clearly, not the type of performance desired in a defensive rifle.

The other option is a non-adjustable drop-in trigger kit. The triggers are fully adjusted at the factory and require no adjustment from the end-user. They are truly a "plug and play" setup. All of the important qualities of a good trigger pull are set by the factory and permanently "locked" into position. Once the hammer and trigger pins are withdrawn and the factory trigger parts are removed from the lower receiver, the entire trigger kit is literally dropped into place. Depending upon the manufacturer, the unit is secured with either the original factory hammer and trigger pins or pins that are supplied with the aftermarket unit. Once installed, the trigger kit will provide a quality trigger with a pull weight in the 3-5 lb. range that will in most cases outlast the rifle, with a very remote chance of ever coming out of adjustment. A quality trigger is an essential item on a defensive rifle and the non-adjustable drop-in trigger kits offer the three features we look for in any accessory: performance, reliability, and durability. We consider this item an essential accessory for your defensive rifle.

LUXURIES TO CONSIDER

Now that we have optimized our defensive rifles for speed and performance, let's examine some of the luxuries that are not necessary on a properly configured defensive rifle, but may offer some measure of performance enhancement through operational and ergonomic improvements.

FLASH SUPRESSORS, COMPENSATORS, & HYBRIDS

Most AR-15 style rifles are equipped with either a flash suppressor or a compensator at the end of the barrel. Flash suppressors are one of those evil features that anti-gunners love to hate. They literally do what their name implies. They suppress or diffuse the flash of the fireball at the end of the muzzle when a rifle is discharged. The fireball occurs as a result of unburned powder exiting the barrel and then igniting in the oxygen-rich environment. The intent of the design was to reduce the size of the fireball to prevent our soldiers from giving away their firing positions when shooting in lowlight or darkness and to help our soldiers maintain their dark adjusted eye vision. As barrel lengths have gotten shorter, flash suppressors have gained in importance. The shorter the barrel, the larger the

Figure 20 A compensator like this offers some serious advantages in settling the dot during recoil, but beware of the incredible noise and gass pressure that is emitted when used. If you shot with a compensator like this close to someone's head, bad idea!

amount of unburned powder being ejected into the air in front of the muzzle. The more powder, the bigger the flash. While the standard A2 flash suppressor offers sufficient all-around performance, there are several aftermarket styles that were specifically designed to perform better in shorter barrels and they offer a noticeable improvement in short barrels over the A2 design.

Compensators are actually a group of specific designs that get lumped under the name "compensator." A true compensator is a device that has ports or holes drilled into the unit with the purpose of redirecting the expanding gasses that propel the bullet down the barrel in an attempt to counteract the recoil of the rifle during the firing process. A compensator vectors the expanding gasses in an upward direction, which has the effect of pushing the barrel downward during the firing process, allowing the muzzle to stay relatively level. This allows the operator to begin the second shot process quicker than when compared to a rifle without a compensator.

Figure 21 One of my rifles with a Templar Tactical Suppressor. I used to ignore the idea of a suppressor on a home defense rifle, but now think they are an excellent idea if reliability is not compromised.

Another type of "compensator" is called a muzzle brake. A muzzle brake is a device that usually has large rectangular lateral holes machined into the device that extend through the center of the device along the 3-9 o'clock planes. This creates large walls or baffles. Muzzle brakes usually have two to four baffles in a single device. As the expanding gasses pass through the device, those gasses impact the baffles. For a fraction of a section, those gasses impart energy on those baffles with the effect of pulling the rifle forward. This action reduces the recoil imparted to the shooter. This reduction in recoil has the effect of reducing the disturbance the operators "sees" in his sight picture and allows for the next shot process to begin sooner.

It should be noted that just about all designs that are classified as "compensators" are actually a combination of both designs. As with any product, some designs offer outstanding performance while others are clearly inferior. The performance gains are significant enough that every professional competitive shooter's "3-gun"[2] rifle is equipped with some type of compensator. Compensators offer serious recoil reduction performance but that performance comes at a serious price, increased noise and concussion. All those baffles and ports that are redirecting gas

---

[2] 3-gun is a common term used in today's practical shooting competitive community that denotes a competition using three guns, the handgun, rifle and shotgun.

also redirect the noise and concussion, some of which is directed back towards the shooter. When installed on shorter barreled carbines, even just one shot without hearing protection can cause hearing damage. Many users feel the obnoxious concussion and blast is not worth the performance gained from a compensator's use. Should you choose to equip your defensive rifle with a compensator, place electronic hearing protection next to the rifle and integrate their use into your homes defensive plans to avoid permanent hearing loss.

A relatively recent development in muzzle device technology is the emergence of hybrid designs. Hybrids seek to combine the recoil reduction of compensators with the suppression ability of flash suppressors. To some degree, hybrids have been successful in merging the two technologies, but combining the best of both designs may just be the proverbial "unicorn in the wild." The reason for this is the physics principals of each design. Basically, the science behind compensator performance design is on the opposite side of the physics spectrum from the science behind flash suppressor design. Think of a number line from zero to 100, with a flash suppressor on one side and a compensator on the other side. When you are at 0 on the number line, a design is 100% flash suppressor and 0% compensator and vice versa. For every number you move away from the flash suppressor side and closer to the compensator side you lose a little bit of performance from one side and gain a little bit of performance on the other side. Hybrids seek to find that perfect balance of 50% flash suppressor and 50% compensator. Some designs perform better than others with respect to suppressing flash and others perform better at compensating. There are also those who feel that hybrids are the worst of both designs, offering the combination of both poor flash suppression and poor compensation. Regardless of where your personal views lie, education and research is your path to making a wise selection should you choose to equip your defensive rifle with a flash suppressor, compensator, or a hybrid muzzle device.

OPERATIONAL CONTROLS

The AR-15 rifle has several critical operational controls. Operational controls are things like safety selectors, magazine buttons, bolt releases, and charging handles. Mastering the manipulation of these controls is critical to effectively operating your defensive rifle in a stressful situation. The techniques for manipulating operational controls should be trained until their use becomes reflexive and instinctive. Pay particular intention to this part – *there are no shortcuts to training.* Far too many people try to purchase performance instead of putting in the training time needed to become profi-

Figure 22 These rifles have enhanced operational controls, one with a Phase 5 bolt release and one with a Magpul BAD lever. Both great options, but neither necessary nor replacements for good training.

cient. Various aftermarket parts companies offer all manners of oversized and ambidextrous operating controls. Some of these designs are very good and will improve your personal performance with a defensive rifle, but only if you have put in the training time to use the basic controls first. Don't be the guy that shows up to a training course with every aftermarket operational control available on his rifle without the skills to even use the basic ones. Spend the money to learn how to properly use the rifle first. Later, when you have developed your skill set, you'll be able to make a better decision as to which operational control changes will improve your overall performance with your defensive rifle.

Figure 23 This rifle has a Magpul Grip with the large rear panel. The grip is both comfortable and allows the ambidextrous safety on the other side of the gun to travel freely because it pushes the users hand slightly to the rear.

ERGONOMIC ENHANCEMENTS

A large portion of the success of the AR-15 platform is due to the outstanding ergonomics of the rifle. Ergonomics is the science of integrating human and machine to operate more efficiently and until recently, no rifle in the history of firearms development has come close to the ergonomic efficiency of the AR-15 design. Great effort was made to ensure that the operational controls on the AR-15 rifle were positioned in the best possible location for the human element to operate those controls in the most efficient manner possible. The use of straight-line stocks, handguards, and pistol grips, positioned the human head, hands, and shoulders in such a manner as to be extremely comfortable and an aide in managing the recoil of the rifle. As good as the ergonomics of the AR-15 rifle are, there is no such thing as "one size fits all." Fortunately, there are a myriad of options for replacing stocks, handguards, and pistol grips on the AR-15 rifle. These options allow the end-user to truly fit the rifle to their individual dimensions. Not only does this make the rifle more comfortable to shoot, it's also a key aspect to improving personal performance. As before, there are no shortcuts to training. Seek out quality training and learn to properly mount and shoot your defensive rifle. As you hone your skill and technique, you'll learn how to configure the er-

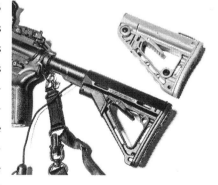

Figure 24 Aftermarket stocks made by Magpul and Safariland (Bill Rogers) are nice additions to a rifle that give the user the ability to adjust stock length.

gonomics of your defensive rifle until it's an extension of your body; improving performance and confidence. While we don't consider ergonomic enhancements an essential part of configuring a Defensive Rifle, don't overlook the benefits to such enhancements. They are the intangible part of what makes a rifle "feel" right when you pick it up.

Hopefully, these concepts will guide you in your quest to configure a defensive rifle that will serve you well and protect your family and loved ones. Remember that the rifle is only a tool and that the real weapon is your mind. Train hard with both and never forget that the world is full of evil…and one day it will find you.

Figure 25 This "battle belt" with handgun holster is a combination of a High Speed Gear Suregrip belt, Safariland holster, and ITW Fast magazine pouches. A great set up for quick access after a bump in the night.

Support Gear

Support gear for a rifle is completely context and situational driven. A Marine in Afghanistan is certainly going to operate very differently than a home defender in Casper, Wyoming. The Marine likely has a plate carrier with numerous magazine pouches, additional weapons, medical gear, etc. The home defender likely slings her rifle and might have time to place a spare magazine in a rear pocket. A patrol officer would probably have time to snap on a single rifle magazine pouch to his belt and deploy with one spare magazine.

One thing I see in my rifle classes is the predominant attitude that gear solves problems, which is incorrect. Skill solves problems and is supplemented by good gear. This section is relatively short because if your rifle is accessorized properly, there is not much you will need to go along with it. In any case, train with the rifle in the

Figure 26 Another great option is a quick sling bag that has several rifle magazines and possibly additional ammunition or medical gear. Something like this can enhance your ability to react to a situation quickly.

manner you will use it, so if you are the Marine mentioned above, set your gear up in a consistent manner and train with it. If you are a home defender or maybe someone who carries a short rifle in your vehicle for defensive use, then your rifle deployment and gear will be significantly different.

I normally train with one single Safariland magazine pouch snapped onto my belt, or place a magazine in my rear pocket. Often times I have a dual magazine cinch in my home defense rifle, giving me a total of 60 rounds in the gun. The point is that is how I will likely deploy my rifle, and that is how I train.

Some things to consider:

- Set up your gear in a consistent manner, and keep it that way. In your initial training and experimentation, change things up and modify gear type and placement until you find something that works. Once you choose the best set up however, keep it the same and train with it!
- If you carry numerous magazines in several locations, make sure you practice with each location, and also test to see if you can access each magazine with either hand. You might be shooting the rifle from the other arm!
- Consider testing your gear with the one-handed only operations (see one handed survival shooting) and see if you can access magazines while operating with only one hand/arm.
- Perform your rifle practice drills with your handgun in the location you carry it, if you are going to be armed with a handgun. This will ensure all of your gear works together.

Training Note: Very often I have students show up at a class with their handgun in some sort of tactical drop holster thigh rig. I ask them if that is where they normally carry their handgun, and 90% of the time I get a "no." My question is then, why are you training with it like that (in a different location and holster)? There are rarely any good answers that follow. The point: train like you plan to fight! If your handgun is carried in a certain place and manner during normal daily wear, train with it like that.

Chapter Summary and Action steps

1. Selecting a rifle includes choosing a model, operating system, and length. Choose one that meets the needs of your particular situation.
2. Consider both the Direct Impingement (DI) and Piston Driven (PD) systems, as both offer pro's and con's. Select the best option and make sure you maintain the systems properly.
3. Use extreme caution when selecting a rifle length of less than 14 inches. Short Barreled Rifles have a purpose in some applications, but consider the downsides before purchasing.
4. Accessorize your rifle properly, with priority placed on key items.
    a. A good operational sling.
    b. A high quality Red Dot Sight.
    c. A permanent weapon mounted light (at 6 o'clock) with a pressure switch that is accessible with either hand when shooting from both shoulders.
    d. A quality drop-in trigger system, if needed.
    e. Back-up iron sights.
    f. Ergonomic and operational enhancements as necessary.
5. Select support-related gear such as magazine pouches, etc. Keep this support gear consistent and train with it.
6. Lastly, make sure you integrate and train your rifle skills while wearing your handgun in a consistent location with where you normally carry it.

CHAPTER 4

Mental Preparation For The Fight

A large majority of individuals that have some level of preparation with their firearm through practice are not mentally prepared for a fight. This section will prepare you. For those experienced warriors reading it, I believe it will give you some additional tools to toughen yourself mentally as well. Remember, if you are not mentally prepared, nothing else matters.

The topics I will cover in this chapter:

1. Mental Preparation for the Fight
2. Mental Toughness vs. Mental Connection
3. The Mental Toughness Routine
4. Active vs. Passive Visualization

Mental Preparation for the Fight

Preparing mentally for battle might be as important, if not more so than preparing physically. As a trick question I ask students in my competition classes what percentage of successful performance can be attributed to the mental side of the game. Often I get answers like 90%, 75%, etc. The truth is that the mental game is 100% of success, because the brain controls the actions. The physical side of any skill is a result of a mental command that guides the action. Whether the command is executed at the conscious or subconscious level is irrelevant, because there is no "physical" without the mental. Training results in learning by way of myelination, a process that coats the nerve pathway with a substance that speeds up the electrical signal as it travels down the nerve pathway (more about that later). Training for a fight mentally requires that the individual has prepared by doing the following:

- Mentally making the decision to use lethal force prior to the event.
- Writing the correct subconscious skills programs to execute during the event.
- Controlling or mitigating the mental stress pre-fight or during the fight.

- Developing a "mental toughness" that helps one continue to fight even when things get really bad.

Mentally making the decision to use lethal force prior to the event

This one is relatively easy, and if you are reading this book you likely have already made this one. Simply ask yourself if you believe you have the ability to point your handgun at someone and pull the trigger. Can you? If not, you need to make that decision now and look at other defensive options, rather than find yourself in the situation and freeze. I recommend you delete the hero scenario and really make sure you can do what needs to be done in the time of need. If you do, you are taking a very big responsibility on your shoulders. You are willing to do violence to others, and this is hard for some people to swallow. The risk of missing and hitting an innocent bystander, lawsuits, and serious bodily injury or death are all very possible, yet the alternative is to do nothing and join the sheep in the slaughter. If you choose to accept this responsibility, I applaud you and the rest of this book will help you to train. Make the choice.

Writing the correct subconscious skills programs to execute during the event

This step is going to take considerably more work than making the decision above, in regards to time. This is where you will develop the skills needed to respond correctly during a lethal encounter. Skill programs are written during your training, and include decision-making skills at the conscious level, and technical shooting skills at the subconscious level. For example, a decision-making skill developed in training might be turning toward the threat (posturing), and beginning a verbal command (tape loop) to an unknown person approaching you in a dark parking lot. The stimulus-response is: threat approaches and alerts you/posture, and begin verbal commands.

Now compare that to the subconscious act of drawing the gun and beginning to pull the trigger *during the shooting* when the proper stimulus has been received that warrants lethal force. This action might be purely subconscious at that point, since the decision to shoot has already been made. The stimulus-response is: visual recognition of a threat that has the means, opportunity, and intent *plus* (from the mechanical aspect of shooting) the correct alignment of the gun on the threat. The act of shooting during a lethal encounter will probably happen completely at the subconscious level (with a handgun at close range) once the decision to shoot has been made. It might also be noted that the actual decision to shoot may also happen unconsciously (pre-programmed) by previous training. An example of that would be someone who had been trained that a person (threat) who had a gun in his or her hand could raise it, fire and hit them faster than they could return fire and neutralize them.

I have a vivid memory of a time in the police academy when I was being taught how to do a car stop in Spanish. The Spanish teacher (a female police officer) was playing the role of the driver of the car I was stopping. During the stop, while I had her at gunpoint (red training gun only) and was giving commands in Spanish, she jumped out of the car with a gun held at her side. I continued commands while she failed to comply and she began to raise the gun toward me. Without any conscious thought whatsoever, I began to fire at her. It surprised me how quickly my subconscious took over and began to engage her based on previous training, while my conscious mind just sat there idly. The key is that the subconscious mind will automate actions much faster than the conscious mind, and that is a key to your survival. Writing correct subconscious skills programs will be a big part of this program, and will be broken down into skill developing drills (live and dry fire training), and mental training concepts (mental visualization, and imagined scenario training).

Controlling or mitigating the mental stress, pre-fight or during the fight

This is a matter of learning that the stress is going to happen, and learning that there are methods to help control it. None of us can completely avoid or make the stress go away, but there are things you can do to reduce it and its physical effects. A good example is to use *combat breathing* to reduce the heart rate as things are starting to get stressful. While this may not always be possible during a spontaneous attack, the technique works well if you have several minutes of recognition before it happens. Combat breathing techniques can also be used during a fight and directly afterward to reduce heart rate and stress levels. The bottom line is that controlling your heart rate will directly affect how you make decisions and operate, which is critical. The mental side of this equation pairs well with the physical side of training for a fight found in chapter four.

Developing a "mental toughness" that helps one continue to fight even when things get really bad

This part of mental preparation will primarily be done with visualization, but there are key physical parts of this process. An example is developing mental toughness and a never quit attitude during physical fitness training sessions. One place where you can really push yourself safely is during hard physical fitness sessions that tax the body to its limits. Elite athletes learn early on that their bodies often quit first, and that their mind is where the real strength lies. You must realize the same thing, and hard physical training is a great place to develop that mental toughness.

Another way to develop this mental toughness and "never quit" attitude is during skill training sessions with environmental factors that make training very tough. Extremely hot or cold temperatures might be a good example of a time when it takes real mental toughness to continue to train. During the physical preparation for the fight section in this book I will address training in combatives (martial arts, etc.). This is another area that will push you to your limits, and often times are the closest thing to a real fight that you can find.

Mental Training Routine

To develop the skills discussed, I have designed a mental training routine to help you prepare. The routine will be performed each time you train (and part of it during other times) and will increase your mental preparation for the fight, as well as your ability to perform under extreme pressure. Performing well after some practice at *your* range while you are *alone* is not a problem for most of us, but when we enter the extreme stress of "game day," things usually change. Most mental preparation material out there is great, but difficult to apply. I have taken the time to distill the best mental training tips I have found and incorporated them into this short mental toughness routine.[3,4,5] This is basically the same routine that I assign to shooting athletes who are training to win state and national titles. I have made some small modifications for the combative environment. Remember, mental preparation means being ready to make the decisions you will need to make under extreme stress, as well as having developed the skills necessary to ensure your survival. This mental training routine will address both areas. Before discussion of the program tools, I want to introduce some of the mental development fundamentals. I want to educate you about these principles before I give you the routine.

General Discussion/Introduction: "Theory of a Miss"

Some time ago, while trying to figure out why I was making mistakes while knowingly making them (observing the mistake happen yet not being able to stop it), I developed an idea called "theory of a miss." The term "theory of a miss" describes the mental system breakdown causing the common "miss" under stressful situations. "Miss" can certainly be used interchangeably with any mistake made during stress, but in this case I used the term because my mental errors caused me to miss the target. Most shooters understand the physical dynamics behind a mistake under stress, but few know the mental factors involved that led to the mistake, or how to correct them. This section will cover the material that will help you find the key to flawless performance (on demand) under extreme stress.

The Root of all Mistakes

The word mistake implies that a wrong decision has been made. The "miss" (i.e. mistake) in a stressful event happens at high speed, within the sub-conscious level of one's thought processes. Thus it can't be controlled, even though you may recognize you are making the error as you make it. Why can't it be controlled or stopped consciously? The same reason you type the incorrect password into your computer, while consciously knowing you are doing it right after you have changed it. The subconscious has automated that process because you do it so often,

---

[3] Lanny Bassham, <u>With Winning in Mind</u> (Wilsonville: BookPartners, Inc., 1995).
[4] Jason Selk, <u>10-Minute Toughness</u>, Vol. 1 (New York: McGraw-Hill, 2009).
[5] Gary Mack, <u>Mind Gym</u> (New York: Contemporary Books/McGraw-Hill, 2001).

and when you change it, the subconscious runs the old program. The subconscious mind is entering the information through your fingers and the conscious mind can't keep up!

Often times I observe shooters on the range repeatedly making mistakes that they consciously know about. Keep in mind that in relation to making a shooting error, if it happens, it did so likely because you have trained yourselves to make the error. When training repetitions are repeated multiple times a "program" (a process called *myelination*) is written into your subconscious to control those physical skills in the future. The root of this uncontrollable mistake is the subconscious mind and how it works. Let's take a closer look at the subconscious and conscious mind by comparing the conscious mind and subconscious mind (also called the unconscious by some):

Conscious and Subconscious, A Comparison

Comparing the subconscious mind and the conscious mind is like comparing an adult to a infant. The infant, prior to the age of about two, does not have the ability to differentiate between right and wrong. After the age of two, and increasing in age, children and adults have the ability to make decisions based on information at hand and can determine between right and wrong in general terms.

Now let's compare that to an infant, somewhere around the age of one. At that age, the infant has the ability to process and record information, but for many different reasons cannot assess whether the information is "right or wrong." The infant simply processes the information and records it for later use in life. The infant does not have the ability to screen that information and store the good stuff and reject the bad.

When comparing the conscious and subconscious portions of the brain, the conscious brain is like the adult. It has the ability to reason and reject incorrect information. The subconscious portion of the brain is like the infant, unable to reason or reject information. Each and every small detail is stored because it has such a capacity for knowledge (similar to an infant's brain that is stimulated more when it encounters more information). The conscious portion of the brain accomplishes analytical or logical thought processes. The subconscious portion of the brain accomplishes automated and automatic processes. Think about it, the last time you drove home, did you consciously have to think about turning on your blinker, or even hitting the brake? Probably not, as these actions are all handled with relative ease by the subconscious mind after being prompted by the conscious decision making process (see stop sign, decision to stop, hit the brake).

A Shooting Example: Some time ago as I was working with a shooting athlete at the range, I watched something that I've seen time and time again. I had very good shooter working on a drill that involved managing his trigger and sights on two types of targets, forcing him to utilize varying trigger and sight management in one string of fire. To accomplish this I had set up two targets at about five yards from the athlete and spread about two yards apart. In between those two targets, about twelve yards away, I had placed a small pepper popper. The drill was simple:

draw and fire two shots on the left paper target, one shot on the steel, and then two more shots on the other paper target, perform a reload, and repeat that array of targets with the same number of shots. To accomplish this task, the shooter would have to modify how he was pulling the trigger from the close paper target to the difficult shot require on the steel target.

This particular athlete was going to be repeating the drill approximately ten times. At about the fifth or sixth time, I stopped him and pointed out the fact that out of those six runs, he had fired two shots on the paper, one shot *at* the steel, two shots on the other paper all while missing the steel target each time. Sometimes he proceeded to make up his miss on the steel, and other times he didn't. When asked, the athlete had no problem telling my why he had missed the steel target repeatedly.

His Mistake: His mistake was a simple timing error coupled with poor sight alignment. The athlete could easily answer the question, "Why were you missing the piece of steel?" But what did not stand out to him was the fact that over those six repetitions he had already began to program his subconscious mind to perform a mistake. Think about it for a second, every time he fired at that piece of steel, he fired at it with either misaligned sights or a trigger pull that was incorrect. So visually, he must have seen something incorrect, and that visual input was transmitted through his optic nerves to his brain, which prompted him to do something, i.e. pull the trigger. He sees the sights, which keys his brain to continue to manipulate the trigger to the rear causing the gun to go off. The problem is that the sight alignment was incorrect and instead of fixing the issue he fired the shot.

This means that he was training the subconscious area of his brain to manipulate the trigger with the wrong visual stimulus. His subconscious mind did not understand that the sight picture and timing of the shot was wrong, although consciously he knew he was making a mistake. The problem is that now his subconscious mind had six repetitions of this improper technique written into it. When I asked him why he was missing the steel he replied, "Because the front sight is nowhere near the target!" "Well," I said to him, "if you have repeated that same sight picture six times in a row, or let's say for the sake of discussion one hundred times in a row during a given training session, then what are you training your subconscious mind to do?" He answered, "I guess I'm training myself to miss."

You see, even a simple drill in which we're firing at targets or a piece of steel can cause us to write the wrong program into our computer (subconscious). Once this program has been written it will take double the work to correct and rewrite it correctly. Remember, the act of repeating a skill allows us to improve that skill through a process called myelination.[6] This process coats the nerve pathways with a substance called myelin, which is a fatty substance that helps the nerve transmission travel faster. The more a skill is practiced, the faster that nerve transmission is, hence the improvement that comes from repetitions of any skill.

The big problem is that once a nerve becomes coated with myelin, it cannot be "unmyelinated," and the only way to correct a bad habit, is to create (myelination) a new and

---

[6] Daniel Coyle, <u>The Talent Code</u> (New York: Bantam Dell, 2009).

stronger habit. So, if the initial skill took five thousand repetitions to write (myelination), then the new one will take at least that many and then more so that it becomes the primary path that is selected to run a skill. Now this shooter went through multiple repetitions of missing the steel, and as I have discussed, this trained him to miss.

Another problem is that if he missed a piece of steel during training on a regular basis, what do you think that did to his self-image? It could create a negative self-image and belief that he cannot hit a piece of steel of that size at that distance. Imagine what a training scar like that would cause in relation to a gunfight!

Subconscious Skills

The example discusses above speaks to the critical importance of training the subconscious to execute correct skills with proper stimulus. In this section it is important you understand more about that how the subconscious works. One great author[7] calls the subconscious part of the mind the "skills factory," and rightly so. The subconscious portion of the mind is where key components of a specific skill set are stored for use in an automated fashion. This includes common repetitive tasks such as those related to driving a car; along with skills that might be part of your self-defense plan (i.e. shooting a gun).

Ingraining skill happens at the subconscious level, and is necessary in order for you to perform complex movements at extremely fast speeds. If you are training for a fight, then the correct response under stress is obviously very important. When you build subconscious skills you are in essence writing "skill programs." Performing a complex skill at high speed requires subconscious skill programs because the conscious mind can't accomplish such tasks.

The programs that the subconscious will draw from are all written during your training sessions. These small programs will run all or portions of a skill from start to finish as dictated by a conscious thought (information processing). In the sports world it has been said that the best performances are completely subconscious, but the truth is that the conscious and subconscious minds work together in concert to solve problems. A gunfight is a perfect example. We must have the ability to make decisions consciously (communicate, observe, decide to fire, etc.), and then execute skills subconsciously once the decision has been made to act.

The truth is that the decisive thought process and sub-conscious must be in concert. A strong balance of conscious decision making combined with properly ingrained skill program combinations will help you survive a lethal encounter.

Self Image

Your self-image is who you believe you are. Your self-image dictates your level of confidence or lack thereof in your ability to act a certain way or do certain things. It is built as a result of your life experiences. It is one of the most powerful things you can manipulate in your

---

[7] Lanny Bassham, <u>With Winning in Mind</u> (Wilsonville: BookPartners, Inc., 1995).

training that will impact your performances in a positive manner. Your self-image will cause you to believe in yourself or not. Thus it creates an emotional state that is either positive or negative. While the actual beliefs in your self-image are important, I don't believe that they alone affect your performance. Think about it for a second, what you believe doesn't literally affect the outcome of a performance. The *emotions* you experience <u>because</u> of your beliefs *do* affect the outcome, because your emotional state will actually change the physical state the body is in. Let me explain more about what I mean by emotional state.

Emotional State

Your "emotional state" is the mental condition you are in when performing a set of complex tasks. It is the often-overlooked piece of the puzzle in the competitive world that truly paints the picture of whether a performance was true and repeatable, or just luck. Those top shooters who perform well, in what some call "the zone," do it while they are in a positive emotional state. They feel confident and in control. I feel that this emotional state, while less controlled, will have the same impact during a fight. I have found elements of this theory in my own experiences and almost every single training resource I have ever read or interview I have done. Elite athletes and top shooters call it "being in the zone,"- gunfighters call it "coolness under pressure." Either way, it is an emotional state where the individual feels in control, relatively relaxed (as much as can be experienced during a fight), and in the moment. Eliminating negative emotional triggers and creating a positive emotional state is largely the goal of mental training, and what I believe to be the true secret of performing well. I pay particular attention to my emotional state (control zones) when training and performing.

You might be wondering how you can have this level of control during a lethal encounter. I admit the environment is much less controlled than a sporting event. But I also know that with the right training one can increase their ability to stay in a positive mental control zone and maintain that level of coolness. When doing research for this book, I found many different cases of individuals involved in multiple gun battles, as well as physical confrontations. The one common denominator in their assessment of their performances during the fight was that they believed the factor that led to their success was "coolness" under pressure and their ability to keep from getting rattled. Where did they get this coolness under pressure? They got it from their training, as well as previous experiences. One thing you will find is that almost 100% of warriors who have been in numerous battles hone their ability to be cool under pressure as they add those experiences. So how to we mere mortals develop it if we have not been in a dozen gun battles in Mogadishu or the streets of New York? Luckily the mind can be trained to believe it has experienced something without ever doing it by the use of vivid visualizations (imagining) of the scenario. I will discuss the use of passive and active visualization later in this chapter. Additionally, the use of scenario or integrated type training with real role players is a great way to develop this experience without having to pick a dozen gunfights with terrorists in Baghdad.

I believe this is the same concept as attempting to stay in a positive mental state when performing. Don't confuse nervousness with negativity by the way, as many shooters perform exceptionally well when they are nervous and/or scared. Obviously there is going to be fear and nervousness experienced in a fight and I have not found a single person that has been in a gunfight or any kind of a fight that had told me they did not feel some nervousness or fear during that fight. They simply controlled it and operated within that chaos of nerves and fear. The really experienced individuals tend to feel calmer as the number of incidents they are involved in increase. This is simply a process of them building confidence in their abilities and learning how to maintain a positive (in control) emotional state during the fight.

It is very possible to program the brain and convince the self-image to believe that your best performances are when you are nervous or scared, while at the same time feeling in control. During the visualization section, I will address visualizing your own fear, yet operating well within it to build this mental response when the real deal happens. Emotional triggers can be either positive or negative and will result in a corresponding emotional state. Common negative emotional triggers are as follows:

- *First Experience Memories*: These are memories created during your first experience(s) of a particular event. Those new to shooting often feel an incredible amount of stress and anxiety during their first range session. This occurs because of a lack of self-confidence in their ability. In our first experiences we will often see things that seem to be repeatable and "easy," but they are far from that. This is also the case for those in law enforcement and the military that have never shot before and have watched most of the shooting they have ever seen on T.V. They watch actors do things with guns that are unlikely and actually wrong and then try to repeat this skill. When they fail the first time at the qualification range, then this first experience might be a serious negative emotional trigger during a time when they need to use their firearm in the line of duty. The only way to fix first experience memories is to override the experience with positive ones. Sometimes, this memory or experience is so strong that it is carried with us for years. This trigger can be overcome by experience and skill development. Positive self-talk can aid in reducing this effect on performance, but hard work and developing the skills is the solution. You can't lie to yourself about your performance. If you are reading this book and have some negative first experience memories and might have to rely on your skill with your firearm to save your life, please take the steps to fix this immediately.
- *Self-Image*: Your own self-image is a huge emotional trigger that can have catastrophic effects on your performance. "Getting over" ourselves is sometimes the hardest thing to do. A poor self-image is largely a result of previous failures, or more so the lack of self-forgiveness. Shooters should hold themselves accountable for their mistakes and take corrective action via hard work, not self-punishment. You must take every step necessary to build up a self-image that says you can succeed when the time comes. Unfortunately, many of today's law enforcement officers that end up barely qualifying with their firearm know that they do not

have the skills they need to survive, and are in my opinion a ticking time bomb in relation to using their weapon in the line of duty. When you punish yourself internally and hold yourself to impossibly high standards of perfection, you set yourself up for failure. Self-image is the key to unlocking full potential, and without a strong self-image individuals may do well but will never do their best. Keys to building a positive self-image are positive visualizations, self-talk, and most importantly, self-forgiveness and an aggressive attitude toward skill development. Mistakes happen - get over them and find solutions to the errors. Look at a mistake as an opportunity to learn "why" something happened and improve.

- *Fear of Failure*: This is probably the most common emotional trigger and it is linked directly to self-image. The fear of failure resides deep in most competitive individuals and stems from a mentality that failure is not an option. We develop a fear of failure because we have all failed at one time or another and it is disturbing. Realistically, a fear of failure can be tamed by changing the way an individual thinks. Failure to accomplish a certain goal or level can be looked at as something so positive and powerful that, if used correctly, will drive them to certain success. Here is the key: failure must be understood as the single propellant that has driven all great successes to the levels they reached. If failure is experienced during training, then this is the best place for it to happen right? You would certainly rather fail during training and correct the problem than fail during the fight. I have yet to find a person, company, or story of a great success without repeated failures first, sometimes hundreds of failures! The key is to change the way you think, and continue to move forward.

- *Laziness*: Laziness may not seem like a common emotional trigger but it is. Laziness in a training program results in lack of self-confidence. Those that do the work deserve to reap the rewards, and when an individual slacks on their training they cause internal doubt to start growing inside the recesses of their mind. The only cure to this emotional trigger is the work. When an individual does their homework and has put in the time, they will have an incredible amount of confidence when placed in a situation where a high level of performance is required.

Training for Emotional Control

In order to rebuild emotional control and place yourself in a positive emotional control zone, there are several key steps you can follow. Remember, learning emotional control is a key part of the personal improvement process of learning how to do anything in control. Here are some things that you can do to learn or rebuild how to place yourself in a positive emotional control zone:

- *Do the Work*. Nothing puts us in a better emotional state than solid preparation. The only person you cannot lie to is you. If you have done your homework and prepared well then that is the first step in placing yourself in a positive emotional state and boosting your self-image. This entire book is about developing your skill through well-designed training sessions that will allow you to excel. You can check this box if you are reading, learning, and acting on the guidance you have read. Doing the work facilitates physical performance and in turn also builds mental confidence under stress.

- *Acceptance.* Accept that there may be some setbacks when trying to un-train certain negative processes. Just taking the time to slow down and learning to perform techniques in control is incredibly difficult. I spend most of my time on drills that twist my brain in knots because I mix easy and hard shooting skills together, and then I force myself to slow down enough to perform the technique I am working on correctly. If you are training for combative purposes you may actually have a do-or-die performance standard, but if you allow it to dominate your mind you will not perform at your best. If you have done the work (step one), then don't worry; your performance will match your preparation.

- *Baby Steps.* Take one step at a time when rebuilding emotional control. Start by fixing practice routines so that they build proper skills and thus confidence. Move to applying those skills in practice scenarios and mini-tests, always striving for the emotional state of being in control, even while under extreme stress. Further that by applying those learned skills and emotional zones during small training exercises that simulate the real event with N.L.T.A. (Non-Lethal Training Ammunition) and then graduate up the chain all the way through to game day. The point is, use the crawl-walk-run principle.

- *Positive Self-Talk.* One of the best ways to retrain your brain and turn a negative primer into a positive one is to change your self-talk. It is believed that we have tens of thousands of conversations of self-talk each day. Imagine if you used these self-talk conversations for positive purposes.

- *Expanding your Control Zones.* When you are training, "expanding your control zone" should be your primary goal. This simply means that you should be working on executing a given technique as fast as you can perform the skill correctly, while maintaining a measured level of accuracy (depending on the mission/situation you are training for). Then during training repetitions of a given drill, push the pace and attempt to perform the skill correctly.

Mental toughness

Mental toughness is a term I have heard throughout the years as I have competed against the best shooters on the circuit or from elite level operators that know if they make a mistake they could cost someone their life. You also hear this term on a regular basis on sports shows when announcers are talking about the ability of some of the great players to perform when the pressure is overwhelming. Mental toughness is primarily made up of confidence acquired through training, which is critical if you want to succeed. Whether you want to win a sporting event or survive a combative situation, you will need to be mentally tough to succeed. Anyone of us can perform well when we are at the practice range; the trick is to keep those skills honed to a degree required to ensure success in the high-pressure arne. You will develop mental toughness in this program by doing a mental training routine each time you train that includes things such as perfect execution of the drills (to develop confidence in your skills), visualizing yourself succeeding (to develop confidence in your abilities under pressure), and focusing on positive images and using positive words (to put and keep yourself in a positive mental state).

Mental connection

The term "mental connection" means that you have to commit to connecting mentally with every skill you train in practice, thus improving your ability to ingrain the skill properly and completely. *One of the biggest mistakes I see people make when training is that they go through the motions during their training drills, instead of mentally connecting with each and every repetition.* To get mentally connected in this program, you will perform active visualization exercises during your practice sessions. There are key points included on each training drill sheet that will remind you of the technique, visual, and mental skills that are important during that drill. Pay attention and use them and this will maximize your learning experience. If the learning occurs properly, then the subconscious skill programs will be developed right, and applying them on-demand and under pressure will be second nature. When I train, often times I push myself to the point where I make mistakes. This is intentional, because I want to find the limits of my performance. When this happens though, or even if I find myself making a small error, my first step to fixing the mistake is to stop and mentally "connect" to it via visualization (I will cover visualization later in this chapter). Before I attempt to do it correctly physically, I mentally fix the mistake, and then begin the training drill again. This mental connection really improves my ability to fine tune a skill or fix a mistake. Try it the next time you are at the range.

Your Mental Training Routine[8,9]

The following routine can be done as one short 10-15 minute routine, or can be done in pieces. I want you to follow this routine before your live and dry fire training sessions. You will also use the passive visualization techniques outside of training sessions (really any time you want - the more the better). Following this mental routine before and during training sessions will ensure you build mental toughness each time you train. There are four main components to your mental routine are: the *focus breath/combat breath cycle*, *performance statement*, and *visualization techniques* (active and passive). Each of these components will be written onto 3x5 cards that you place in your range bag, or training areas as a reminder to go through your mental routine each time you train. I recommend getting some 3x5 cards ready now, as you will be using them soon.

---

[8] Jason Selk, <u>10-Minute Toughness</u> (New York: McGraw-Hill, 2004).
[9] Lanny Basham, <u>With Winning in Mind</u> (Wilsonville: BookPartners, Inc., n.d.).

Lets break each component down:

Utilize The Focus Breath/Combat Breathing Cycle to lower your heart rate. This breathing technique will allow you to control your heart rate and stress levels. It is obviously not going to be something that you will have time to do if you are spontaneously attacked, but it is incredibly valuable in times when a fight might be imminent and predicted, during the fight, or after the attack has occurred. I originally learned "combat breathing" from a martial art instructor who used the technique to focus his mind and lower his heart rate before and during sparring matches.

Normally, arousal level and heart rate will increase when you feel stress due to the physiological design of the body. An increased heart rate increases the blood flow to major muscle groups, and allows increased strength to facilitate "fight or flight". For example, if I told you to shoot and hit a head shot on a threat target(s) target at five yards, most of you could do it easily and your heart rate would probably stay pretty close to your resting heart rate levels. However, if I took your five-year-old child or significant other and had them stand very close to the target you were shooting at, do you think your heart rate would increase? Of course it would, even though the shot was exactly the same. Because of the potential risk to your child you would place much more importance on that shot for fear of hitting the wrong target.

When you feel stress, your heart rate increases and this can impede performance. While an increased heart rate is not always a bad thing, as some heart rate increase is important to perform well. The problem is that too much of an increase decreases performance. Visual skills, fine motor skills, decision-making skills, etc., have all been shown to degrade. This normally begins to happen when you increase your heart rate to more than about 200% of your resting heart rate. The following chart shows how the heart rate affects performance. The numbers on the left are the heart rate. Resting heart rate is probably around 50-70 beats per minute, and as you can see too low for good performance. The performance zone is about 110 bpm up to 140 or so, and anything above 150 causes skills to begin to seriously degrade. Heart rates above 170 may cause irrational behavior and serious deterioration of fine and complex motor skills.[10]

See the chart on the following pages for a visual on heart rate and performance.

---

[10] Bruce K. Siddle, <u>Sharpening The Warriors Edge</u> (Belleville: PPCT Research Publications, 1995).

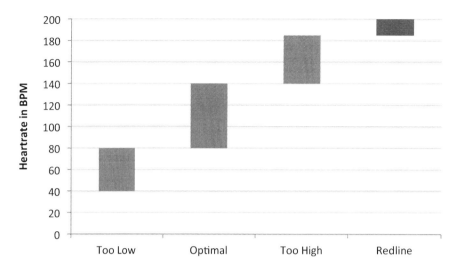

Figure 27: Heart rate and Performance

So how do you control and lower your heart rate? The answer is simpler than you might imagine. Just breath! More specifically, use a certain type of breath pattern and technique to begin to lower your heart rate. When would you use the technique in relation to a fight? Anytime you can - before, during, and even after the fight. Imagine yourself in the Wal-Mart parking lot with a man approaching that is obviously not right. As he approaches you notice his hand inside his coat pocket, and the look on his face tells you he means to do you harm. You begin to raise your hands and give verbal and physical cues for him to keep their distance, but they keep coming. Do you think your heart rate is going to rise due to fear? You bet it will. Now is the time to begin to control it.

When the situation first began and you realized that the man was probably intent on doing you harm, you could have been going through your combat breathing cycle. How will you remember to do this and allow it to become instinctive? Because you will do it during your training sessions and this will allow you to ingrain the technique for use anytime you are in pre-fight mode.

Remember, we are going to train these things regularly, so following this "routine" will be second nature if you practice it. After the fight (that you WILL win), you will be beat up and breathing hard. Now is the time to stay cool and think clearly. So once again your combat breathing cycles will help you regain the balance you might need during that stressful time. Other than lowering the heart rate and stress to a manageable level, a great side benefit to these exercises is better oxygenation of the blood. Oxygenated blood helps one's reaction time and visual skills, as these systems all rely on higher oxygen levels in the blood. The more you practice this technique, the better it will work when you need to call upon it in stressful situations.

Here is how it works:
- *Breathe through the nose (if possible).* Breathing through the nose is key to lowering your heart rate. For several reasons, when you breathe through the nose you automatically

begin to lower your heart rate, because your body is designed to breathe through the nasal cavity versus the mouth. Mouth breathing causes a variety of stress related responses because during a fight or flight response, humans tend to breathe through the mouth to get more oxygen and activate their survival instincts that are designed to increase gross motor function and heart rate

- *Breathe deep from the diaphragm.* Diaphragm breathing requires very deep breaths, which allows the diaphragm to expand. Sometimes this is called "belly breathing." When you do it right your belly tends to expand rather than your chest expanding, which is what most of us do when we breathe. The truth is that most of us breathe wrong. To increase your success in breathing with the diaphragm, you will use a technique that forces you to breathe deeply and fill the lower lobes of the lungs with oxygen. To do this, you will do one of the following breathing cycles selecting either the 4-4-4 or the 6-2-6 pattern. Here is an example of using the 6-2-6 pattern:
    o *Inhale for a count of 5-6 seconds (through the nose)*
    o *Hold the breath for a count of 2 seconds*
    o *Exhale for a count of 5-6 seconds (through the nose)*
    o *Repeat this pattern as many times as necessary*
    o *Note: make sure to let your belly expand when you do this as this helps you breathe with your diaphragm (hence the term belly breathing)*
    o *An alternate to the 6-2-6 cycle is to use the 4-4-4 cycle which would be done by inhaling for 4, holding for 4, exhaling for 4, holding for 4, etc. This cycle might be more applicable during physical activity such as a fight, and will help you keep yourself from hyperventilating.*
    o *Really force the air deeply into and out of your lungs and be careful not to hyperventilate.*

This long 12-15 second breath circuit will force you to breathe deep, if you follow it correctly. It will lower your heart rate and increase your fine motor functions. It will also oxygenate your blood and increase your information processing and visual skills. Once again, you will need to master and practice this during training repetitively in order for it to work while you are under stress.

Your task… write the following on the top of one of your 3x5 cards: *Focus Breath 6-2-6 or 4-4-4*

Develop a performance statement that will help you control your thoughts under stress

Your *performance statement* is a short, powerful statement that will keep you in the present and remind you of what you have to do to succeed. More specifically, your *performance statement* is a simple and concrete statement that will help you control your thoughts under pressure. This will help keep you in a positive emotional state. I strongly believe in using a performance statement in the competitive environment, and hesitated teaching it in this book but then realized the concept was at least as, if not more important for a fight. I believe this because during a lethal encounter, most of us will experience short random thoughts where our brain is searching for solutions to the problem at hand. The higher the stress level, the more random the thought process might be. The use of a performance statement will help center you and reduce the stress you feel as well as remind you of key actions that might be important. Once again, this statement is probably best used in the pre-fight timeframe, but I think it can be used anytime, even during the fight itself.

A perfect example happened to me the other day during some training I was doing with one of the instructors I work with. We were working on combative techniques, specifically ground techniques. My training partner is better than I am and caught me in a chokehold. I thought I was done but I remember thinking, "relax and breathe," which is my performance statement in defensive situations as I tried to fight my way out of the hold. I escaped. Now, I am not saying that using my performance statement allowed me to escape. It simply focused my mind and calmed me down for a second during a time where I wanted to panic and tap out. If you are in a fight for your life, "tapping out" will not be an option.

My statement, "relax and breathe," is simple and reminds me to do the two most important things during a fight: *relax,* so I don't use all my energy and burn out and *breath,* which is critically important to keep the oxygen levels in my blood up and reduce or control my heart rate. Most importantly, since I use this performance statement all the time in training, it helped center my mind and bring some positive emotional control into a situation where I was choking and about to panic. Your performance statement should be used regularly in training, to build the habit of controlling your thoughts and focusing. When you use your statement try to visualize yourself executing what you need to do to be successful.

Your Task: To write your *Performance Statement*, do the following:

Ask yourself what the two or three most important things are that you will need to do in order to perform under stress. Think about what a good instructor, coach, or mentor may tell you to get you through a high-pressure situation. Take a piece of paper and write those two or three things down. If you have more than three, go ahead and list them all. Now take that list and form those things into a statement that will simply remind you what to focus on under pressure. Your statement should be short and to the point, with no more than two to three key action sentences or words. What do you need to tell yourself to survive?

Once developed, you will use your performance statement(s) during training and high-pressure events to control your thoughts and focus your mental state. For now, go ahead and write it down on your 3x5 index card, right below where you wrote your focus breath details. Title your card: "*Performance Statement*". During training take your index card out and remind yourself of what your statement is. Take a moment to visualize yourself doing the things in your statement. Imagine how you will feel during your high stress encounter and envision the control your statement gives you. Remember the mental connection you are trying to create during training. Make a habit of reciting your *performance statement* during training, especially when you are pushing yourself and things are getting tough.

Visualization Techniques

Visualization is mental imagery. Seeing yourself doing something before you do it is an incredibly powerful tool, and is one that I see neglected by many shooters out there. There are two types of visualization: *active* and *passive,* and they both have a different purpose and timeframe for use. How will visualization help you? It will help with that "mental connection" to the drill while you do it, and if you incorporate realistic visualizations during your training, your brain will have a familiarity with whatever you imagine. Think about it. What if you could prepare for a real fight with hundreds of practice fights first? You would really be ready for the real thing, which is why I strongly advocate the use of visualization during your training. So how will visualization be applicable in real world self-defense situations? It can help you in two key areas. The first is to increase your training effectiveness and "mental connection" by giving you a tool to visualize all or portions of your training drills before you do them. This will increase your mental connection to the drill, and enhance learning. I actually use visualization during my training to correct mistakes I am making if I catch an error during a drill. I simply repeat the visualization of me performing the skill correctly in my mind before repeating the drill again. Secondly, proper use of visualization will allow you to experience a lethal encounter before it actually happens.

Operationally an example of this process might be visualizing and creating that same "pathway" for a future high stress situation, and running a successful outcome in your mind over and over. A great example of using active visualization during a real world event would be a time I used it during an extremely high-risk arrest on a drug trafficker while I worked for the Knoxville Police Department. We had been assigned to assist a Federal agency on a take down that involved a suspect with a large, powerful truck. The suspect was to have a large amount of cash from an undercover agent who was purchasing narcotics from him. The suspect was also know to be heavily armed, and likely to flee, using his large vehicle to ram police cars. I was assigned as a blocking vehicle, and armed with a shotgun. My role was to place my S.U.V. police vehicle literally against the front bumper on a key signal, and then deploy my shotgun and give cover until other officers could arrest him. This required a complicated process of waiting for the signal, and then driving at high speeds right up to the suspect's vehicle without crashing into it and then positioning myself with the shotgun. If I failed any task, I might allow the suspect to flee, or worse get shot if I did not deploy the shotgun and provide good cover. I can remember sitting in my vehicle for an hour waiting on the signal, all while rehearsing the entire sequence in my mind: "Signal, accelerate, brake, shift to park, door, shotgun safety." It may not sound complicated to you, but believe me there were a bunch of moving parts. In the end, my actions and the arrest went perfectly. The suspect never had the chance to move his vehicle due to our blocking actions, and I hope my shotgun, deployed in quick order, helped him make the decision to go back to prison versus shoot it out. Visualization worked great during that event.

The next level in visualization techniques is to envision the same scenario, and add the "if-then" variations, which means that you would run visualizations of what you would as the situation played out differently. "If-then" is simply a process of programming that *if* X happens, *then* you will react this way (whatever the proper reaction is). I have spoken to several elite pilots and tactical team members who use the skill of visualization to improve their chances in a high-speed fight or room entry. If they can employ it effectively and feel it is worth their time, then I think it is of great benefit for you.

Professional shooters have two primary reasons for doing visualization. First, they use it to help them remember and follow through better with their plan on the stage. Second, they visualize themselves performing well which increases their performance on the stage, even though they have never shot that specific stage before. Your see, the brain will follow a visualized "mapped" route much more efficiently than an unplanned (un-mapped) process. This means that every time you visualize something, your brain treats the visualized experience as if it were real. It gains an "experience" each time you use a vivid visualization, and this experience is one of the things it will draw from during a lethal encounter.

Active Visualization:

- Active visualization is mental imagery that should be used when you are actually training. It should be used to increase your mental connection to what you are doing, and in most cases will be best used during training. Every one of the professional shooters I surveyed for my other book (Your Competition Handgun Training Program) used visualization techniques in training and during competition. What do they know that the average shooter can learn from? They know that the mind is a very powerful tool, and that they can increase their chances of success when performing if they can see themselves successfully do something, before they physically do it.
- *Use the first person view.* This means that you should visualize as if your eyes are cameras and you are watching the action through these cameras.
- *Use all the senses.* When you visualize, you should visualize more than just visual input. Visualize information such as touch, sound, smell, and yourself experiencing emotion while performing the actions. Visualizing your emotion during the shooting is important because it will allow you to visualize yourself performing while still feeling calm and in control. Emotion is the one area most miss when they visualize.
- *Visualize at the correct speed.* This is critical, and is something that can really hurt you if you do it wrong. Your subconscious mind does not know the difference between what happens in visualization and reality. Therefore, if you see yourself doing something at the wrong speed, you will likely perform the action at the speed you saw yourself doing it. Make sure you visualize yourself doing the action the same speed that you really want to do it.
- *See the skill from start to finish.* If you are visualizing a drill in training, see yourself doing it from start to finish, which may include your post engagement actions such as the scan process. This will increase the reality of your visualizations, and the learning experience it will create.

- *Pay attention to the details.* Similar to the speed concept above, remember that you really need to pay attention to what you visualize. Your brain will learn and repeat what you program into it. Make sure you visualize all details correctly.

Using Active Visualization in this Program:

- *Actively visualize each drill repetition before you do it.* This is for both dry fire practice and live fire drills. This might be new to you and you will have to make yourself do it at first. Write it in your training logs as a reminder if you need to. Make absolutely sure you visualize all drills before you do them. If you make a mistake during a drill, stop and take the time to visualize yourself doing that particular action right several times before you do the next drill. I always tell my students to "See yourself do it, then do it". Your training sessions should look like this: visualize it, do it, visualize it, do it, etc.
- *Actively visualize a scenario, as you are shooting.* This means that instead of just shooting at paper during your training sessions, you should convince yourself that you are engaging a human threat that is attempting to take your life, or the lives of others. Make it as real as possible, and use realistic targets. These two things combined will lessen the "surprise" effect that actually pointing your gun at someone and pulling the trigger may cause. Remember, you are training to do the opposite of what most of your actions have taught you. I'm talking about violating rule one: *never point a gun at something you are not willing to destroy.* The more you visualize the entire scenario and make it seem real in training, the more your mind will be prepared to deal with the real situation. Remember, your subconscious mind does not know the difference between a vivid visualization, and the real thing.

> *Key tip:* *If you are a member of a unit/team/etc. that plans out operations in advance, use the details of that operation in visualization and run it multiple times before the event. I have used this technique in a team setting and verbalized the plan, while running an internal video of the upcoming event. This will ensure you will perform better due to mental preparation and the positive effect it will have on your actions. Take what the professional shooters use for each game and apply it to your world!*

Passive Visualization

Passive visualization is more about self-image and mental preparation than a direct memory or performance tool like active visualization. Your use of passive visualization will be different than active in that you can do passive visualization anytime, anywhere. In this program I want you to do a short passive visualization exercise each time before you train, and you will also do at least one visualization per day during your normal life activities.

Passive visualization is best done in a combination of first person and second person views. First person is like viewing what the action would look like through your eyes. Second person would be watching yourself perform from the perspective of having someone else take a video of you. I recommend using both angles in whatever manner that seems to come natural to you.

I want you to create your own *success visualization* (like a video in your mind), and here are the steps to doing it:

- *First, create a series of "success videos" of yourself.* These success videos should be of situations you may encounter in different environments. Here are some examples:
    - A lethal encounter in or around your home such as a home invasion by armed intruders.
    - A lethal encounter in or around your vehicle, such as a carjacking by armed intruders.
    - A lethal encounter in or around your place of employment or another key area of your choice.
- Key details of each clip: Each clip will be 30-60 seconds in length, and you should see yourself in a positive manner, performing all actions exceptionally well during the three scenarios. Each clip should be a complete scenario of someone attempting to harm you or a loved on in the key areas outlined above. Why those areas? Because statistically you will spend more time in them than anywhere else. I am also going to ask you to create and visualize yourself in a lethal encounter in one of those three areas once per day. Each visualization should be as detailed as possible, and include every detail that you can imagine about the incident. Make sure you follow the rules of experiencing emotion, sounds, smells, etc. Try to think of all of the elements that you would find important during a lethal encounter and include that in your scenario. For example, if a good tactic for your home defense plan is to use a key area or angle for cover against an armed intruder, see yourself moving to and using that area. The important part: Visualize yourself succeeding each time and performing extremely well. See yourself executing your tactical procedures, shooting techniques and following through all concepts perfectly. Make sure you visualize your calmness under pressure. The total time spent doing this can be well under 3-5 minutes, but if you have more time, feel free to really create a powerful video and mentally view it several times. Visualize yourself surviving the encounter.
- *Now, write a couple bullet points about each clip* in your success video on the same 3x5 card that has your *focus breath*, *performance statement*, and *self-image booster* on it. You might want to write this on the back, so you can be relatively detailed about it.

<u>Bad Day</u> - *Run one "bad day" scenario a couple times per week.* For this visualization, I recommend picking a location other than the three you use during your training sessions, and include a scenario of some sort of injury. What I want you to accomplish is seeing yourself fighting through an injury and prevailing. See yourself winning the fight no matter what, no matter how bad things seem.

By now you should have developed a performance statement, self-image booster, and mental success videos including a "bad day" scenario. They, along with a quick reminder about your focus breath should be written on a 3X5 card. I recommend duplicating a few of these cards, and placing them in your other training areas, and one in your car in case you forget one. Place one in your dry fire area too. When you find it, you will use it to go through your mental routine, and use the mental tools during your training session's. Use these tools consistently along with the other mental tips in this section and you will be well on your way to some serious mental toughness.

Chapter Summary and Action steps:

1. Use a special breathing technique to lower your heart rate and arousal state, increasing your fine and complex motor skills:
    a. Before each training session you will go through at least one repetition of the 6 in/ 2 hold / 6 out breath (or 4/4/4 cycle), through the nose.
    b. Every time you feel stress, an increased heart rate or heightened arousal state, whether before, during or after high-stress events (especially fights), remember that you can use your focus breath to control yourself.
    c. Any other time you want to lower your heart rate and increase the mental connection.
2. Create a performance statement that will give you something simple and concrete to think about before and during high stress situations:
    a. Read or say it before repetitions, or during training to increase the effectiveness of it while under stress. Use your statement in conjunction with your breathing cycles.
    b. Use it anytime you feel negative thoughts coming into your mind. Repeat it as many times as necessary to keep yourself calm and focused.
3. Use active visualizations any time you train to increase your ability to execute drills and stages better. Consider using active visualizations during real world events if you have the opportunity.
4. Use passive visualizations each time you read your self-image booster by running your success video and bad day scenario in your mind. Always see yourself "winning the fight."

CHAPTER 5

Physical Preparation For The Fight

Good mental preparation is critical, but lacking without a commitment to the physical side of the equation. Simply practicing with a rifle is physically hard, so consider what fighting with one might be like if your heart rate doubles due to stress and adrenaline. Now add a physical fight for your life, long sprint, or positions that are physically hard and imagine what your heart rate would be then? The point is that each of us has the ability to improve our fitness levels. This chapter will get you started.

Covered in this chapter:

1. *Wake Up Call*
2. *Fighting Fitness*
3. *Fighting Fitness Attributes*
4. *Fitness Program Recommendations*

Wake up call

This chapter may serve as a wake up call to some of you. It will also be non-traditional in nature, and I will give you my realistic recommendations on getting fit, and staying fit for the fight. To put it bluntly, if you are one of those people that think you will just be able to "shoot someone" if someone threatens you, think again. I have been exposed to far too many concealed carry holders who pay little or no attention to fitness, because they carry a gun. They argue that the gun they carry is the great equalizer, and will even the odds. Unfortunately if those same individuals are involved in a fight for their life, and the situation begins by someone punching them in the face or grabbing them, they might realize that accessing a firearm is very tough, or nearly impossible.

Even in situations where there is no physical contact with the threat, most gunfights are physically taxing from the stress. The point is that if you plan to carry and defend yourself with a rifle, and fail to take the act of getting physically fit serious, you might lose. I have met and trained with some of America's elite warriors, both in law enforcement and the military and one thing that I have found in common is their fitness level. These guys and gals are fit, and they work on their fitness daily. Fitness is critical to your survival. If you have not addressed your own fitness level, consider this your wake up call.

General Concepts / Physical Fitness Basics

The training program in this book is designed to increase your ability to perform well in a fight for your life. One of the things that I want you to incorporate is physical fitness in your training program. As stated above, I believe strongly in the benefits of physical fitness for any activity and I guarantee that you will increase your chances of survival if you are physically fit. In this section I will discuss some of the basic elements of physical fitness. I will also attempt to utilize this space to teach you about the elements of physical fitness that are important to your shooting goals. I do strongly recommend that you seek other books and resources on improving your physical fitness to the highest levels possible.

Definition: Fighting Fitness Vs. Traditional Fitness

Hopefully you're sold on getting fit, and have a desire to travel down that path. How do you develop your fitness for a fight, and what is important? In today's age there seems to be a new fitness gimmick or workout that comes out every day, but most are simply repackaged materials that you could have found fifty years ago. Some experts believe that the most significant fitness strides in history were made during the 80's, especially in the competitive arenas like powerlifting. I have experimented with a variety of workout programs and exercises and will recommend some things that I have found to work. One thing that I want to point out is the fact that exercise alone will not give you what you need. In order to be truly prepared, you need to learn how to fight. This means finding someone who can teach you the basics of physical self-defense. If you follow my recommendations, you will gain a significant level of fitness development *during* combatives training, without doing traditional exercise.

Figure 28 Spend time doing truly "functional fitness" like striking a heavy bag or strike dummy. The results will both accomplish your cardio goals, and let you work a skill at the same time.

Most people interested in getting in shape approach fitness like this: Build a base of strength, flexibility and cardiovascular fitness in the gym, often with bodybuilding type movements and _then_ supplement that base with combative/martial arts training. I am going to recommend the opposite: Build a base of strength, flexibility, and cardiovascular (cardio) fitness that is directly relevant to fighting as well as inclusive of technique (by training in combatives), and then balance/supplement that with strength training exercises and a focus on flexibility. The key word in that last sentence is "strength," more on that later in this chapter. Also, notice that I did not include cardiovascular fitness as a supplemental exercise, simply because you will develop a high level of cardiovascular fitness during your combative training. If your idea of cardiovascular fitness is standard cardiovascular exercise done on a machine, I strongly recommend selling the elliptical or treadmill and buying a heavy bag instead. Try punching a bag for thirty second intervals with short rest periods in between rounds for 25-40 minutes and you will get a great cardio workout that benefits you much more than running on a treadmill.

To put it bluntly, I can take someone who is really fit and strong from traditional methods of exercise and place them in a three-minute round of medium intensity sparring and they will be extremely exhausted at the end of it. Some won't even be able to last the three minutes, and will gas around the midway point. There is a big difference between a medium intensity sparring session and a real fight, so imagine how fast a fit person will become exhausted during the real thing. The person with no fitness level at all has really no chance unless the fight ends extremely fast.

One thing that really stands out to me is how different fighting fitness is from traditional fitness. Consider this example: over the years at different times I have suspended my combative training and maintained my fitness through a variety of exercises and programs. Even at my fittest levels, when I get back to combative training, I am always amazed at how fast I get tired and "redline" while doing drills or sparring. What does this mean? It means that maintaining a level of fighting fitness requires prioritizing those methods and sticking to what best effects the end result, i.e. if you are training to fight-fight in your training. In my opinion, this is the true definition of "functional fitness."

Figure 29 Tire slams with a 10lb sledge are non-traditional, but build incredible grip strength while raising the heart rate by working the whole body. And you get to beat on something, what's not to like!?

I have used the term combatives multiple times, and should define that term. I began training long ago in a system called Okinawan Freestyle Karate (we called his system "bare knuckle" full contact Karate) taught by Tommy Mossman in Jacksonville, NC. I considered myself a martial artist, and trained religiously. I thought I was prepared for anything until I had the opportunity to train in a system called Gracie Jujitsu in Torrance, CA. You may recognize the Gracie name, as Rorion, Rickson, Royce, and a variety of others in the Gracie family modified a system of Jujitsu to suit their needs and developed a revolutionary method of teaching their system. Rorion Gracie helped start the first UFC as a testing ground for his system of Gracie Jujitsu. His brother Royce fought and won in the first several UFC's, demonstrating the effectiveness of the system, and the lack of ground fighting knowledge by most of the mainstream martial artists.

I had the opportunity to train with Rorion and Royce in 1997 and 1998, only a few years after Royce's multiple wins in the UFC. Thinking I had some skills, I was humbled by the newest students at the Gracie academy when we "rolled" (grappled on the ground). Even though I was still very confident in my striking skills, I knew immediately that if I were to end up on the ground with anyone skilled in this system I would lose. And this began a lifelong search of training that would help me reach an endpoint rather than focusing on a certain "art" or regimented method of training. My endpoint goal was surviving and prevailing in a real life fight. So for the purpose of this book, when I use the term "combatives", I am referring to all skillsets that will help you win a fight. Combatives consist of defensive skills (defending against an attack), striking skills (to counter attack), grappling skills (both standing and on the ground), and "in fight weapon access" skills. This is the often-overlooked area that even most hard-core fighters do not train, and that is the inclusion of training weapons during combatives training (such as red guns and training knives).

Specific Fitness Requirements For A Fight

So what fitness specific assets are required for a fight? Other than generally getting in shape, what matters in a fight? Pavel Tsatsouline, Chairman of StrongFirst and former trainer to the Soviet Spetznaz (www.strongfirst.com) makes a point of focusing his students on strength before anything else. The name of him company says it all. The reason behind that is strength is the foundation to anything that relates to athletic (i.e. warrior) performance. Pavel is well knows for being one of the first to introduce the kettlebell, a serious yet simple strength training tool to the west. He and many of his athletes possess a level of "wiry strength" that is unsurpassed by many of the heavily muscled bodybuilders you would find in a gym.

Figure 30 The infamous kettlebell, one of the tools of Soviet strength training over the years.

Pat McNamara, former Delta operator (U.S. Army Special Forces) calls it "a performance-focused approach to maintaining your combat chassis" in his first article in Recoil magazine (Recoil Magazine, Issue 9). McNamara talks about the missing links in his article and states that while Crossfit and other fitness approaches have changed the way we view fitness, but that they still miss the mark. He advocates circuits that work the neglected areas, and recommends learning the Olympic lifts for their strength building benefits as well as caloric challenges and increased hormonal responses (testosterone and human growth hormone) they give you. Pat takes a slightly different approach to his workouts and breaks them down into: Speed/Quickness, Power, Strength, and Hypertrophy workouts respectively. You can find out more about Pat at (www.tmacsin.com).

Everyone has a slightly different approach to fitness, even when you study elite level trainers. Don't get caught up in trying to find the "perfect workout" when it comes to developing fighting fitness, as there are many different ways to reach the end goal. Instead focus on attributes and the principles behind those attributes that will help you reach your goal.

I can distinctly remember a day on the range with a student group that was made up of various students from the Naval Special Warfare community when one of them noticed a long aluminum pipe lying on the range. He looked at me (I am relatively muscular and think of myself as fit) and challenged me to do a "get up" with the pipe in one hand. I am not certain of the weight of the pipe, but it was relatively heavy and long which made it awkward. I asked what the heck a "get up" was and he basically said to lay down and put the pipe in one hand, and then to stand up while keeping it higher than my head. Now, understand there is a much more sophisticated way of explaining and doing a "get up" (Turkish getup), but those are the basics. Anyway, I laid down and grabbed the pipe and managed to make it almost to my knees before giving up. The truth was that even though technique is part of that equation, pure whole body type strength is the other. I did not have it. My buddy then demonstrated the move perfectly with the pipe above his head. The point is that my strength training had something missing, and the pure strength this frogman demonstrated on the range that day played out well during the combatives portion of the class later in the week. Lesson learned: strength rules in a fight!

Key fitness attributes (and principles) that will greatly increase your ability to fight are:

- *High strength to weight ratio.* I am talking about pure functional, whole body strength that should be trained with a variety of methods, but most importantly the focus should be on getting strong.
- *Grip strength.* This is an often-overlooked key area that has specifically helped me in real fights, and in training.
- *Midsection (core) strength.* This was really what I was missing most in reference to the Turkish getup lesson I learned on the range. I had plenty of power on certain planes, but my midsection was weak and this limited my ability to use that strength. I can attest to the fact that every time I return to grappling (usually jujitsu) I find myself incredible sore in the midsection for the first week, even though my gym routine often includes abdominal exercises.
- *Cardiovascular energy systems strength (specifically applicable to higher heart rates).* Now, don't picture yourself having to get on a stationary bike to develop this, instead use your time wisely and develop this strength while getting stronger or improving your combative strikes.

Figure 31 Grip strength is very important. This is an example of it's benefits in action during a weapon retention technique.

Developing the above can be accomplished in many manners. Most of us do not have the time to spend hours in the gym each day, and even if you could it would not be necessary. Thirty to sixty minutes of training each day will easily allow you to build the fitness levels you need. Use your time as wisely as possible, and focus on functional training by actually doing the things you want to get better at.

This section is not meant to replace the advice of a good trainer, so first I recommend you invest time and money researching products or people you can use to help take your fitness levels to the next level. In the end of this section, I will introduce you to three programs that I recommend doing in whole, or part to increase your fitness levels. Before discussing them though, I want to give some thoughts about the fitness areas discussed above, and what I believe your focus should be in the simplest terms. The key areas are: *high strength to weight ratio, grip strength, midsection (core) strength,* and *cardiovascular system strength*. The following are the principles to focus on in each attribute mentioned above, and potential methods of training:

High strength to weight ratio.
- Bodyweight and/or functional movements rule. This means if you are pushing, pulling, or pressing your bodyweight (or more) in the different planes of movement, you will be heading the right direction.
- Repetitions should be kept in the 3-5 ranges, and failure on any exercise should be avoided. Strengthening the muscle is the goal, so more sets of a lower repetition ranges will accomplish this better than higher bodybuilding type repetition ranges. Keep in mind that muscle without strength is functionally useless and burns energy needed for the fight. Additionally, working the muscle during sets to the "burn" or complete failure is regarded as a bad idea by most strength trainers (including Pavel Tsatsouline, mentioned above). Trainers argue whether training to failure is ever a good idea, and the science is a bit blurry in that area. One thing they are pretty consistent about is that training with lower rep ranges, stopping several repetitions before failure, and piling the weight on will make you strong.
- Pick movement functional exercises that require the use of the entire body and midsection at the same time. Examples are the getup, kettlebell swings, deadlift (sumo), muscleups (if you are strong enough). Additional selections would be movements where you have to push, pull, or press your body weight up without the support of a bench or device. These include push-ups (and variants), pull ups, pike presses, etc.

Grip Strength.
- This area will be greatly enhanced by your heavy bodyweight exercises, as well as time on the range with your rifle. Just drilling for a couple hours (dry fire or live fire) with your AR will wear your hands out and strengthen them.

- Pavel recommends working the grip with the IronMind (http://www.ironmind.com) grippers by using a method he calls "greasing the groove." This basically means that you pick a gripper (or any hand strengthening exercise) and perform about 50-60% of the total maximum of your repetitions numerous times per day for numerous days per week. So if you for example can close the number 1 gripper ten times, then you would do five to six repetitions numerous (ten) times over a given day, and repeat that several days during the week. I have been using this method in the off-season (when I am not shooting competitively) for years now with success.
- In addition to finger (grip) strength, I also work on forearm and wrist tendon strength with a 10lb sledge hammer and a variety of exercises. One of my favorites is one I call pot stirrers. The method is simple; I grab the sledge on a specific area on the handle (the farther toward the end of the handle you grip, the harder it is) and hold the hammer end out in front of my body. I then move the handle in a manner like I am stirring an imaginary pot with the handle.

Midsection (core) strength.
- A large majority of your midsection (core) strength can and should be developed while you are working on other areas. For example if you follow on of the programs recommended below (Kettlebell Simple and Sinister), the key exercises in the program would strengthen your midsection. If you follow my recommendation and begin to train in any type of MMA gym, then the ground fighting (grappling) develops those muscles as well.
- Keep the tension up and repetition range down. Most people working their "abs" focus on high repetition for the burn they think will give them that six-pack. While this method has some merits, it does not work as well as keeping the repetition ranges low, tension in the abdominals up (squeeze and keep the abdomen pressurized), and focusing on form. You can literally do half the work and get twice the results.

Cardiovascular energy systems strength (specifically applicable to higher heart rates).
- The vast majority of my cardiovascular work is done while actually training (with a partner, or in a MMA/Jujitsu type gym, or practicing my strikes. I like to focus on a minute or two of high-level work followed by a rest set that allows my heart rate to recover. Your training doesn't have to be complicated, just push the pace (safely) and rest in between sets. I wrote up a simple, yet functional interval program that you can use or modify if you like (http://blog.shooting-performance.com/the-ultimate-functional-fightingshooting-cardio-circuit/). Each set focuses on a skill area I want to work on, and in between each set while I am resting and letting my heart rate return, I focus on stretching the muscle group I just worked.
- The second area that you can use (as I do) to work on your cardio is while on the range. In the live fire drill section, the Moving Mount Drill is one where you will be sprinting and

mounting your rifle to practice putting those two things together. I usually do this drill for distances of 75-100 yards, and repeat it five times. After each repetition of the drill, I jog back to my starting point (allowing heart rate to return somewhat). Once again, and way to strengthen your cardiovascular system while doing something functional.

- One last point on the cardiovascular system is that (per Joel Jamieson in his book Ultimate MMA Conditioning) it is important to do sessions of lower intensity cardio work one or more times per week. This means that the heart should be kept at 130-150 BPM (beats per minute) for 30 minutes or more. Why do this type of exercise? Because the Aerobic energy system is worked at this intensity, and with improvement of this system, the body is capable of generating much more total energy. This increases the overall effectiveness of all energy systems needed for a fight (Aerobic and Anaerobic Energy Systems). For more information on the different energy systems and how to train them, I strongly recommend his book (Ultimate MMA Conditioning, www.8weeksout.com).

Developing Your Program

So now that you understand the key ingredients and principles behind functional fighting fitness, you have to select your path to get there. Your options are to follow the rules outlined above or to follow a pre-designed program, or possibly a modification of either. It might be simpler for me to give my recommendations broken down by experience level. Some of you reading this chapter might already be in very good shape and using these principles to keep you there. If so, that is great! Continue down the path you are already on. For the rest of you, read on.

Option 1- If you have no experience.

1. Pick one of the three programs below and follow them. I suggest that you cycle through each eventually to get the benefit and education from each. When following them, keep in mind that you can still focus on and mirror the principles discussed above. For example, if you follow the Core Performance or P90X programs, beware of pushing to failure in the exercise if you want to focus on the *strength* principle discussed above.
2. Supplement with grip exercises as needed. I suggest ordering several grippers from IronMind and working on this by following Pavel's principle of "greasing the groove" discussed above. Add pot stirrers with a sledgehammer if you have the time. If you are avidly training with your rifle as well as handgun you may not need to add much more to your total workload because remember you are working your grip while shooting.
3. Replace the standard cardiovascular machine type training with either:
    a. Striking or MMA type practice with interval paced workouts (1 minute up and 1 minute of rest or something similar)

b. Shooting type interval workouts using a drill like the Moving Mount or Movement Offline type drills done for numerous sets.

Option 2 – If you have some experience.

1. Consider mixing and matching pieces of each of the programs listed, based on your needs and personal desires. If you have not worked with kettlebells or done some of the specialized whole body strength training, I suggest you start with Pavel's program, and then work through pieces of the Core Performance and P90X programs. Since you are intermediate, you will probably enjoy and be challenged by the bodyweight exercises demonstrated by Tony Horton in the P90X program.
2. Validate the program you choose by testing it against the principles listed above. Remember, those are the keys that will really benefit you in a fight.
3. Use as much functional training as possible doing real motions that you could use in a fight (moving drills or MMA type training)

Option 3 – If you are very experienced.

This is a suggestion that might guide your planning, but let's be honest, if you have this much experience you are already on the right path. My suggestions will hopefully help you prioritize differently if you are focusing too much on fitness skills that are not as useful in a fight. I have had this problem myself, the key is to simplify and focus on what works.

1. Pick each of the attributes above and develop your fitness training to meet each objective. Select one at a time and build your program, choose the exercises/methods you will use, and schedule the frequency you will use them. For example, in strength training you might select three days to train and use a combination of bodyweight, compound, and functional whole body strength exercises in the rep ranges of mostly 3-6. Since you have experience, I would recommend mixing it up as needed.
2. Switch it up every six weeks or so. I think that the key to staying as focused as possible is to make sure that you are mentally engaged during your training. The more your body gets used to a certain stimuli, the more you will need to change it up.
3. Focus on function as much as possible.

Fitness Training Schedule

To reap the rewards of your fitness program you will have to put in the effort. This means dedicating 30-60 minutes three to five days per week, and making those sessions as focused as possible. If you decide to follow the P90X[11] or Core Performance[12] programs you will be train-

---

[11] Tony Horton, "P 90X," P 90X, DVD, prod. Beachbody Inc. (Los Angeles, 2007).

ing up to six days per week. Be wary of working hard that many days per week if you are not up to the task. Recovery is going to be a concern, thus if you want to stay healthy you will need to ensure you are not pushing your body too hard too fast and that it has enough time to recover (heal) from the workouts. Remember, your endocrine system only has so much bandwidth, and if you push too hard you will over-train and injure yourself. Based on my recommendations above, you will be combining combatives and supplemental fitness moves to get fit. So how do you balance them and develop a good schedule? I have tried every combination you can think of and have found that the simplest and most efficient method is to alternate sessions. Remember, you can only do so much per week and still recover, so alternating sessions has been the most beneficial for me. Here is how my week looks:

Day 1- Strength exercises/lower body
Day 2- Combatives at dedicated gym or Strike Session (Heart rate- high-HIIT) /Flexibility
Day 3- Strength exercises/upper body
Day 4- Combatives at dedicated gym or Strike Session (Heart rate- medium rate) / Flexibility
    Note: Sometimes I use the combative circuit I designed for this session.
Day 5- Flexibility/Recovery open session (I vary this one depending on what I have that weekend, i.e. if I am shooting a competitive match, I will keep this day less intense)
Midsection/Core- I address this at the tail end of each combatives training section, if I feel the need. If for example I grappled for an hour at the gym with my training partner, I have no doubt I worked my midsection. A Strike Session workout in my home gym would be followed by two-three midsection and neck strengthening specific exercises with as perfect form as I can muster and low repetitions.

Grip Strength- During the competition season I handle a handgun daily, and a rifle a couple times per week. This works my hands and forearms enough where I will usually add one day of grip strength specific stuff to one of the strength workouts I have. In the off season when I handle firearms slightly less, I add one or more day of grip strength focus using the "grease the groove" method discussed above.

Figure 32 Pot "stirrers," one of my favorite grip/wrist strength exercises.

Note: I will soon be trying the minimalist total body program designed by Pavel Tsatsouline in his new book *Kettlebell Simple and Sinister*, but I cannot comment on such a program at this time because I have not com-

---

[12] Mark Verstegen, <u>Core Performance</u> (Tempe : Rodale, 2004).

pleted it. I believe it will allow me to reduce my time spent training yet give me a very solid level of functional strength and movement.

This is how my workout week is structured, and notice that my strength and combative sessions are alternating. This seems to allow me to recover better. Notice that I don't have "cardio" anywhere on my schedule. As stated above, I know that I need to be as efficient as possible, and my end result is to be fit for a fight. My combative sessions, whether I am working strikes on my strike dummy or ground fighting with my partner are the best cardio sessions I can get. They are functional, efficient, and allow me to be accomplishing two goals at once (combative training and cardiovascular fitness). These are just my examples and what work for me. Once you get into your program you may find a better way to lay out your week, just keep it as efficient as possible and stay focused on the goal: fighting fitness.

Finding a Good Combatives Gym (or something similar)

MMA stands for mixed martial arts, and is the result of the first UFC's that demonstrated how traditional marital arts were lacking certain skill sets. If you are a traditional martial artist, please don't be offended and think I am saying your system is lacking, just understand that most traditional systems are. If you happened to train in a system that addresses all elements needed for real self-defense, then you are way ahead of most martial artists who are wasting their time scoring points in mock sparring matches. Most martial arts systems have gotten too far from real combat, and have been watered down into somewhat useless techniques. MMA training is generally focused on MMA type competitions, which are semi-realistic full contact fights that allow most strikes and techniques to be used. While MMA is not completely realistic combat, it is as close as you can get and offers an excellent base of skills that can be directly applied on the street. Once you find an MMA gym in your area, jump right in and begin training. You will probably find that if you do not have a strong base of fitness already that these training sessions will be very tough physically.

There are some other systems (such as Sayoc Kali and Martial Blade Concepts) out there that are just as good and maybe better than an MMA gym. The problem is that the martial arts world is as complicated and watered down as the fitness world it, and it would be very difficult for me to recommend something specific in the limited scope of this book. Keep it simple and select a place that uses aggressive, simple techniques that will work in the real world without years of complicated training. Once you have a good base, branch out from there.

Integrate Your Combative Training with multi-level weapons training

This is the next logical step in relation to your MMA training and fitness development, and requires that you have a place to do it and like-minded individuals. Multi-level weapons training is like MMA on steroids, and simply means that instead of traditional sparring, you will arm yourself with **safe training weapons**, and integrate them into you sparring. This will bring a whole new level of awareness and realism into this type of training. If you are new to combatives, and have not been to this type of training before you will need to find a qualified academy or instructor to train with. Some MMA instructors may not understand the integration of weapons into the free sparring, and will probably not be able to teach you what you need to know.

Training Programs

This section will have two recommended programs as an option for those of you who would like to follow a dedicated program. These programs are intense, and each twelve weeks in length. I would recommend them to anyone who does not have the experience to develop their own program, or wants to use the workouts to supplement their normal week. If you follow my advice and begin training in combatives, you might be wondering how you are going to do both. My recommendation there would be to train in combatives one or two times per week, replacing the "cardio" element of whatever workout you choose with the combative session. Eventually you will be able to take the best from those programs and build a schedule that suits your needs.

I recommend a couple different physical fitness-training programs, which I have personally used to elevate my fitness levels. I highly recommend that you investigate both programs and utilize them as you see fit. One of the programs is predominantly done as a DVD video-based follow along program, and the other one is in book format. I don't have any association with either of these companies, and they do not sponsor me to say nice things about them. They are simply the best and most diverse workout programs that I have found that will help you elevate your fitness levels without spending hundreds of dollars on personal trainer or exercise equipment. The key is that they are total programs, which address all of the key fitness areas, and they are relatively simple to follow.

Keep in mind the fitness related principles discussed above when using any of the below programs.

Kettlebell Simple and Sinister

This program is your minimalist approach to training. The book is written by Pavel Tsatsouline, Chairman of StrongFirst and former trainer to the Soviet Spetznaz. The book per Pavel is one of his greatest works and an incredibly simple program to follow. Keep in mind that while I am listing it as one of the programs because I do have experience with Pavel's material, I have not completed this program from start to finish like I have the others. More about the book directly from the website:

- *Simple & Sinister will prepare you for almost anything life could throw at you, from carrying a piano upstairs to holding your own in a street fight.*
- *Simple & Sinister will forge a fighter's physique – because the form must follow the function.*
- *Simple & Sinister will give you the strength, the stamina, and the suppleness to play any sport recreationally – and play it well.*

- *If you are a serious athlete, Simple & Sinister will sve as a perfect foundation for your sport-specific training.*
- *If you are a serious lifter, Simple & Sinister will build your strength, rather than interfere with it.*
- *Simple & Sinister will achieve all of the above while leaving you plenty of time and energy to do your duty, your job, practice your sport, and have a life.*

Website: http://www.strongfirst.com Recommendation- Get the program and follow it. Strongly consider instruction in some of the kettlebell exercises if you are a novice.

Core Performance Workout[13]

This program is a very detailed and spans twelve weeks. It incorporates elements of everything needed to perform one's movements well. It is a very detailed program and can be a bit complicated to follow, but it is well worth it. The workout requires relatively little equipment and can be done at home with a few simple pieces of gear. This workout was designed and built upon the premise of developing core strength called "pillar" strength. The author of this program believes and demonstrates that all movements originate around that pillar area consisting of the midsection, lower back, and hips. If you strengthen this area, then the result is better movement mechanics for the entire body. I used this program as a pre-nationals routine several years ago. I did the program later than I should have, and consequently I had to work through the heat of the summer inside my garage home gym during temperatures exceeding 95 degrees. This may have limited the effectiveness of the program a bit, but it sure got me acclimated to the heat. Overall, I felt the strongest I have ever felt, and moved better than I have ever moved after completing this program. I also have a series of CD's made by the designer of this program called "Core Essentials", and find those CD's useful, but not necessary if you desire to do the 12-week workout in the book.
- Website: http://www.coreperformance.com/
- Recommendation- Get the book Core Performance and follow the program.

P90X Workout[14]

This program in my opinion is the easiest to follow along and I recommend it for beginners. One thing I like about this program is that it is primarily a bodyweight program. While some of the exercises are probably not ones I would focus on, the large majority are. Don't mistake what I just said as meaning the program itself is easy, just that it is easy to follow along due to its design. This program is an intense 12-week program that can be followed via DVD. It incorporates a very diverse group of workouts and principles that will increase fitness levels in all key areas. The program requires absolute minimal equipment and will work well to increase strength to weight ratios by reducing body fat. The great thing about P90X is that the workout is packaged in a series of twelve DVD's that you just pop in your player and follow along. The

---

[13] Mark Verstegen, Core Performance (Pheonix: Rodale, Inc, 2004).

[14] Tony Horton, P90X, 01 01 2004, 01 01 2009 <http://www.beachbody.com/p90x>.

main trainer, Tony Horton, is a gifted trainer operating at an incredible fitness level. Trying to keep up with the trainers on the DVD is very inspiring and fun for those wanting a challenge. If you are new to fitness or have some physical limitations, you may want to start with a preparatory program of some sort before starting this program. Make sure you start in the off season for this one, as you will want to have the time to dedicate to building a good base of fitness.

- Website: http://www.beachbody.com/category/p90x-online.do
- Recommendation- Get the P90X program and follow the DVD workouts.
- Note: There is now a P90X2 program out there, but I recommend starting with the base program first.

This chapter is meant to get you motivated about the importance of fitness in a fight. I also wrote it to reject the theory that "I'll just shoot them" when a high stress incident goes down that comes from some. Fitness is the key, so use the material I have given you in this chapter to develop your own system of getting fighting fit. Your life may depend on it!

Chapter Summary and Action steps:

1. If you are not doing something to address your fitness now, don't wait. Even those of you that may have physical challenges to overcome can improve your fitness. Start now- do something!
2. Learning how to defend yourself with a firearm involves much more than just shooting, if you are not skilled in combatives, find a place to train in your local area and "just do it".
3. Focus your training time on real functional activities that will keep you fit and give you the right kind of fitness.
4. Recommended reading on these areas:
    a. Ultimate MMA Conditioning by Joel Jamieson: A scientific approach to training for fighting fitness (he trains professional MMA fighters and the concepts he uses are revolutionary)
    b. Train to Win by Martin Rooney (motivational principles)
    c. Training for Warriors by Martin Rooney
    d. Ultimate Warrior Workouts by Martin Rooney
    e. Core Performance by Mark Verstegen
    f. Kettlebell Simple & Sinister by Pavel

CHAPTER 6

High Performance Rifle Manipulation and Marksmanship Techniques

This chapter will teach you how to objectively analyze and select the techniques that will best serve your needs. This is a critical component in the process of training yourself to a high level of performance. It will also contain material that will help you effectively execute the training drills, as there are key components of technique that must be mastered in each one.

Covered in this chapter:

1. An expanded view of what technique is, and how it should evolve.
2. How to find and assess good techniques to add to your "toolbox."
3. The current Shooting-Performance defensive rifle techniques.

Assessment and Evolution of Technique

When someone enters my coaching program, I require that they attend at least one technique assessment session with me so I can determine whether or not they understand and can demonstrate proper technique on many critical skills. You see, without this session, there is no way I can possibly assign them a training program or coach them along the way. Giving someone a training program to follow is easy but ensuring that they are doing the drills correctly and training the skills correctly is the critical ingredient. In this chapter I am going to discuss how to objectively analyze techniques to select and use in your program. This book is about designing your own training program to maximize your performance. It is not designed as a technique book. The reason for this is that technique is evolutionary, and I am constantly experimenting and changing things. I feel that to really learn technique, a book is barely adequate as a teaching modality. Video is better, and a class is best. Even so, I included a technique section in this book so you have the knowledge and a reference to understand and properly execute the drills. If you are a new shooter, before attempting to follow this program, or design your own, I strongly recommend that you get some instruction from an expert first:

- *Take a class.* I strongly recommend you find and take a class at an established training institution or from a known expert. I am very particular who I would tell you to train with now due to the large amount of so called instructors and training classes out here that lack credibility and professionalism. Make sure you do your research and find a professional instructor that is certified to enhance your learning experience. Unfortunately there are dozens of completely unprofessional instructors and institutions out there. It seems that there are now more than ever before, dozens of individuals who have spent time in the military or law enforcement that decided to open up their own school. While some of them are exceptional and I would highly recommend training with them, others should not be teaching. Rarely do these instructors possess the skill and knowledge to actually teach you something. Select your instructor wisely.
- *Buy a video/DVD.* There are actually some very good training videos out there today that will greatly enhance your learning experience. I strongly recommend starting here if you cannot afford to take a class. One great thing about videos/DVD's is that you can hit the rewind button as many times as you like so that you really get a chance to review the technique you are watching and learn it thoroughly. There will be a DVD that will compliment this book that demonstrates each drill and all techniques in detail; **I strongly suggest you invest in it**.

> *Note: When I produced the DVD's that support my competition book, customers raved at how much more usable the program was. Books are great, but DVD's/videos offer so much more information. The only thing better is real instruction on the range.*

- *Books.* My research library is awesome and I never fail to buy a good book on shooting if I see one. I own pretty much every book out there and strongly believe in gaining knowledge and a cross section of techniques. Be wary of the author though, and don't forget to do your research and analysis on the techniques presented in the book.
- *Hit the forums.* There are a ton of "arm chair" shooters out there on Internet forums; there are also some very skilled and knowledgeable shooters who will share what they know with you for free. Take what you read on them with an open mind, and critically analyze what you read before "buying into" the concept completely. Use common sense and try to validate the information you find.
- *Take a Good Shooter to Lunch.* If you can't afford a class or the other things listed above, find the best shooters in your area and link up with them. If you are a police officer or member of the armed forces you may try to find one of the local competition shooters, unless you have someone in your department or unit with a high level of skill. One thing I had to learn when I started competing (I was active in the U.S. Marine Corps) was that the civilian competitive shooters possessed some really serious skill. Top competitive shooters really helped push the evolution of firearm skills. I needed to listen to what they have to offer. So find a good shooter, hopefully someone at the master class level in a practical shooting sport and offer to buy him or her lunch. Or even better, bring them lunch on the range, and just happen to

have your gear with you when you meet with them. (Warning: Some good shooters may also like to be bribed with beer. Be cautious, as these shooters tend to become addicted to free beer and may become a nuisance.)

Selecting and Analyzing Technique

Now that you have some source options to learn technique, how do you separate the good from the bad? Think of how much stuff is out there on technique. It seems that every time you turn around someone else has "invented" and is promoting some new sort of high-speed technique. While some of these techniques are cutting edge and should be incorporated into your training sessions, many of them offer no real return in terms of an applicable skill you could use in a fight. Remember the way it works – you will get *out* what you put *into* your subconscious memory. If you select and train a technique that is wrong, unfortunately you are stuck with it until it is retrained correctly! My goal is to give you guidance on how to figure out what you are going to add to your training toolbox and what you will throw away.

How do we objectively analyze technique? Well, the first thing is to understand that technique is constantly evolving. I would strongly recommend that you think of technique as something that can and will change on a regular basis. Technique is the one thing that I don't get tied to rigidly because I know in the future I will probably have evolved and made slight changes to any technique that I use. You will find yourself doing the same thing as you advance through your training programs and continue to gain skill.

If you ask the ten top shooters in the world today how they do a specific technique with a handgun, you may get ten different answers. If ten of the best shooters can do things ten different ways, then obviously technique itself is not the difference between performing well and performing poorly. When coming up with the concept for this book, I made a decision that I would talk about technique, but that it was probably more valuable for you as the reader to understand how to objectively look at techniques and select them or reject them based on your needs. Sure, I can and will show you some great techniques that I have learned over the last twenty years, but that won't help you when you encounter a new technique.

My goal is to teach you how to objectively look at something and analyze whether or not it will increase your individual performance. If it won't, then I would advise you to reject it. However, if it will help you reach your goals, then obviously that is a technique you need to add to your training program. There are several steps to objectively analyzing technique – let's break each one down in detail:

1. Is the technique from a valid source (someone who has excelled at what you are trying to learn)? This step alone will weed out many hair-brained techniques. Now, this does not mean that you must train with the ninja of the day, who has been in 43 gunfights and "seen the elephant" to learn a good technique. It simply means that good instructors will have researched and validated the techniques they teach. They will constantly strive to find a better

way. Don't forget that talking to some of the instructor's students will often tell you a lot about an instructor. Good instructors will have students that are willing to say so. If you find a technique from a source that is unverifiable, use caution, but proceed to the next step.
2. Will the technique allow you to perform better under the circumstances you will encounter on game day (the fight)? If not, then reject the technique. If yes, then move to the next step.
3. Validate the technique by testing it against some set performance standards. Time or accuracy standards are best, and try to test the technique in the circumstance and environment you will use it on game day.

> *NOTE: This validation may not prove anything if you do not know how to perform the technique yet. Make sure you ingrain some skill with it before testing to ensure you can objectively assess it. Reject the technique if you invalidate it by testing (find it doesn't work). If you can validate the technique or if you can't perform the technique (because of lack of skill with it), move to the next step.*

4. Ask yourself if the technique can be trained in a reasonable amount of time? If not, then you will need to decide if it is valuable enough that you should add it to your program and ingrain it into your skill. If you decide it is, then move to the next step.
5. Break down the sub-skills within the technique and design *skill development* and drills to train those skills. Prioritize the technique/drills and plug them into your training program at appropriate times. Then you will begin the process of learning the technique.

There you have it. A logical way to assess and accept or reject a technique you see from a source that you have not yet validated. Once you find a good instructor, and validate the material they teach, it is reasonable to assume that most of the material they teach is probably relevant and worth your time to learn. Don't accept this as the rule though, and no matter what, always question and validate the technique. This will ensure it will work for you when the chips are down.

Remember, you are not insulting an instructor if you question his or her methodology, you are just ensuring that the insurance you are buying will cover you when you need it. All good instructors will welcome a student that logically and politely questions what they are teaching, because that is how instructors grow and evolve. I have changed many of the things I have taught because of a student questioning something and allowing me to modify and improve upon what I teach. I don't own any technique and don't feel compelled to teach something that could be changed and improved upon. I recommend that if you do find an instructor who will not listen to your questions about their techniques, move on. You will be better off in the long run.

Terminology Discussion

It is important that you understand the terminology and difference between marksmanship and manipulation. The simplest way to define them is to say that marksmanship is the management of the three key areas that directly effect the aspect of shooting the rifle and hitting the target. Manipulation skills are everything else. To be even more specific, let me give you a different visual:

If you can manage the sighting system, trigger system, and hold the rifle on target (manage the recoil), you can hit anything repeatedly. That is marksmanship.

Conversely, the aspect of getting the rifle into position, loading or reloading it, and fixing malfunctions is the skill of manipulating the rifle. Those skills, while supporting of the marksmanship skills, actually have little to do with hitting the target. They instead keep the rifle fed with ammunition and able to go "bang."

The reason you need to know this is that these skills can and will primarily be developed in different areas of practice. For example, rifle manipulations (or manipulation of any weapon for that matter) can and will occur primarily during dry fire practice. Marksmanship skills however are best developed in live fire practice drills because we need the stimulus of the sights, trigger feel, and recoil to really develop the skill of shooting better.

The third key area I will discuss in the technique section is movement. There are many times when some sort of physical movement is required in order to get into a position so we can apply the proper marksmanship and manipulation skills needed to get hits on target. Some of these movements include pivots, stepping movements, sprinting movements (and mounting while doing so), and moving while shooting (applying marksmanship principles *while* moving).

Rifle Deployment

Before discussing technique, I want to address the issue of deployment. Specifically, if you are going to use a rifle to defend yourself, then you have to address the issue of getting your hands on the rifle first. If you are member of the U.S. Military deployed overseas, then this is a no-brainer, but if you are a chiropractor who plans on defending your home with a rifle, access is a consideration. If someone violently kicks in your door in the middle of the night, do you think you will have the time to open that safe, get the rifle, load it, and engage the intruders? Probably not unless you prepare ahead of time, and place some things in your favor. Let's discuss the issue and break down deployment by area, the home, a vehicle, and in between.

Figure 33 Gunvault AR Safe.

Home Deployment

The key here is going to be getting the rifle into action quickly. While I do not advocate leaving a loaded rifle lying around, neither do I recommend having one locked up securely in a safe that is very slow to access. What are your options? First, consider using tactics and home security to your advantage. Secure doors, motion lights, and a early warning alarm system will buy you enough time to deploy a rifle from a quick access safe. Keep your bedroom door locked if possible to buy even more time to access your rifle.

My personal option is to use a handgun secured in my favorite quick assess safe made by GunVault (www.gunvault.com) that would buy me enough time to get to a safe area in my home, where I would load and sling my rifle. In fact, the quick access safe I have has both a handgun (loaded with a weapon mounted light) and one 30-round rifle magazine. An option like this would allow me to have an unloaded M-4 staged that I could load if I have time. If time does not allow, then I defend my home with my handgun. Gunvault is also making (I am not sure of the release date) a quick access device called an "ARVault" that is the same quick access finger pad system that my handgun safes use. It will be a perfect solution once on the market.

Whichever home deployment system you decide on, make sure you spend some time practicing getting to the rifle. For example, if you choose a quick access safe with finger pad, practice opening it in the dark, with both hands. I strongly suggest staging a light near your safe or buying one with a keypad system that can be manipulated in complete darkness. Several quick access safes have lights built into the keypad area. Additionally, if you are planning to deploy an unloaded rifle, make sure you add loading practice to your training drills. Spend some money on dummy training rounds, clear all live ammunition from the room you are in, and practice getting the rifle out and loading it. The more practice, the better.

Vehicle Deployment

Carrying a rifle in a vehicle is nothing new. I grew up in Idaho and Wyoming, and it was rare *not* to see a ranch rifle of some sort in a window rack in most trucks. While it worked for many years, I am certainly not recommending having a visible, unsecured rifle in a vehicle. That would be a recipe for disaster. Instead, I recommend a hidden rifle in some sort of securing device. You might opt for a magnetic locking mount similar to what most patrol officers' use in their cars.

Figure 34 American Security Defense Vault DV625 sliding safe meant for under bed use (another great option) would also work in the bed of a SUV or car trunk.

Another option might be a lockable box or rack that allows you to lock the rifle up. Most of these products have some sort of key access, so once again time is not on your side when accessing. Again a good reason to always carry a handgun as well!

The bottom line is that there are many different options for vehicles, but each is very specific to what you drive. Research your options and more importantly, train with them. If you plan to deploy a rifle from any given mount quickly, plan to spend some time going through the motions.

In between Access

What does "in between" mean? It simply means a method of deploying a rifle when you are not at home or in your vehicle. If you are in the military or law enforcement, slinging a rifle and carrying it openly is your job. Not so with most of you civilians out there. While open carry laws allow us to openly carry a defensive rifle in some states, it is certainly not recommended unless the zombies have attacked and we are in all out war.

Figure 35 This is the smaller Vertx backpack I carry with a quick access area I have a handgun stored in. The same concept could be applied with a slightly larger pack holding a rifle with a folding stock.

Options for having a rifle with you, yet still having it hidden are pretty limited. With the invent of the "arm braces" that are being sold for AR style "pistols" it is possible to have a rifle-like system in a backpack. Just remember that the extremely short barrel lengths on a system like this might compromise its reliability (read John Paul's section on SBR's). There are also some new folding stocks sold for AR's on the market that might offer the ability to carry a short barreled rifle with the stock folded in a backpack, but I have not tested these setups yet so can't necessarily recommend them.

Rifle Marksmanship

My goal in this section is to teach you the critical aspects of marksmanship for defensive purposes. The context for what I am teaching is typically going to be closer range shooting, that most of you would use. I will however cover the other distances as well, for those of you that might have the need to hit a target at much farther ranges. It is not my intent to repeat what you might read in other books or documents. The principles of marksmanship have been covered thoroughly for more than one hundred years in numerous sources. What I want to do is to give you a different twist on what you might think is the best way to put rounds on target fast. Think about that last statement, "put rounds on target fast." The key to defensive shooting whether you are defending your living room in Cookeville, Tennessee or a compound in Afghanistan is to place rounds on the threatening/attacking person as fast as possible. That means that there is always going to be a balance of speed, and accuracy.

Keep in mind that speed will be somewhat instinctive when the problem presents itself. You don't have to travel overseas and spend three years in the Special Forces to learn this – simply *google* "gunfight." Then watch the videos you find. Are the people on those videos shooting controlled and slow in most cases? Probably not. They have a sense of urgency to put bullets inside the attacker because they want to live. The same urgency applies no matter what our context is. Just think of it like this – the technique that I will relay to you will always focus on putting rounds on the effective area on target "as fast as possible within the ability to control those shots".

When you are practicing, you will focus on key skills in certain sessions in this program, but realize that there will be some overlap of skill development. An example of this would be the Transition to Handgun Live Fire Drill where you will work on reacting to a "dead rifle." During the drill you would be working on aspects of both marksmanship and manipulation.

Let's label the elements of marksmanship, and then I will break each down in detail. They are: *rifle mount and management (recoil), trigger management, sight management*. Some of you might be wondering where the classic elements are, such as follow through, breath control, etc. Those principles are actually parts of the primary three, and I will address them within those areas.

> *In the following sections I offer all of the techniques along with photo's that will guide you during your training. Understand though, that it is very difficult to capture that information in a photo. Video is the key, and again, I strongly recommend the DVDs if you want a much better visual guide.*

Rifle Mount and Management (recoil control)

Do you control your rifle? More specifically, can you shoot it accurately, yet very rapidly, at distances of twenty-five yards or more? The goal is to develop a high-performance stance/mount system that will ensure that you can not only shoot accurately with your rifle but also get it on target quickly and shoot it with superior speed. Once the decision has been made to use deadly force, the faster you can neutralize the threat, the greater your chances of survival. This means that you need to get the first hit as fast as possible and follow-up hits even faster.

How do we control recoil? First, let's compare how a rifle recoils in comparison to a handgun. Handguns have a higher axis to bore ratio, which means that the recoil will travel in an upward direction. A rifle's recoil will travel in a more linear path straight backwards because the bore on an M16/4 system is actually in line with the stock, which is mounted on the shoulder. This is one of the reasons that a rifle can be shot so much faster than a handgun in most cases (at distance).

In a situation where life and limb are at stake, speed and accuracy must always be balanced, yet prioritized. This means that while hitting is the first priority, specifically with the first shot, quick follow-up shots are extremely important to ensure that the threat is effectively neutralized quickly. To fire quick follow up shots, recoil control must be maximize, to improve your recoil control, follow these steps:

1. *Square the body and weight forward.* Most shooters want to blade the body off more than necessary. Squaring up with the strong foot only slightly back allows one to mount the rifle more centered on the chest (see step 4) while staying centered offers the benefit of keeping the pelvic girdle as square as possible to the target improving the stability and mobility of the shooter. "Weight forward" simply means that the nose should be over the toes. To test this, go ahead and stand square to a friend, drop the strong side foot back slightly, unlock the knees, and stand upright. Have your friend push back on the center of your chest. Now, lean forward (without bending the knees much more) and place your nose just barely in front of your toes. Have your buddy push on you again. You (and he) will find that simply shifting the upper body weight forward of your center of balance offers substantial recoil potential due to the weight shift.

2. *Grip the gun high with the strong hand.* This is a phrase we often use with a handgun, but it applies to a rifle too. Your shooting hand--the one on the pistol grip that controls the fire systems--should be as high (or forward if using a standard stock) on the pistol grip as possible. Once you find this position, ensure you apply grip pressure and pull the rifle straight back into the chest (where the stock is mounted) when shooting. Simply resting the shooting hand there will not do the trick.

Note: A key point with the strong hand position on the AR systems is to ride the safety with that the thumb. If you are shooting with the left hand and do not have an ambidextrous safety on the rifle, you will have to either switch your thumb to the other side of the gun, or use your index finger to manipulate the safety. This ensures that the safety can be clicked off quickly as the rifle is mounted into the shooting position. I have had students fail to disengage the safety many times during training, simply because they did not pay attention to this key point.

3. *Grip the hand guard as far forward as feasible with the support hand.* This is an area that I often see taught and executed wrong with the biggest mistake being actually moving the support hand back to grasp the magazine well. When mounting the gun, ensure that your support hand is gripping the hand guard as far forward as possible while pulling the rifle straight to the rear. Gripping forward on the hand guard like this will do several things. First, it will increase the recoil control of that hand due to having greater leverage on the front of the gun. Secondly, it offers a better mechanical advantage if one has to snap the gun to a new target, once again due to leverage. Lastly, the shooter will have

Figure 36 The farther the hand is forward on the handguard, the more leverage the hand has against the gun. The finger pointing forward is optional.

much more control if they are forced to retain their gun from a surprise close-range attack.

4. *Mount the gun as centered as possible.* This is a big key to controlling recoil and one that almost everyone I have worked with misses to some extent. I, like many of you, was taught a standard bladed stance (by both my father and the U.S. Marine Corps), which is more traditional and places the stock on the outer portion of the shoulder. The problem is that this placement of the stock allows the gun to turn the body as the rifle pushes backward. This causes the sights (or dot) to cycle high right or left (for a left-handed shooter). To find the proper centered spot on your chest, stand mostly square to the target with head erect and looking forward. Now, grab the stock of the rifle and place it on the center of your chest and drive your chin down onto the stock until you find a good cheek weld spot that allows you to see the sights or through the scope. As you drive your chin down, the rifle will have to move slightly to either the right (for right-handed shooters) or left (for left-handed shooters) but will stay relatively centered on the chest. You might find that this places pressure on your cheek in relationship to the rifle, which is good. Anytime I am shooting a rifle, I focus on "pressuring" my cheek into the stock to increase my control on the gun and minimize dot movement.

Note: Another great side benefit of centering the gun while squaring up is that, while shooting on the move, the gun will move MUCH less compared to mounting it on the outside of the shoulder. Since, the shoulders move while walking, movement translates to the gun, and therefore centering on the chest minimizes the gun's movement a bunch!

5. *Drop the strong side elbow and drive the shoulder forward.* Once you have mounted the rifle in the manner described above, your next focus will be to drop the strong side elbow and drive the shoulder forward. This will do a couple things for you. First, it will flex the front deltoid and pectoral muscle on that side of the chest, which will solidify the rifle's position and increase the pressure of the stock mounted to the chest. Go ahead and test that now by placing your hand on your deltoid/pectoral area with the elbow out to the side and dropping it straight down. Secondly, it will keep the elbow low and out of the way so that it is less

Figure 37 Drop the elbow as low as possible. This solidifies the position, and keeps the elbow out of the way (when using cover).

likely to get hit by bullets when shooting around cover or to bump into obstacles or people when you are moving.

6. *Minimize and press.* Now that you have mounted the rifle into a secure "platform," all you will have to do is minimize the movement and press. The pressure on the gun should be substantial, but also neutral in a sense – straight to the rear except for the pressure required to hold the rifle upright. Therefore, be careful not to pull the rifle off to one side or another.

Once you have established this stance/mount, it is imperative that you practice manipulating the trigger while moving NOTHING else. From the ready position the mounting process includes the above steps combined with manipulating the safety and lastly pulling the trigger. If the stance and mount are correct, controlling the rifle will take very little work, but you will have to learn not to "overwork" the recoil. Let your body weight and leverage control the recoil while you focus your attention on managing the sights and trigger.

Focus on the above principles to greatly increase your ability to fire faster while maintaining your "acceptable level of accuracy" with your rifle. Modify the techniques slightly if needed to work around body armor, gear, or position (covered later in the technique section), and strive to improve your ability to shooter better in each practice session!

Figure 38 The fully mounted stance. This is the basic, high-performance platform.

Prone and Kneeling Positions

Once you have mastered the standing position it's time to look at other positions that you need to add to your toolbox. I am not an instructor that teaches classic positions or a huge number of positions simply to teach them, and instead offer simple solutions that work. The more you train and work your shooting skills in different situations, the better you will be prepared to use a non-standard position if needed. Make sure to keep the principles discussed above (square stance, elbow down, stock relatively centered, etc.) in play as much as possible, and keep the recoil control mechanics consistent. The following positions are useful:

Prone: The prone position is a superior position of stability. It is probably less likely used in a closer range situation that most of us will be in, but is a critical position to know if you have to stabilize the rifle as much as possible for a long range or extremely tough shot. Key points, lay flat and spread the legs. Make contact with the rifle on the ground at three points, the strong and support elbows, and magazine. Build a good cheek weld on the rifle and literally lay your face down onto the stock. Breathing will cause the rifle to move, so shoot during a paused portion of the breathing pattern. I suggest breathing in, then out with most of your breath and pausing for the shot. Don't hold your breath for any length of time or the lack of oxygen will distort your vision.

Figure 39 The kneeling and squatting positions. Notice how the upper body is nearly identical to what you would see in a standing stance. The principles are the same.

Kneeling: Kneeling positions should primarily be used for increased stability or use of cover. Additionally kneeling might be used to lower your profile and expose yourself around cover from a different position than the enemy expects. Kneeling is simple – maintain the same square stance and simple kneel with attention focuses on keeping your upper body forward and weight behind the gun. You have the option of kneeling down on your support side knee and resting the support side elbow on the knee, or kneeling on the other knee and supporting your gun side on that same knee. Regardless of which you use, make sure to make contact with the knee with the upper portion of the elbow versus the elbow tip. The elbow tip will move around and be very unstable. If you feel your arm and run your hand down your triceps toward your elbow, you will find a relatively flat spot where your triceps meets the elbow. This is the position you will want to rest on your knee.

Squatting: Squatting is similar in profile to kneeling, but offers a much faster platform to build, if you are athletic enough to pull it off. Squatting into and out of a position is very fast, and my preferred short term use of low cover technique if I can get low enough. The position is very simple – just squat down maintaining a wide stance and shift your body weight forward.

Sight Management

Sight management with a rifle set up like I recommend will entail placing the dot or crosshairs of the scope in the aiming area while allowing for mechanical offset if the threat is at very close range. That said, for those of you that have iron sights of some variety the aspect of sight picture and alignment should be discussed.

- *Sight alignment*: is defined as the alignment of the front sight in the rear sight notch, with the top of the front sight being even across the top of the rear sight, and equal space on both sides of the front sight. With a peep type rear sight, the difference would be that the front sight alignment is verified by centering the top edge of the front sight in the rear peep sight. With standard irons, another way to remember this is there should be equal light and equal height between the front sight and the rear sight. With a peep rear sight, try to imagine a line both horizontally and vertically through the sight, and the key is to have the front sight on the intersection of those two imaginary lines. In traditional marksmanship, time is taken to perfectly align the sights for every shot; however, it must be understood that necessity for perfect alignment increases or decreases depending on the distance to the target. The greater the distance to the target, the more perfectly the sights have to be aligned; conversely, a closer target requires less sight precision. You must learn what level of sight alignment is necessary to successfully hit at different distances.
- *Sight picture*: This is the relationship between the aligned sights and the target. Typically the aligned sights with the front sight as the visual focal point will be placed with the tip of the front sight exactly where the shooter wants the bullet to hit.

Threat Based Focus vs. Sight Focus: With a handgun I teach traditional focus and alignment for the purposes of learning how to align the gun and also discuss a threat-based focus. It is understood that a large percentage of humans will experience central nervous system (CNS) override during high stress, which is part of the physiological and psychological effects of adrenaline and other hormones released into the blood. Subsequently, this process will have numerous physical effects on the body, one of which is dilation of the pupils and the increased inability to focus on the front sight or anything other than the threat in front of us. You are hard wired to look at what is going to hurt you during a fight.

This is one of the main reasons that I like a daytime bright optic like the Aimpoint or Eotech one power scopes for defensive use at closer ranges. The fact remains that the rifle is superior to the handgun in that it is much easier to point at the target and maintain alignment. It is however, entirely possible that the visual focus will be pulled toward the threat while under stress, and if you have iron sights on your rifle you must have the ability to align the gun with sight focus alignment *and/or* threat focus alignment. Do not confuse this threat-based focus shooting as point shooting because it is not. Keep in mind, that although our focal point may not be the sights (front sight specifically), the sights and rifle are still in front of us and can be seen and visually referenced.

Figure 40 The Eotech holographic sight. Notice how the reticle is centered in the scope, but realize this is not necessary with modern parallax free optics like this one.

The rifle itself is an alignment tool and true alignment can be achieved at ranges of three to five yards by aligning the gun itself like pointing your finger. One thing to consider though, for those who argue against training with the sights, is that sight focused training teaches us to become kinesthetically aware of the guns alignment through many repetitions of pointing the gun at the target. We "learn" where the gun is pointed via the sights as a visual reference, even when we may not have a hard focus on the sights. This will allow you to learn the kinesthetic feel of aligning the gun in situations where you may not be focusing on the sights. In your training, use the sights to teach you how to properly align the gun, but experiment with a "threat focus" and simple alignment of the rifle at closer ranges. Learning what you need to see to verify the shot should be one of the main goals of your training.

Mechanical Offset

Keep in mind that no matter what optic or iron sights you have on your rifle, there will still be some mechanical offset between the bore and aligned sights. This will make your point of impact low at close ranges. The reason you need to train with and know your mechanical offset is so that you have the ability to hit a specific shot at close ranges should the need arise. An example is a headshot taken with a hostage or something that might obscure the shot. If you have 1.5 inches of mechanical offset at five yards and place your aiming point on exactly what you are trying to hit, then you will shoot 1.5 inches low. If the innocent hostage (your child!) is in front of that target, then that offset is something you will want to know, and be able to work around.

Trigger Management

Proper management of the trigger is one of the most important factors related to hitting a target under stress <u>at high speeds</u> *once* a solid mount is established within the parameters of the situation. I want to make this distinction about the proper mount because I have heard and disagree with the "trigger control is all you need" thought process. Trigger management is critically important, but remember the importance of building a solid base first.

Why are we concerned with speed? <u>*Because faster hits equate to faster neutralization of the threat*</u>. Improper management of the trigger will result in slower shot to shot times, as well as unintended movement of the gun during manipulation causing errant shots. Pay attention to the following factors while manipulating the trigger during training sessions.

- *Trigger Control*: Trigger control is defined as a constant directly rearward pressure on the trigger that allows the shot to be fired without disturbing the alignment of the gun. Proper trigger control will allow for accurate consecutive shots.
- *Trigger Isolation*: The shooter must isolate the action of the trigger finger to avoid milking the gun. "Milking the Gun" can be defined as increasing the grip pressure with the entire strong-hand while pressing the trigger. In order to counteract this process the gun-hand should remain motionless, and locked into place during the trigger press, and the training goal is to learn how to pull the trigger with the trigger finger while keeping the rest of the fingers motionless.
- *Trigger Direction*: The trigger must be pressed straight to the rear and there should be no pressure applied to either side of the trigger (apply pressure only to the front). The concept of pulling the trigger straight to the rear allows the shooter to fire the gun without pulling it off alignment left, right, up or down. This is critical.

Full Trigger Manipulation. Proper trigger manipulation can be broken down into one of two types of manipulations, the *Accelerated Pull (AP)* and the *Controlled Pull.*

Figure 41 Trigger finger placement on the trigger. Also notice how the thumb has manipulated the safety into the fire position. This happens each time the rifle is mounted into the shooting position, and the opposite when brought off the shooting position.

In my research and training over the years, I have come to the conclusion that manipulating the trigger on a rifle (or handgun) in a close range fight is not done like we teach in so many classic academic settings. For example, when I taught at the federal level, more often than not we focused on teaching trigger manipulation that helped students pass a qualification test. This was normally a slow, steady squeezing manipulation of the trigger under very liberal time constraints.

In most current Law Enforcement training (at the state, local, and federal level) the focus is to get the shooter to accomplish their hits and score well on targets that often times do not represent the dynamics that most rifle fights occur. Unrealistic times (too slow) are also problematic in most of these courses. This has lead to the development and teaching of only a *CP* (controlled pull) type trigger manipulation, which as discussed previously is applicable in only certain situations.

Except for rare circumstances law enforcement officers and civilians will generally be engaging within room distance or possibly a bit farther. I strongly recommend that shooters train for the dynamics that are both possible and most likely in the fight, and this means a shift toward more of an *AP* trigger manipulation, combined with a moderate amount of practice using the *CP* manipulation. Let me break each one down.

Accelerated (AP) Trigger Pull. The AP trigger manipulation technique is similar to a "slap" (although it bothers me to use that term because it is misunderstood as a jerk) but more so an accelerated press on the trigger when contact is made with the pad of the finger. The old adage of "slow steady press" does not apply during a high stress, close range encounter. To keep things simple, just remember that the closer the target, the faster you can manipulate the trigger to the rear and less time you need to "fix" the gun alignment before the shot goes off. It can be described in these steps:

STEP 1: Make contact with the trigger
STEP 2: Accelerate through quickly (straight to the rear)
STEP 3: Repeat (until the threat is neutralized)

Controlled Pull (CP). The CP trigger manipulation technique sometimes referred to in my classes as "prepping and pressing" is a method that allows the shooter to accurately engage smaller or farther targets with as much speed as possible. A key to manipulating the trigger like this is the concept of resetting the trigger during recoil, rather than "pinning" and resetting it after recoil as some instructors teach. Key steps:

STEP 1: *Prep (Take the slack out) the trigger.* You are pulling the trigger back to the point where you start to feel clear resistance. This usually happens as the gun is extended toward the threat, and after the grip is formed. Trigger movement should never be stopped once started (if shooting is still warranted), even though the movement may have to slow near the wall area due to the increasing pressure required to fire the shot. Never stop the finger movement at the wall hoping to fix the sights perfectly before firing, as this will cause an errant shot due to improperly timing the trigger pull.

STEP 2: *Verify sight alignment and placement.* This step will be should be happening as you are accomplishing step one (prep). Line up your sights make fine adjustments to the weapon's sights to ensure a straight line across the top and equal light and space on the left and right side of the front post in relation to the rear sights. This trigger manipulation is used during harder shots, so the vision should be focused on the top edge of the front sight.

STEP 3: *Press to fire the shot.* Break the shot by pressing the trigger straight to the rear until the firearm discharges. As soon as the shot breaks, allow the trigger finger to relax which will facilitate the next step (resetting during recoil).

STEP 4: *Reset and begin to re-prep the trigger.* The trigger should immediately be reset for each additional shot, during recoil. To fire multiple fast shots, resetting the trigger must occur during the cycling of the weapon, allowing the shooter to fire as soon as the muzzle returns to the correct spot on the target. There is rarely an acceptable reason to "pin" the trigger to the rear during recoil with a rifle, unless extreme accuracy is needed.

Alternatively, *Pinning the Trigger.* During the rare case where the target is at very long distances, pinning the trigger might be necessary to ensure that hits are made because it forces the shooter to focus exclusively on follow through and keeping the rifle absolutely still until the bullet has left the barrel. In this case, due to the distance and likely use of cover, time is irrelevant, and follow through is absolutely necessary. In a huge percentage of cases though in the defensive setting, this type of follow through is not useful, and will actually slow the trigger management process down. Beware of which technique you train, and make sure you have a purpose behind the skills you ingrain.

> **TRIGGER MANIPULATION:** *Which trigger management is best for combat? You don't get to decide ahead of time. The situation that occurs dictates this! But what is important is to understand that you must train yourself to do what is necessary to hit the threat in a variety of circumstances. An accelerated pull as described may not work for a situation where the shot requires more accuracy and control. In the end, your brain will select the solution necessary to hit the target, as long as you give it the proper input during training. This means you must train on targets and/or distances that require both.*

Rifle Manipulations

This section will address the manipulations necessary to make the rifle shoot, and keep it shooting (or move to a secondary weapon in some cases). The key to practicing manipulations is to first select ones that are the most functional in terms of being consistent and saving time. Remember that speed and accuracy are most likely very balanced and interrelated in a gunfight with a rifle. Being able to manipulate your rifle at speed, while under stress is a key skill you need. The under stress part is the reason why you want to choose how you manipulate the rifle wisely, and consistently, because anything you do under the effects of the adrenaline and other chemicals dumped into your blood stream during fight mode is going to be potentially more difficult than when you are relaxed and stress free.

In each of the sections below, I will address the reason behind the manipulation as well as the method of doing them properly. Like everything, there are different ways to accomplish each technique, so consider that my way might not necessarily be the best if it does not work for you. That said, I strongly recommend you listen to what I am teaching you, as there is a reason for everything I do. Try and test what I offer, and do your best to use the technique as I lay it out. Keep in mind that it might not feel as comfortable as the way you have done it in the past, but what *new* technique ever feels right the first time you try it?

The Dead Trigger and Transition

Before I teach you how to reload your rifle or clear any malfunction, I want to discuss the context of the situation and make you think about a few things. Dealing with a malfunction or emergency reload situation requires that the operator think about what's going on. The common answer is to perform a reload as quickly as possible, but think about it for a second. If you happen to be defending your home or maybe you're a law-enforcement officer and you're doing a warrant in a house and you're in a gunfight, when the gun runs empty you're likely very, very close to the person you're shooting it out with.

If you break the fight down into time, a full reload with an automatic rifle such as an AR-15 or AK-47 platform is going to take you two seconds or more to perform. If the person you're shooting at is within at 20 to 30 feet, this means that they can close the distance and make contact with you, or shoot their gun several times well before your reload is done. Another consideration when the gun goes dead (i.e. pull trigger and no bang) is that you may not know exactly what's wrong with it. You don't know if it's a serious malfunction or possibly that the weapon has been shot and damaged beyond repair.

Therefore in a situation where you're at room to yard distance (3-10 yards), I strongly recommend that you immediately transition to that handgun if armed with one so you can guarantee that you will quickly be able to get rounds on target again. Think about it in terms of time and risk. While a reload with the rifle and transition to the handgun might require very close to the same amount of time, the fact that you have a dead trigger on the rifle does not always mean you can fix it with a reload. What if that dead trigger signifies a catastrophic bolt override malfunction or something similar? Most rifle malfunctions that cannot be cleared with a tap, rack bang will take much more time to fix than you have to spare. If the rifle is damaged and shot up as referenced above, then it is now a viable club, but not

Figure 42 Teaching a rifle transition to handgun in a class in Alaska. The weird looking war face is optional.

much more. If armed with a handgun, your automatic response should be getting it out and into the fight anytime you have a dead trigger on the rifle. Dump the rifle and transition to the handgun! Steps to the transition:

1. Try to pull the trigger on the rifle (this could happen during a series of shots), and get either a click, or nothing at all.
2. Recognize the rifle is dead and if the distance is appropriate, not behind cover, and you have a handgun…
3. Sweep the rifle out of the way and to your side with your front hand (the one that was on the front handguard/stock) while building the grip on your handgun in the holster.
4. After the front hand sweeps the rifle out of the way make sure it ends up near your chest in a good area to meet the hands together and build a two-handed grip on the handgun.
5. Engage with the handgun as appropriate.

See the following photo sequence.

Dead Trigger

Guide the rifle/grab the handgun

Grip the Handgun

Extend and shoot

Keep in mind that the handgun is now your primary weapon, so finish the fight with it and then follow your post engagement actions. Consider:

1. Finishing the shooting.
2. Scanning the threat and all areas around you (with the handgun as the primary weapon, remember the rifle is dead).
3. Retrieving and looking at the rifle once the fight is over and assessing if it is a problem you can fix (*reload or clear the malfunction). If so…
4. Holster the handgun and fix the rifle.
5. The rifle is now your primary weapon again.

Finish the fight

Assess the rifle (handgun still out)

Holster handgun

Fix the rifle

Figure 43 Reload sequence

So let's assume that the distance is great enough that transitioning to a handgun is not feasible or you don't have a handgun transition to. In this case during the fight when the rifle goes dead your options are to fix it by performing a reload or clearing the malfunction. Additionally, let's say you're at a very close range and you don't have a handgun, consider defaulting to combatives and strike the threat with the rifle. Trying to touch their brain with the muzzle with a full power weapon strike might shift the fight in your favor. If the distance is too great, another option is to use explosive movement to get to a safer spot like a piece of cover, or at a minimum put distance between you and the threat before attempting to reload or clear the malfunction.

One last thought I want you to consider – if you are transitioning, that does not always mean you are transitioning to a handgun. Consider your other weapons, such as a knife if you carry one. The point is that you are transitioning to another weapon system; so don't forget the tools you possess. Train with them so that you respond reflexively based on what is happening!

The next sections will cover reloading the rifle, and clearing malfunctions. As you probably know by now, these are appropriate techniques that will be done as necessary based on the concept of transitioning discussed above.

Reloading techniques

An emergency reload is defined as any time when the chamber is empty and there is absolutely zero ammunition in the weapon system. Most rifles will have a bolt that will lock to the rear, but not all rifles will do this. The complete lack of ammunition, and the fact that the rifle ran out of ammunition while you were still actively shooting it defines the *emergency* reload situation

Let's break down the reload process:

1. Release the old magazine and retrieve the new one.

    a. AR Systems: Right-handed shooters will use the index finger to release the magazine by pressing the button and letting the magazine fall, left-handed shooters will use the thumb.

b. AK Systems: Use the left thumb to release the magazine while you pull the old magazine out of the gun. Left-handed shooters revers this procedure. An alternate method is to use the new (full) magazine to hit the magazine release and "wipe" the old one out with the new one.

c. Other Systems: Those of you that use something other than an AR/AK type system will have to figure out the most consistent method to use with either hand that works well and saves time.

MAGAZINE GRIP: While you're releasing the old magazine and initiating the retrieval of the new magazine I recommend you grab it with the beer can type grip however, there is a second option often taught by other instructors and it mimics the exact method you would normally grab a handyman magazine. I'll call this method the index finger method because you're basically going to place your index finger along the front of the magazine and base pad in the palm of your hand. I don't use this method because I find it harder to control the magazine well. Whichever method you use, I recommend setting up your magazines in your pocket or in your gear so you can easily grab them and use the method of your choice.

2. Once you have the new magazine guide it up in the magazine well of the firearm with enough force to make sure it is seated well. A quick tug before you take your hand off the magazine is time well spent to ensure it is seated.

RIFLE POSITION: When reloading your rifle (or clearing a malfunction) you have two positions you can keep your rifle. Number one, you can keep the rifle on your shoulder if you're strong enough, or number two you can tuck the butt stock several inches under your arm and clampdown on it with your arm. Option number two will give most people more control over the rifle, and this is the option I recommend if you're not strong enough to keep the stock in your shoulder. Clamping the rifle is also a good technique to use while you are moving, because it keeps the rifle secured and easier to manipulate.

3. Once the new magazine is inserted, you have two primary methods to release the bolt or work it if it did not lock to the rear. First, you can rotate your thumb up and onto the bolt release button and press it, and then slide that hand back into position on the front handguard. Another option is to release the bolt by reaching up and

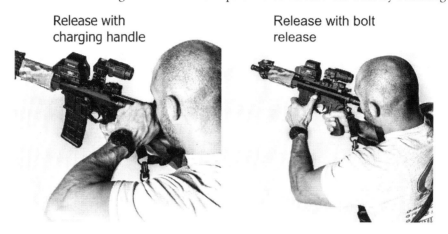

Figure 44 Charging handle or bolt release? Either one is a viable option, but be consistent whichever you choose.

grabbing the charging handle and pulling it directly and fully to the rear. This method seems to be the method of choice for some instructors who argue that it's more of a consistent movement that mimics the same movement used on other rifle types as well as to clear malfunctions. I find using the bolt release is faster and very consistent, as well as designed for that purpose, so I use the release in most cases.

4. Reassess and re-address the threat if it's still a shooting situation. If you used the tuck method with the rifle ensure you get the stock if you talk to stock back on your shoulder. Drive it forward and slightly up your body back to a good cheek weld position. Don't forget the lead hand needs a slide forward to that consistent spot on the handguard as well so you can reacquire a good mount and if necessary fire more shots.

TRIGGER FINGER: During the entire time you're performing the reload process make sure you're taking your finger off the trigger placing it outside the trigger guard. <u>The last thing you want to do is have a negligent discharge after performing the reload.</u>

Malfunction clearing techniques

Before I break down the specifics of clearing malfunctions I want to remind you that the same concept applies as discussed in the emergency reload section and that means that if you were in the room to yard distance I strongly recommend training yourself to and practicing transitioning to a handgun as your immediate response to a dead trigger.

One of the things we discussed briefly in the reload section was timing and malfunctions are unique in that a simple rifle malfunction that can be fixed with a tap (of the magazine) and rack (of the bolt) is very fast to fix the problem. It is as fast as transitioning to a handgun in most cases. But remember the issue is that if the malfunction is a serious one, the clearance procedure could take much longer. It's for that reason that I advocate always transitioning to a handgun if you have one as your immediate response. Let me break down each malfunction type and the general clearance steps:

Tap

Rack

Slide (hand forward)

Shoot

Figure 45 Phase I sequence

1. *Phase I Malfunction.* The defining factor of a phase I malfunction is that it can be fixed with the simple tap, rack procedure. Key steps:
    a. Try to fire the rifle, get no response (dead trigger).
    b. Tap the bottom of the magazine to ensure it is properly seated.
    c. Rack the bolt with the charging handle or bolt handle, ensuring it is pulled all the way to the rear, and released. Roll the gun to help the bad round come out of the chamber.
    d. Ready to fire is necessary and warranted based on the situation.
2. *Phase II Malfunction.* The defining factor of a phase II malfunction is that it CANNOT be fixed with the tap, rack procedure. Key steps:
    a. Try to fire the rifle, get no response (dead trigger).
    b. Perform a tap, rack procedure if possible and unaware of what the problem is (this can also be skipped if you know the problem will not be fixed with tap, rack.

c. Lock the bolt to the rear if possible but moving the front hand back to the bolt release and pressing on the bolt lock nub while using the rear hand to pull the charging handle to the rear.

d. Reach up inside the magazine well and if you can feel any brass or live ammunition, try to sweep it out.

e. Work the bolt at least twice, which will pull any stuck rounds out of the chamber.

f. Reload the rifle with a spare magazine as done during a normal reload.

CONSISTENCY: I recommend using a clearing method that works every time during the daylight or darkness and one that you can perform with your eyes closed. While some steps above can be skipped and the clearance still be done successfully, I recommend sticking to the steps. For example, some instructors do not teach the "lock the bolt" step, but I have found that not locking causes more problems than the time saved by not doing it. Remember, saving time is important, but not so much that you want to short change the process and cause another malfunction.

3. *Phase III Malfunction.* The defining factor of a phase III malfunction is that it cannot be fixed with a phase I or II clearance. The other defining factor is that the bolt, when pulled to the rear is stuck and can't be moved enough to clear the chamber. This malfunction is unique and caused but problems internally such as a malformed piece of brass or something stuck in the chamber. This manipulation will use a combination of the standard techniques and momentum to fix the problem.

    a. Try to fire the rifle, get no response (dead trigger).

    b. Perform a tap, rack procedure if possible and unaware of what the problem is (this can also be skipped if you know the problem will not be fixed with tap, rack). During the "rack" step, you will not be able to pull the bolt to the rear.

    c. The ground is the best option to use momentum on the following steps, so kneel on the ground. Another option is find a position around the ve-

Lead hand slides back

Lock the bolt

Rip the mag out

Finger sweep

Work bolt (2-3 times)

Figure 46 Phase II sequence.

hicle, table or other solid obstacle that you can utilize to drive the butt stock of your rifle in to.

d. If you have a collapsible stock I recommend collapsing that stock down so you don't break your stock during the momentum clear. I will say that I have never broken a stock even during times I did not collapse the stock, but be advised that you might want to collapse your stock before trying this technique.

e. Roll the rifle over so the magazine is pointing toward you while pointing the muzzle away from your head. The opposite will be done with the AK platform as the charging handle is on the other side of the gun.

f. Hook the charging handle with your thumb and depress the latch if you have one on your rifle (all AR's).

g. While keeping the muzzle away from your head, take the entire rifle three or four inches off of the ground and then drive it aggressively into the ground while at the same time pulling hard with your thumb on the charging handle. This will create some momentum and most of the time on the first strike will cause the bolt to release and extract the stuck round. If not, repeat this step.

h. Continue to pull the bolt always the rear to make sure that you extract that round completely out of the chamber and if the bolt is moving and you feel like you have good extraction, continue the clearance technique as described in the phase II clearance.

Figure 47 Hook the thumb on the bolt release, and tap the buttstock on the ground while pulling the charging handle hard (make sure you have it unlatched!).

i. Remount and ready to shoot if the threat still presents itself as an active threat.

> *BOLT OVERRIDE: One anomaly type malfunction that you might run across is what's called a bolt override malfunction. I have personally not experienced a true bolt override but I actually learned about how to clear a bold override and the possibility of one in Kyle Lamb's DVD so I want to give credit where credit is due. A bold override is where you actually get a piece of brass or round stock up in the charging handle between the bolt and the front end of the charging handle. When you try to attempt your clearance and pull the bolt to the rear, locking it will feel like a short stroke. The bolt will feel like it's not coming all the way to the rear. The reason for that is because the brass is stuck up in the charging handle and is not allowing you to pull the bolt to the rear with that piece of brass in front of it. The key to getting that rounds out of that area is to lock the bolt rear and then drive the charging handle forward which will normally take the tension off the round and allow it to fall out and out of the chamber.*

Movement Techniques

Moving while manipulating the rifle is going to allow you to react to threats in a much more effective manner than standing still. Movements include pivoting to address the threat, movement offline to cover, and moving while shooting or manipulating your rifle.

90-Degree Pivot

In this section, I will describe a 90 and 180-degree pivots but the same mechanics will be used when performing pivots at varying angles from your front. Pivoting 90 degrees or more may be necessary when a threat appears somewhere other than directly in front of you. A combination of target acquisition and body mechanics will allow a shooter to turn and engage a threat with about the same speed as they could engage a threat to the front. The proper method to engage a threat to the right or left is to use the target acquisition technique of turning the head and eyes toward the threat first. While the eyes acquire the threat, the weapon is presented to the threat with the same mounting technique previously discussed. To perform a correct pivot you will pivot your head, then your body to face the threat by pivoting the foot on the same side as the threat and pointing your toes toward the threat. Then step with the other foot in the same direction (note: this is a forward step; try to avoid stepping to the rear, into the unknown). Pivoting should be done on the ball of the foot while the other foot will step forward completing the move and reforming the stance in the direction of the threat.

180-Degree Pivot

Pivoting 180 degrees may be necessary if you need to engage a threat that appears to your rear. Pivoting 180 degrees will be done very much like the 90 degree pivot, with the exception being the distance pivoted. The proper method to engage a threat to the rear is to use the target acquisition technique of turning the head and eyes toward the threat first. While the eyes acquire the threat, the mount process and pivot is initiated as taught in the mount process discussed above. Some shooters may find it easier to step and pivot rather than pivot and step as described above. If so, you should step with the opposite foot of the direction they wish to turn. That foot should cross the other foot and step about the same distance as the normal stance. The other foot will naturally pivot to mirror the foot with which you initially stepped.

Offline Movement Techniques

Movement offline while manipulating a weapon is a skill that is critical during extremely close engagements where the need to create distance is imperative. For example, when a person finds themselves a step or two away from cover. Movement offline should be to a position of cover or an obstacle of some sort. If there is no close cover available, moving offline to outrun bullets will not be very effective, and shooters will be better served using a sprint step technique to run to a distant obstacle or piece of cover. It is also a key technique that integrates with movement offline from an attack with a knife or blunt weapon. Shooters can move offline in any direction, but two common directions are left or right offline movement.

One Step: Used to move one or two steps to cover. Movement in any direction should start by moving that foot first (the one in the direction of the desired movement). If moving to the right, move the right foot first, and the opposite with the other foot. The feet should not cross and movement should be natural and steps should be about the same distance as a normal step. Both feet should move

Figure 48 Mounting and moving offline. This picture does not depict it, but the bigger the step the better.

about the same distance, and if the shooter moves a certain distance with his/her right foot the other foot should move the same distance. The ending stance after movement should be a good fighting stance, with good balance and weight distribution. The mounting or draw process, reloads, or malfunction clearance can be done during this movement. Remember, explosive movement is the key to move the body offline of the attack.

Sprint Step: Used to move offline to a distant piece of cover in an open area where the only option is to move quickly out of the line of fire. Pivot toward the direction desired and explosively push off the foot opposite of the direction to be traveled. This is similar to a cutting movement used in sports. The body turns and faces the new direction; then explosively sprints to cover. Mounting or drawing during this movement is less important than getting to the piece of cover and not getting shot.

Shooting while Moving Techniques

In the dynamic environment of a gunfight, engaging a threat while moving might be necessary in certain situations. The absolute best option is to stop the body's movement and then shoot, but this cannot be done in all situations. Therefore, I recommend practicing shooting (and learning to stabilize the gun) while moving. The proper technique for shooting and moving:

- *Center the gun.* This was discussed in the mount/stance section but I want to remind you the importance of keeping the stock as centered as possible on the chest. This will help minimize the gun's movement. The farther out on your body the stock is placed, the more the pivoting movement of the shoulders will move the gun.
- *Bend the knees.* Lowering the center of gravity and keeping the knees bent will help minimize movement by using the legs as shock absorbers.
- *Narrow gait.* Keep the feet closer together if possible when moving, similar to walking along a 10-inch board. This will minimize movement of the rifle left and right.
- *Short steps.* Short steps will keep the muzzle from raising and dipping as you step. Keep the steps short
- *Steps should roll from heel to toe and toe to heel.* When walking, this rolling of the feet will help keep the gun more stable than stepping and "slapping" the feet onto the ground. Move forward by placing your heel on the ground first and rolling from heel to toe.

KEY TIP: *Watching the gun movement and changing the lower body dynamics to minimize that movement is the simplest way to learn how the lower body should act.*

Rearward movement

While engaging might be necessary in certain situations, and more specifically might be a viable technique when a shooter needs to create distance while engaging a threat at the same time. The technique used to engage while moving to the rear is very similar as moving to the front except that as the foot moves to the rear, the toe touches the ground first and the shooter rolls their feet from toe to heel. By distinctly placing the toe on the ground and rolling to the rear, the shooters foot will also likely "roll" over an object on the ground rather than trip on it. The body position will remain low with the knees bent and all of the other principles will remain consistent.

Moving mount

At times when using the sprint offline technique described above, or when simply running from one place to another, you locate a target to shoot. This requires that the rifle be mounted and fired as quickly as possible. When running, I like to use a technique that places the stock over my shoulder, and allows me to swing my arms when I run. Remounting the rifle is simply a matter of driving the rifle forward while sliding the stock back into the optimum position on my chest and then finding a good cheek weld. Remember, when drilling a technique like this, if you plan on running with the safety engaged (recommended), practice disengaging it while mounting the rifle. See the next photo sequence to see this in action.

Figure 49 This is a great example of using a stock over shoulder dismount and remount in addition to footwork to safely move around a friend to address a threat on the other side of him.

One-Handed Manipulations

I am an avid believer in practicing skills that might be considered extreme, such as one-handed survival shooting skills. These days, with ample high quality training available, it is common to find instructors teaching one-handed manipulations with a handgun. One-handed manipulations with a rifle are an often-overlooked skill that should be addressed, especially for those who may only be armed with that weapon. Back in my Marine Corps days, the only weapon a private through Staff NCO (Non-Commissioned Officer) would be issued was a rifle. Transitioning to a handgun during a fight was not an option because we did not have them!

Even these days I run across members of the U.S. Military that might only be issued a rifle, or, even more common, may choose not to carry a handgun on an operation for some particular reason. And how about the civilian gun owner who chooses to grab a rifle to defend their property? They certainly might have a need to know how to manipulate their rifle with one hand!

> *Question:* Ok, so if I am selling one-handed manipulations with a rifle (or even a handgun for that matter), how often is this skill required and is it worth your precious training time and ammunition to practice them?

The statistical answer is not much. So why train it? Because this survival skill must be possessed if the worst case occurs, and if it is not, your life may be in jeopardy. You don't have to practice one-handed skills each time you shoot, but I *strongly* recommend that you learn them and then practice them routinely enough so you are confident you could perform them under stress. I strongly believe in dry fire practice as a means to a higher level of skill, and the good news is that almost everything that is required (from a skill perspective) can be practiced with some dummy rounds in a safe area of your home (remember the dry fire rules).

> *Safety Note:* One-handed survival shooting is a high-level manipulation skill that must be practiced correctly and safely. If you do not have the knowledge to practice these techniques, please find a qualified instructor to teach you the skills allowing you to practice them safely. Training with one-handed survival techniques allows for the possibility of pointing the muzzle in an unsafe direction, so please ensure you get quality instruction.

Lets get into the details of manipulating and shooting your rifle with one hand. First, if you have not addressed one-handed handgun manipulation, please do so since using a handgun with one hand is the first option I will guide you to if you are carrying one. This is simply because using (shooting and manipulating) a rifle with one hand only is very difficult because of its weight and length. Secondly, please understand that I am writing this section to address the M-4/16 rifle system and its variants simply because that is what I think most readers will be carrying. If you are carrying another rifle, the principles taught in this article should be followed, but you might have to experiment with your particular rifle to refine your techniques. Please do so safely with non-live dummy rounds before using live ammunition!

The following techniques all incorporate some of the same items such as where to secure the rifle while manipulating, how to manipulate the bolt with one hand, how to release the magazine with one hand, etc.

So, the worst has occurred, you are in a fight for your life and injured, allowing you to use only one hand to shoot the rifle. The following techniques will allow you to fight through the situation and survive.

One Handed Shooting Techniques

The first thing I want to discuss is actually shooting with one hand only with a rifle. Due to the fact that effectively using a rifle normally requires the use of both hands, how do we shoot with one hand only? I will give you two options (both of which I recommend testing and training with on the range):

- *Tucking the buttstock under the arm to control the vertical movement of the rifle.* This is often the best choice if you are smaller or lack significant upper body strength. Tucking the buttstock under the arm and maintaining control with the hand on the pistol grip is the best way to control the rifle. This position is limiting in that it does not allow you to mount the sights (or optic) in front of your face.
- *Mounting the rifle to your shoulder and using your chin (strong cheek weld) to control the rifle.* This option is my personal choice, and it allows me to continue to use the sights on the rifle since the buttstock is mounted to my shoulder. It does take a bit more strength than the other technique, but is effective if you can make it work.

Shooting the rifle with one hand only. Tuck it under the shoulder, or mount it and drive your face down on the stock.

Okay, so not you are in the middle of the fight with only one arm and the rifle stops functioning. What now?

Transition

Depending on the distance to the threat and the situation, transitioning to your handgun might be your best option. If you are fighting in your house or a building, this is probably the case. The transition sequence with two hands is described previously in this chapter. Remember, learning how to draw and manipulate your handgun with the support hand is also a key here, so please ensure you have that skill too. Its possible you may only have your support hand available. To transition, simply draw the handgun after guiding the rifle out of the way. If you are using a rifle without a sling, that could be problematic and you will have to accept the fact that retaining the rifle is impossible. Remember that the rifle is no longer operational, and until you survive the immediate fight is useless. If cover and distance is available, then attempting to get the rifle running will often be the best option.

If transitioning is not a logical option, then fixing the rifle or reloading it is your best option. Lets discuss the techniques for these options.

One-Handed Malfunction Clearance

There are two malfunction clearances that I will define as a phase I and II malfunction, and each will fix almost any malfunction you might have. Lets cover the Phase I first (Tap, Rack, Ready):

- Tap the magazine in the gun by bringing the gun down with some force onto the top of the leg. This should secure the magazine in the gun if that was the problem. (Photo: Tap the Magazine)
- Secure the rifle between the knees (bring it around your leg versus covering your foot with the muzzle). I recommend securing it with the magazine well pointing to the right (see photo) when you are operating the rifle with the right hand. This will allow the brass coming out of the chamber to fall out easier. If operating the rifle with the left hand then the magazine well should be pointed straight down if possible. See the illustration below.
- Now reach over the gun with the operational hand and work the bolt with the charging handle. Don't forget to pull hard and slingshot the bolt versus riding the bolt forward possibly causing a worse malfunction.

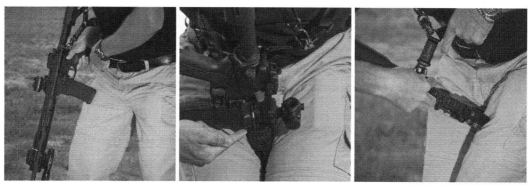

Figure 50 Tap, Secure (between legs), and Rack the bolt.

Phase II (Lock, Rip, Work, Tap, Rack, Ready) (assuming you already tried a Phase I, or observed a malfunction that you knew a Phase I clearance would not clear):

- Lock the bolt (this step is optional, but often clears the malfunction from the rifle). This is best done by using the knife-edge of the hand to lock the bolt to the rear (see photo on right).

- Rip the magazine out by pressing the release with either the index finger or thumb and pulling the magazine out.
- Work the bolt at least twice to extract any remaining brass/ammunition from the chamber. You can also use a finger sweep during this step if you find a piece of brass stuck in the chamber area.
- Follow the TAP/RACK/READY steps to tap a new magazine in the gun (don't forget to tug!), rack the bolt with the charging handle, and now you are ready to shoot if the situation still warrants it.

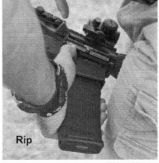

One-Handed Reloads.

Performing a reload with one hand will require the same securing method (between the knees) to maintain control of the rifle. Another option that works if mobility is a concern is simply letting the rifle hang from the sling while performing the following motions, but be aware that using this technique offers much less support of the rifle, and the muzzle direction might be unsafe when operating the bolt. Reloading key points:

- *Releasing the magazine with the right hand in operation*: Simply hit the magazine button with your index finger and let the magazine fall out of the gun before securing the gun between your legs.
- *Releasing the magazine with the left hand in operation*: Secure the gun between your legs and grab the magazine while pushing the button with the thumb. Pull the magazine out of the gun. (See the photo above)
- *Access the new magazine and reload*: Grabbing the magazine might be more or less challenging depending on where you keep your extra magazines. (This might cause you to modify your gear a bit) When inserting the magazine with one hand, ensure that you secure it firmly and tug to ensure that it is seated in the gun. Release the bolt but grabbing the charging handle and slingshot it to release and cycle the bolt. Remember to do this aggressively and do not ride the charging handle forward. The bolt release is an obvious choice to release the bolt but in some cases it is hard to access, which is why I recommend using the charging handle.

Task Fixation

Don't forget that during any type of one-handed survival shooting manipulation, it is very important that you continue to keep your head and eyes up and in view of the threat area. *It is natural to get fixated on the gun and area where you are working to get it running, and while it is okay*

Figure 51 Keep your head and eyes up! Watch for the threat.

to glance down to assess in certain cases, it is still important to keep your head and eyes in the game so you can react to what the threat is doing. Make yourself look up when training!

Checking your gear

One of the first things we cover in our one handed manipulation and shooting blocks of instruction is gun and gear set up. Obviously, the type of sling, spare magazine placement, etc. that you wear will effect how you are going to operate your gun with one hand. What you *can* do is test your equipment trying different one-handed techniques, so you know their limitations, and then find ways to work around the problems you are having. This takes time and dedicated training, and absolutely must be done to ensure you don't end up having to figure this stuff out during an actual fight.

Selecting the right technique

Techniques are usually best chosen by finding ones that are consistent and simple, but you will have to know several in order to operate with only one hand. The reason for this is that certain techniques simply will not work in all situations. I always teach multiple techniques, and discuss with students when each might be used during our one-handed survival shooting class. Try not to limit yourself to firearm techniques only, and think outside of the box when it comes to surviving with one hand. Often times, I stress that fact that sometimes a gun solution is not always the answer, and it is best for you to utilize some sort of physical technique to shift the fight to your favor before you would try to reload the gun or clear a malfunction with one hand.

Training for one-handed manipulations

I absolutely must stress the importance of getting training from a qualified instructor if you are unfamiliar with these techniques. DO NOT go to the range and attempt any one-handed technique until you have trained that technique with an unloaded firearm with dummy training ammunition first. In classes I teach, I stress lots (hours) of dry practice first, and then a simple live fire drill that allows the user to test all of the techniques during live fire.

In closing, let me point out this very important point: Manipulating and shooting with one hand is a difficult skill to perform under stress. If you are in a situation where a one-handed survival technique is needed, then things have gone from bad (just having one hand in the fight) to worse (now having to fix a non-working gun with one hand). Figure out how to survive the situation in the comfort of your home during dry fire, or on your range during some live fire training before you end up in a fight for your life needing a particular skill. Don't get caught unprepared in this arena!

Close Range Techniques

Shooting a rifle at close ranges (less than 3 yards) might require the use of alternate mount techniques. The range and circumstance might not allow you to shoulder the rifle normally and mount it to shoot. The situation is likely one where you were moving through an area and before you can react the threat is upon you, either grabbing at your rifle muzzle or tackling you. Your goals should be to: a) gain distance if possible; b) retain the rifle (it's yours, you don't want to give it away), and c) engage if appropriate. Gaining distance might be easier said than done, but if you can get away, do so. The following section discusses the technique and breaks it down in order as it probably happens during the event. Weapon retention is covered first, and close range shooting positions are last.

Weapon Retention

Keeping your rifle is certainly a big priority. If you have a high quality sling on, it will help tie the rifle to your body. This is a good thing unless the threat uses it against you. There are some simple steps you can use to help retain your weapon and hopefully gain distance, but keep in mind that all options are on the table, including shooting the person off of your if they are grabbing your rifle. Shooting however, might not be your best option in some cases where you are in close range to others that you do not wish to shoot (like a team or family environment). Consider the following:

- **Step and Pull.** If you can, step aggressively to the rear or offline at an angle while pulling the rifle directly back toward you, optimally tucking the stock under the arm.
- **Shoot if possible.** This stepping/pulling action should pull the muzzle inline with the attacker, and if so and they are still holding on, pull the trigger. Remember, this is a shooting position, so you will have to flick the safety off when building the shooting position.
- **Attack.** If shooting the person is not warranted or your choice, but they are still grabbing the rifle muzzle, you need to get them off it. The first step and act of pulling and tucking the rifle under the arm gives a greater level of control over the rifle, allowing you to take your front hand off the rifle and use it to smash down onto their arms/hands, into their neck or face, and better yet, access a blade with that hand and start cutting them off your gun. Remember, if you are "cutting" them off your gun, you are using lethal force. Some of you might ask, if you can use a knife on them, why couldn't you shoot them? Simple – imagine your young son somewhere near you during this chaos and maybe in a position where he might be hit if you shoot. Sometimes shooting is not an option at that moment.
- **Create distance.** Hopefully the above actions will get the rifle free. When possible, space is your friend so try to create distance as soon as possible. The last thing you want is him or her grabbing the gun again.

I had the opportunity to work with Michael Janich (http://www.martialbladeconcepts.com) on rifle retention and asked him his take on some specific techniques against a rifle grab. What follows is his response:

Michael Janich on Rifle Retention

AR-style rifles and carbines are extremely potent weapons that are adaptable to many different tactical environments. At close quarters, however, their length makes them considerably more difficult to maneuver than handguns and can easily turn any close-contact engagement into a deadly wrestling match. Whether you are a duty-bound officer or soldier or a civilian considering an AR for home defense, you owe it to yourself to incorporate long-gun retention into your training regimen.

Establish Context

There are many different ways of approaching long-gun retention, however, some of them are very dependent upon the context of your mission and both what and whom you have with you besides your rifle. In a military context with clear rules of engagement and a team of shooters to back you up, your tactics may be as simple as controlling your gun's muzzle direction and staying out of the line of fire while your teammates solve the problem for you. If you had to address a gun grab yourself but you still had the benefit of operating in full kit, your defense might be to transition to a pistol or a knife to shoot, stab, or cut the attacker clinging to the other end of your rifle. Full kit often also means you have equipment like ballistic helmets that can turn a simple head butt into a life-changing experience for the gun grabber.

Assessing your mission, rules of engagement, and available resources is critically important to determining the best rifle-retention tactics for your situation, so you really need to invest the time to define the context in which you anticipate having to apply your skills. Obviously a lone civilian using an AR for home defense is going to have vastly different options that a member of a SWAT team. With that said, however, I feel strongly that the fundamental concepts and the mechanics of one's initial response to a rifle grab are very universal. What works well for an individual also works well when that individual is part of a team. And the more universal a solution is, the less you have to think about it under stress.

An Ounce of Prevention

What's the best defense against a rifle grab? Logically, it's to not let the bad guy grab your rifle in the first place. Awareness, good tactics, and proper movement should all be first-line defenses against weapon grabs. However, if an unfriendly does get close enough to you to touch your weapon, you still have an option: the classic "J Stroke."

The "J Stroke" is a defensive movement of the rifle that basically consists of "writing" a letter "J" in the air with the muzzle end of your gun. It is often taught as a counter against a completed grab and is typically done without changing your shooting grip. Although this may work for larger, stronger shooters, I've found the mechanics of it are not adequate against committed grabs from bigger attackers. To be more precise, since most shooters use some form of palm-up grip on the weapon with their support hand, the force achievable by pulling the weapon downward is limited by the strength of your grip. If the attacker achieves a solid two-handed grip, the motion of the "J Stroke" could easily cause your support hand to come off the gun, leaving him with dominant control.

As a preventative tactic, however, the "J Stroke" works quite well. As an attacker reaches for your weapon, quickly angle the gun down, pivoting it from the index of the butt on your shoulder or pectoral muscle. When the muzzle reaches about groin level, rotate your upper body to face directly toward your attacker, stepping as necessary with your rear foot to maintain your balance as you square up. As you do this, circle the muzzle up in an arc, orient it on the attacker's body, and lunge forward to strike him with the muzzle. Use your whole body to power the strike and maintain good trigger-finger discipline as you do.

This tactic works equally well whether the attack is coming from your left or right sides. By applying the basic order of operations described above, you'll actually have a true "J" for attacks coming from the left and a reverse "J" for grabs coming from the right.

Under, Over, Drop, Center, Ram

If an attacker does manage to get his hands on your rifle, it's important that you make maximum use of your body mechanics to retain control of it and ultimately break his grip. To do this, you need to:
- Use your strongest muscles
- Use your skeletal structure
- Use body weight
- Use body rotation

With these priorities in mind, the rifle-retention method that I prefer follows the order of operations of "under, over, drop, center, ram." I guess if I thought harder I could come up with a cool-sounding acronym for this process, but I didn't. If you can trust yourself to handle a loaded rifle, I'm confident that you can remember the sequence without one.

"Under" represents tucking the buttstock under your armpit. To do this, you must obviously pull the weapon back toward you—an action that can, by itself, serve as both a preventive and proactive counter to a grab. This should be as reflexive as possible and ideally should not involve any grip change on the weapon. It should also make use of the first principle noted above, using your strongest muscles. Use the latissimus dorsi ("lat") muscles of your back, not your biceps. Instead of thinking of pulling the weapon, pull your elbows back toward your body. That will naturally bring the right muscles into play. Once the butt is under your armpit, use the same muscles to clamp down, anchoring it under the shoulder (skeletal structure) with lots of surface area working for you.

"Over" signifies wrapping your support hand over the top of the weapon's forend. Unlike the conventional palm-up grip used for shooting, this places the entire skeletal structure of the hand over the weapon. Your hand's grip is the weakest link in maintaining control over the gun, so wrapping your hand over the top eliminates this weakness.

With the rifle tucked under your armpit and your support hand wrapped over the forend, you've created a strong skeletal structure over the gun. This prepares you for the next step, which is to "drop" your body weight suddenly to break the attacker's grip. Rather than simple squatting, think of abruptly picking up your feet to drop your body quickly. As you do, angle the muzzle downward. This sudden drop, combined with the entire weight of your body will make it almost impossible for the attacker to maintain his grip on the weapon. In many cases, it will also force his head to snap forward, creating an excellent opportunity for a head butt. Delivered with a helmet, this can be a true fight stopper.

At the conclusion of the "drop," you should be in a squatting position with your weapon angled downward. From this position, pivot toward the attacker and "center" your muzzle on his body. If he has any grip left on the weapon, your sharp pivot should finish breaking it and point your muzzle at his body's centerline. At a minimum, it will put his hands in an awkward position and compromise his ability to grasp the weapon with any strength.

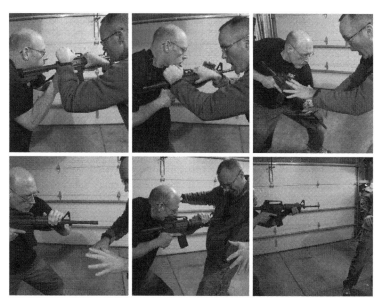

Figure 52 Against an attack from the flank Janich demonstrates the principles of "under, over, drop, center, ram."

The final step in the process is to "ram" the attacker with the muzzle to hurt him and drive him backward to create distance. To do this, maintain your secure under/over grip on the weapon and consciously extend your trigger finger safely along the lower receiver above the trigger guard. Shuffle your lead foot forward and drive powerfully off your rear foot so you strike with the entire force and mass of your body. This method also keeps you from extending your arms and potentially giving the attacker the opportunity to grab your rifle again. Although targeting the sternum typically creates the most pain and distance, depending upon the dynamics of the situation, you can also strike the solar plexus, abdomen, pelvis, or groin.

This method is extremely effective against grabs from both the left and right sides and also works perfectly with typical single and double-point slings. It also works exactly the same way whether it is applied preemptively to thwart an attempted grab or reactively to break the grip of an attacker who has already managed to latch onto your weapon. Additionally, it allows you to decisively control the direction of your muzzle at all times and maintain the ability to fire the weapon if necessary.

Low/High

If a weapon grab occurs in extremely confined quarters—like a hallway—you can still apply the same basic principles and concepts of the technique. The only difference is that the pivoting motion to center up on the attacker may be limited. If this happens, center up the best you can and focus on delivering ramming strikes to the attacker's low-line—including his thighs, groin and pelvis. Once you've "tenderized" him a bit with those, raise the muzzle to the high line and ram his sternum to drive him back and create separation. Be prepared to follow up as necessary.

The Shear

One other release technique worth considering is called the "shear." This technique works best against grabs coming from your support side—especially if the attacker manages to grip toward the center of the weapon.

Like the previous technique, your initial reaction should be the same: to use your back muscles to pull the weapon back and tuck the buttstock firmly under your armpit. Once this is done, release your support-hand grip on the weapon and bring the palm of your support hand to your head. This should place the elbow of that arm close you your ribs. Maintaining a firm clamping pressure on the buttstock with your armpit and a solid grasp on the pistol grip, quickly turn your shoulders, jerking the weapon back as you drive the elbow of your support arm forward to strike your attacker's wrists. The movement of the support-arm elbow should be as linear as possible. This allows the humerus (the bone of the upper arm) to act as a strut, again using structure to get the job done instead of muscular strength. To further reinforce this structure, keep the palm of your support hand braced against your forehead just ahead of your temple.

Again, the key to this technique is to power it with an explosive turn of your shoulders, not a steady push. It should be more strike than push. At the end of the strike, your support hand will be positioned for two finishing options. The first is to hit the attacker in the face with a palm-heel strike to rock his head back and create distance. The second is to quickly slap your palm down on the top of the forend and drop, center, and ram as before.

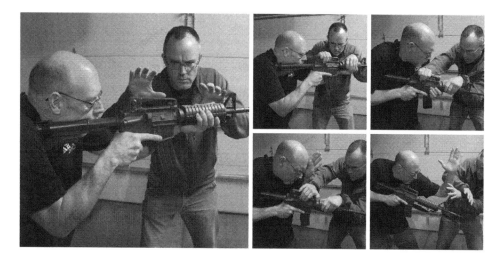

Figure 53 Retract and tuck the gun, tuck the elbow, rotate the shoulders and shear attackers hands off the gun with the support arm elbow as gun is jerked to the rear.

Training Creates Reflex

Understanding the mechanics of these techniques and trying them a few times is good, but it doesn't create the conditioned reflex you'll need to apply them in the dynamics of a real fight. To do that, you need proper training and lots of repetitions. The best way to do that is with a plastic "blue gun" version of your rifle that is equipped with the same sling set-up. Your training partner should wear gloves to protect his hands and you should work slowly at first to get a feel for the mechanics of the technique. As you get more comfortable, work it from different angles and gradually increase the intensity while ensuring that you pull your strikes short to ensure safety. As you improve, add another training partner so you have two "attackers" who randomly grab from different angles to challenge your ability to react spontaneously.

Countering grabs is a necessary part of any good rifle gunfighting skill set. Now that you've got the knowledge, invest the time in the training.

Michael Janich- MBC

Close Quarters Shooting Positions

Shooting from close quarters requires a different approach. The above steps describe tucking the rifle under the shoulder as a good position to help retain it, and shooting from that position is a good option. While it is my preferred position there is another I will offer that can be used if tucking the rifle under did not work. Shooting from these close quarters positions should be practiced so you have the skill down if you need to pull the trigger. Practice the following positions:

- **Tuck the rifle under the shoulder**. Pull the rifle to the rear and try to tuck the entire stock under the shoulder, and clamp down on it with your strong side arm. In the drill section, this is one of the shooting techniques practiced, so make sure you practice flicking off the safety when performing the technique. Keep both hands on the gun when pulling the rifle to the rear. *Remember, the retention technique described above requires that you rotate your lead hand over the top of the gun, so make sure you are practicing that move when you use this technique during live fire.*
- **Retract the rifle over the shoulder**. This technique might be used if the rifle stock is knocked off your body and you cannot get the stock under your shoulder. Simply pull the rifle to the rear aggressively and allow the stock to slide over the shoulder. I like to rotate the rifle slightly clockwise so that the stock is sitting on my shoulder. Be careful not to drive your optic or rear sight into your eye, a mistake you will only make once. Once again, don't forget to flick the safety off when practicing this technique. Additionally, the hand rotation discussed above is consistent with this technique.

Low Light Techniques

Accessorizing your rifle with a mounted light and training with it is a critical step in your skill development. Operating a handgun and light independently are easy to manage, but trying to use a rifle and flashlight separately are much more difficult. As discussed in the accessorizing section, a weapon-mounted light is highly recommended if you really want to be able to use your rifle in low light shooting situations.

Light selection and Placement

I strongly prefer my rifle light to be mounted at the 6 o'clock position on the rifle, with the pressure switch directly below where my thumb would ride on the top of the handgun when my hand is in the right position (see the mount section). Why? Well, during initial testing I thought I would simplify and mounted a Surefire X200 on the top rail in a position where I would activate the light with my thumb (with either hand) at the twelve o'clock position. There were a couple reasons I wanted to test this, actually. First, I don't like to have gear mounted to my rifle at six o'clock because it forces my hand to be farther back (toward the magazine well) on the gun causing me to lose the forward grip I like. As discussed in the mount section, I like to have my support hand as far out as possible when shooting a rifle for increased muzzle control. Second, I had yet to mount a rail to the bottom of the hand guard on this particular rifle, so thought I would test the twelve o'clock position with the Surefire light and simply operate it using my thumb just like I would if the light were on my pistol. This allowed me to skip attaching a pressure activation switch to the light, and it works well when shooting bilaterally (off either shoulder).

Figure 54 The 6-o'clock mounting position (light) with the activation switch on the top of the gun and accessible with either hand is the only way to go. I've tested all of the other positions and keep coming back to this one.

Why not mount my light at three o'clock or nine o'clock positions, or somewhere else on the side? Because the light simply washes back brilliantly when shining on a wall or the edge of a door when working corners, sending light splashing back into your eyes. The three and nine o'clock positions also force the operator to expose the light, gun and himself more so than with a twelve or six o'clock position when shooting from the opposite side of the light.

Time to test my 12 o'clock position. The training session began at about 8:00 p.m., and I spent about three hours testing close-, medium-, and long-range shooting techniques and also worked on using cover by setting up some barricades. Training with this simulated cover was a big part of correct training as well as testing techniques in the contextual situation they would be used thus allowing correct lessons to be learned. I did not exceed 100 yards, as using a light to illuminate and engage past 100 yards would be out of context for me (and most others).

I quickly learned that mounting a light at the 12 o'clock position was a real bad idea. There were some other lessons during the session, most of which reinforced what I already knew. Light position on the rifle and proper use was critical!

The lessons learned

Watch the splashback. During my practice I worked shooting around pieces of cover, which consisted of using some barricades that simulated wall corners or the edge of a door or vehicle. Although I spent a portion of the night training in the open just working on illuminating, shooting and scanning the threat area, adding a barricade demonstrated the incredible importance of ensuring that the light did not splash back in my face blinding me during the process.

Watch the shadows. Another observation in relation the spashback concept is that the shadow caused by the edge of the barricade can easily shadow and hide a potential threat downrange. The light must be used in a manner that illuminates what needs to be seen, without exposing too much of the rifle and operator, all while paying attention to the potential for spashback. Staying a proper distance from cover is a big part of this lighting equation.

Test and Modify Your Gear. This one was the biggest of the lessons learned. While I knew that the twelve o'clock mounting position of the light was not the best option, I had convinced myself that at the ranges I would likely operate my rifle, the smoke obscuring my vision would not be an issue. I was wrong! Even at closer ranges of ten yards, the smoke became an issue with multiple rounds fired, and with the light mounted at twelve o'clock; the smoke issue was huge, especially when using an optic (an Aimpoint C3 in this case).

Figure 55 This is what happens when you mount the light on the side of the gun and do not allow the beam to miss the wall--serious splash back of the light right into your eyes!

Without testing the light in live fire, I would not have realized how much the smoke would obscure my vision. At more than fifty yards, the smoke completely covered the targets and kept me from shooting for a second or so until it cleared enough for me to see the next target. After I mounted the light at the six o'clock position, the smoke problems became almost none existent due to the fact that the light was no longer illuminating the smoke in front of my scope. As stated before, the three and nine o'clock positions are not recommended because of the increase in splashback that the shooter will get from those positions.

Have a backup plan. When I teach low light with a handgun, I always tell students to carry a backup light in life-or-death situations. Most rifle shooters have a weapon-mounted light, but what if it fails? A handheld light is a viable option when your weapon-mounted light goes down, but using such a light is a unique skill that must be learned and trained; don't expect to master it during the fight! During the training session, I bumped the switch on the rear portion of my light causing the light to turn off. When the light failed (due to operator error) I resorted to using my handheld light, which is a skill that is tricky with a rifle because you lose the ability to grip the hand guard the same way as normal. Suggestions for using a handheld light with the rifle:

- Option 1 – Use a modified grip and hold the light with the palm of the hand with the thumb over the activation button. Rotate the hand counterclockwise and slightly under the handguard while wrapping the fingers around it as best as you can (switch this to the opposite hand if you are left-handed).
- Option 2 – Hold the light in the palm of the hand with the thumb over the activation button and switch the hand to the other side of the handguard allowing the rifle to rest on the arm. There is less control of the recoil with this method, but it might be easier to use than the first method discussed.

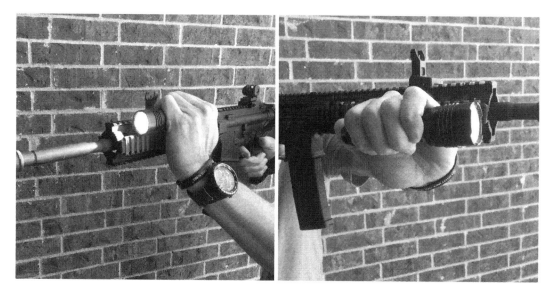

Figure 56 Option 1 on the left, Option 2 on the right. I prefer Option 1.

Using Cover (for protection and bracing the rifle)

The proper use of cover is a critical subject, because it protects you from getting shot. In addition, understanding how to use obstacles to brace on with a rifle is also a very important skill to have when the situation warrants it. The definition of cover is anything that will stop the bullets someone is shooting at you. I had a unique opportunity to learn the benefit of cover during the most intense engagement I have experienced. The good news is that the Amtrak I hid behind stopped the 5.56 bullets headed our way during a dark, oil smoke obscured night while I was deployed to Desert Storm/Shield. The bad news we found out later was that the entity doing the shooting was a sister unit who had mistaken us for an enemy unit. The key is that they were shooting at us with their M-16's and M249's, both 5.56 caliber. I can remember the sound of the bullets hitting the other side of the Amtrak as they engaged us with a large volley of fire. Had they possessed and engaged with a M-2 .50 caliber or something bigger, I might not be writing this.

Understanding what cover actually is will benefit you in more ways than one. First, it's good to know what you can hide behind that will stop bullets, but secondly if you are defending your home from an intruder and have to shoot, it might be nice to know if what is behind the guy will stop the bullets before they enter your child's room or not. Take some time and look over your home and property and figure out what is cover and what is not, and adjust your defensive tactics as necessary.

Shooting Positions While Using Cover

Shooting positions from behind cover must maximize the protection it gives you, as well as maximize your ability to control recoil and hit something. Depending on the distance to the threat, cover can be used to brace the rifle and stabilize it as well. Kyle Lamb (Author of Green Eyes and Black Rifles, an excellent and highly recommended book) refers to a position he used more than any other while being shot at – a braced kneeling position. Bracing is a critical skill that should be practiced on a variety of obstacles, as each is different. The key though, is that when bracing you are likely sticking your muzzle beyond the obstacle, so it might be best used when shooting at threats that are some distance away, so twenty five yards or more. The problem with bracing in a situation where you are room distance away of closer is the danger of someone being close enough to grab the muzzle. The breakdown below will give you a good idea of how to use braced positions on cover, and un-braced positions.

Shooting from both shoulders (Bilateral technique)

Before I break down the close range and braced positions, it is important to discuss the critical importance of learning how to shoot from either shoulder. If you are right handed, you will want to seriously consider learning how to use the rifle from the other shoulder. The biggest reason is that when shooting around a piece of cover to the right (the wall extends to your left) from the right shoulder, it is very easy to maximize the use of cover. Switch the situation though, and try to shoot around a piece of cover to the left while still using the right shoulder and *you will significantly increase* the exposure you offer the enemy. See the next set of pictures.

Figure 57 The photo on the left shows a right-handed shooter working left around cover. Notice the significant improvement and less exposure when the same shooter switches to his left shoulder.

It takes time to train yourself to go bilateral and shoot from the other shoulder, but it might be worth it due to the significant increase in protection from the cover you are working around. Keep in mind that switching shoulders is something that must be practiced extensively before using the technique, and the idea is to use it deliberately as you are working through an area with left and right corners. If the shooting has already started, you might be best to leave the gun on the shoulder you have it on, but if you have the skill at least you can make that choice if it increases your survivability. There are several ways to switch shoulders, but I recommend you pick one that offers you the most control and allows you to work around the gear you carry. I will give you two options to try:

Option 1:

1. Lead hand slides back to grip magwell/magazine.
2. Stock slides off shoulder and over the sling (remember, I use a single point sling).
3. Stock is repositioned on the other shoulder/chest area.
4. Firing hand (the one on the pistol grip) slides forward to the handguard as step 3 is happening.
5. The hand gripping the magwell/magazine slides back to the pistol grip once the hand on the handguard is in position (I also typically switch my feet).

Figure 58 Sequence 1, my preferred option.

Option 2:

1. While keeping both hands in position, stock is removed from body and slide up and over the sling to the other shoulder.
2. Once the stock is in place, pistol grip hand slides forward and grips handguard.
3. At nearly the same time, the handguard hand slides back to the pistol grip.
4. Feet are switched if desired.

Figure 59 Sequence 2, Steve Aryans preferred option.

Shooting from cover at close range

The position I like is a simple modification of the normal shooting mount described in the section "Rifle Mount and Recoil Management." So imagine the standard mount, when shooting from a flat-footed position. Now add a piece of cover you wish to shoot around. If you are shooting around the right-hand side of cover. First, the right foot should be forward slightly so that you can maintain your balance while leaning in that direction. The distance from which you are shooting around must be enough so that you can lean out, shoot and get back behind cover very quickly. Second, to maximize the use of cover, consider sliding the stock out slightly on the shoulder. This stock position is different than the centered position I recommend, but is worth the trade off with the increased protection behind cover. Now, drive the elbow down and shoulder forward as you lean out enough to mount the rifle and shoot. From the perspective of the threat, only your gun, a small portion of your shoulder, and right side of your head should be exposed. Driving the elbow down and shoulder forward will help keep the pressure and bodyweight behind the gun, allowing for faster follow-up shots.

See the sequence below.

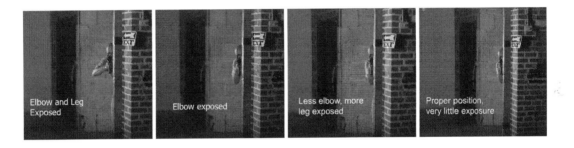

Figure 60 Beware of sticking your muzzle past the cover you are using. You never know who is on the other side.

Shooting from cover at longer range while bracing.

This position is similar to the closer range position, yet different in that the position from cover must be closer so that you can reach the area you are bracing against with your rifle forearm.

Thumb Braced Position

Note: Be very careful not to press your barrel (or handguard of a non-free floating barreled AR) on the barricade, or you can actually move the impact of your round enough to miss the target. Unfortunately I first experienced this in a 3-gun match where I was touching my barrel against a post I was using for rest. I had made the mistake of resting my barrel on it rather than my handguard and spend almost an entire magazine trying to hit a small popper at 80 yards. Not good!

Palm Braced Position

The bracing is done with a combination of the handguard and your own hand. I like two methods, the "thumb" brace or the "palm" brace. The thumb brace is faster for me because I don't have to switch my hand position on the gun, but the palm method is more stable on some items. When bracing to build an effective position you will need to focus on three things. First, you must continue to hold the gun up with the forward arm when bracing. A common mistake is to think that the bracing object (wall, etc.) will hold the rifle up. Second, drive the gun forward into the bracing object with either the thumb or palm method. Third, use your body mechanics and torque your handguard into the braced object, so if you are bracing around a right corner for example, you would torque your body to the left and driving the handguard into the object. Lastly, remember that when you are bracing around an object, using that object for stabilization is a goal, but also using it for cover is a very important goal as well. Keep the body exposure to a minimum and make sure you are driving your elbow down and keeping most of it behind cover rather than letting it flag out in the open.

Chapter Summary and Action steps:

1. Good techniques properly trained will be your key to success. Test and objectively evaluate everything you incorporate to make sure it meets your own personal needs.
2. Use the techniques described in this chapter to increase the effectiveness of the dry and live fire drills. Make sure you pay attention to the details, like manipulating the safety, etc.
3. Strongly consider watching the DVD's made with this book for a focused look at each drill and the technique within it. A second option is to download and use the drills right on the range by visiting my Vimeo page (vimeo.com/ondemand/defensiverifle).

CHAPTER 7

Rifle Skill Development Training Program and Drills

Learning proper technique is imperative, but ingraining those skills into the subconscious mind for future use is the critical part of the equation. It is incredibly important to have a plan (program) and drills that are well designed and executed correctly in practice. This chapter contains your full step-by-step training program and all of the drills you will need to take your skill to the next level.

Covered in this chapter:

1. *Skills Needed For the Fight*
2. *Training Session Execution*
3. *Training Program Overview*
4. *Dry Fire Training Drills*
5. *Rifle Zero Theory*
6. *Live Fire Training Drills*

Skills Needed or the Fight

Developing the necessary level of skill to survive a lethal encounter is obviously a big part of this program, but how much skill is necessary? The answer is: *there is no answer.* You see, I don't believe there is a certain skill level that will ensure that you will survive a gunfight. There is no such thing. Unfortunately, most local, state, and federal agencies as well as the U.S. Military attach a scored number to the skill level of their trainees during their qualification tests. Sometimes that number truly measures skill, but most of the time it is simply a liability factor necessary to cover the legality of arming the individuals. If you compare the specialized team members of elite units and the base level officer or soldier, often times you will see big differences in skill. This is because the elite level shooter knows they are very likely to be involved in a fight, and they train for it. The average soldier or law enforcement officer will only be trained to the level that their agency or unit deems necessary to pass a qualification test. It is up to the individual to take the responsibility of training to higher levels and unfortunately, a significant number don't. This same analogy can be applied to the average concealed carry permit holder. Most wrongfully believe that if they passed the shooting test in their CCW course (if there was one), that they are prepared to carry a gun. Whether you are a civilian or professional, don't be that person. I strongly recommend that you set your own level of success you wish to reach and train to that level. Your life is on the line, so set the bar high!

As the Federal Air Marshal (F.A.M) firearms training Lead Instructor, I used to give a graduation speech to my trainees at the F.A.M academy graduation, and one of my comments was: "Take responsibility for your own survival." My point was that having an excuse for failing during a fight at 35,000 feet is irrelevant, and the bad guy could care less why they did not have the skill necessary to win. Therefore, in this program I will not set a level or score that I want you to reach. I want to challenge you to reach the highest level of skill possible, and then push some more. Once you are done with the mental training and firearm skill development in this program, you will have a solid understanding on how to continue to train yourself to the next level. For self-defense purposes, your training will never end. There is always a "next" level.

Execution of Training Sessions (How to Train)

This step will discuss the critical information that will help you understand the key components of actually executing a training session. I will discuss how you should approach your session, as well as frequency, duration, documentation, and other factors that will improve your learning experience. I would love to tell you that most experienced shooters are on the right path and train correctly, but when observing different individuals train, I have commonly noticed a lack of understanding about how to actually approach a training session.

Training Session Parts - Your actual training sessions can be broken down into three key timeframes: *Pre-session*, *During-session*, and *Post-session*.

1. *Pre-Session*. This is your opportunity to prepare yourself for the best session you can possibly have. This will enable you to maximize the learning that will occur in the session. If you skip this step then you will not be prepared to train effectively. It will not take much time, and can actually occur at home before driving to the range or training area. Before you begin your training session you will want to do the following:

   a. *Review your training logs/notes from the last session.* Your notes should have information that you wrote down that is actionable and critical to your next session. You may have written down things you did wrong and need to change or things you did right and need to try to experience again. ALWAYS review your previous session notes, even if you just scan them for something that you may have logged that will change how you execute the current session.

b. *Plan the session.* Most of the time, if you have followed the steps in this book you will already have a pre-planned session, but if not you will need to take some time to plan your session. If you fail to plan, then you plan to fail. Remember how important your time and money is. Thus, planning your session is critical to your learning experience. Based on what you want to accomplish, there is a drill that will allow you to work that skill.

c. *Set goals.* This is really important. If you are repeating the same drills over and over for consistency sake (and measurement of your metrics) then you should know what your current abilities are. In this case, do your best to exceed these times or scores in the session. Set the bar high and do your best to reach it. NEVER execute a training session without some goals for the session, even if they are small. Concluding a session while achieving your goals is one of the best ways to begin to develop a positive mental state and a strong self-image. I always end each drill by trying to beat myself (best time or accuracy).

2. ***During Session.*** During your training session there are key things you will want to pay attention to. If you are using my drills then all of this information is at your fingertips to use during the session. The critical components are listed for you to review and focus on. Every single repetition should be done as correctly as possible. I can't say enough how important it is to execute all repetitions with attention to detail. When you are going through your training session, you are writing those subconscious skills onto your internal hard drive (brain), and if you make the mistake of writing it wrong, you will have twice the amount of work ahead of you to fix it. Critical components you should be focusing on during your session include:

a. *Paying attention to as many technique factors as possible during each drill, trying to connect with each one physically and mentally.* Remember that you are literally programming your brain to act, and whether or not you act correctly under stress will be written during these training drills. The more you mentally connect with the drill the better. I tell my student to visualize that the paper or cardboard target in front of them is real, and actually a person that has intent on doing them harm.

b. *Constantly monitoring the timer. (If you don't have one get one).* Each time I do a repetition on a drill I get quick visual times for the following: first shot, total time, shots fired, and the split between the last shot and the one prior to it. This data is critical to my training drills and allows me to document each repetition with pinpoint accuracy. Don't think that a timer is only relevant for competitive purposes. A timer is a key piece of gear that will allow you to objectively measure your skills by showing you how much time it took to do them. Even though this does not have anything to do with tactics, it allows you to measure and compare your beginning times at certain skills to your end times. This will help you push yourself during training. The PACT Club Timer III is my personal favorite for training. A shot timer "hears" the shots as they are fired and will give you feedback on how fast you are shooting. A timer is an invaluable training tool.

c. *Complete a thorough analysis of the target between drills.* This will show you where your hits are on the target so you can analyze what is going on. Pay attention visually to what is happening when you fire the shot by watching the sights and then verify that the hits are where you called them. I document bad hits when I see them and when I go to analyze and paste my target I get to check my ability to call the bad shots. If you aren't seeing and calling bad shots, it is likely that you are not looking at the sights when the recoil cycle initiates. When you are watching your front sight or dot, it should "bounce" like a basketball when the gun goes bang. Learning to see this is a key component of your training program.

d. *Correct mistakes as they happen.* Don't get in the habit of just doing drill repetitions over and over when you are making mistakes. If you make an error, fix it on the spot. Analyze it and change something, and then repeat the same drill several (3-5) times correctly to ensure that you ingrain it correctly. Make sure to take a note of what you found and fixed. Remember how I described myself fixing a problem in the mental section? I visualize the problem and solution in my mind several times before I attempt to do the drill again. This usually fixes the problem faster, and increases my mental connection to perfecting the skill.

e. *Document everything.* Tie your notebook to your chest if you have to, in order to always have it close enough to take a quick note. I recommend noting drill times and then the hits on the target when you are done. Again, I also write bad hits down as I shoot them, emphasizing my ability to call bad shots. If you run into a problem you can't fix, write it down for future research with your "lunch expert." Make sure you keep detailed notes about how your gear worked, and if you have problems, document that too. Visit my website or email me and I will send you a link for free logbook forms.

3. *Post-Session.* When you complete your training session it is time to wind down, and solidify the good training you accomplished. Make sure you:

a. *Wipe down your gun and gear.* I don't do a detailed cleaning every time I shoot (much to the dismay of my former Drill Instructor and at least one gun writer), mainly because I don't believe that a detailed cleaning is necessary each time I shoot. I do wipe the gun down, and pay particular attention of the areas of the gun that will tend to wear such as slide rails, etc. I also re-lubricate the gun before putting it away so the next time I shoot I minimize wear and tear. Make sure you take the time to wipe things down and dry them if you train in wet or cold weather (to prevent mold and rust).

b. *Finish your documentation.* The best time to take notes is when you are still fresh from the training session. The information you write down is critical to future training sessions. Check over your log and make sure you have all items complete. My training log forms also have sections that force you to positively find solutions and document those notes which reflects that thought process, rather that writing how poorly you did. Be careful what you write down, as negativity will beget more problems. Consider writing information in a manner that requires you to find a solution.

c. *Analyze your targets.* Even if you are pasting or covering the holes in the target you used you will notice that your overall group is either centered or not. If not, take notes of where it was and try to draw some conclusions as to why. Try to find out if you might be making some sort of physical error or if it might be a sight or ammunition issue.

I suggest pasting the non-center hits on your target when training. This will force you to call the shot from what the sight picture is telling you. A bad habit in training is "hunting for the hole" by looking over the gun at the target each time you fire a shot. With a rifle and good optic like 90% of you will be using, you need to learn to call the shot based on where the dot was when the rifle went bang.

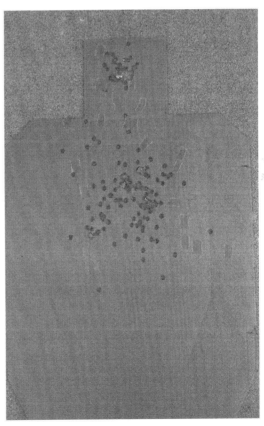

Figure 61 This photo shows larger handgun hits for easy visual reference.

When to Train

This is something that some of you may have no control over, since you will be forced to schedule around family and work. For those who can control when training occurs use common sense and train during the times you are likely to use the skills you are training. Most of you will probably use the skills at different times, so my recommendation is to simply train at different times each day. If you are reading this book, you are training for combative purposes so you might consider training during times when the light conditions are changing. This will allow you to track your progress during different lighting conditions in which you may be forced to use your skills. I also recommend working the most during times when you are feeling your best. To put it simply, if you feel good you will perform well. This helps increase the effectiveness of the training, because you will enjoy the process more and will probably pay more attention to the details that are important. There are also benefits to training when you are not at your best, so don't be afraid to hit the range when you are sick or tired every once in awhile.

Training Frequency and Duration

Training frequency and duration is a critical question in your training program and how often you train will affect your results. You may have heard these terms before when referring to physical fitness training. How often and how long should each training session be? Key research indicates that the number of times we train as well as how long we train will have a definitive impact upon how well we learn. In theory, it seems simple to say that if ten minutes of practice is good, then one hundred minutes must be great right? Not necessarily. Unfortunately, there is no perfect answer to the question, "How long should a session be?" The longer the training session is, the harder it is to pay attention to what you were trying to learn. What is long? My experience is that most people will not maintain focus for more than about 30-40 minutes of focused training at a time (this includes training time, not preparation time).

Keeping sessions shorter, will allow you to focus more intently on the details that we are trying to improve during a training session. Does this mean that I am telling you to train for only 30-40 minutes? No, it does not. It means that I strongly recommend that you take a short break after every 30-45 minutes of intense training. If your training sessions have been designed correctly you will naturally be taking breaks to document and set up a new drill. This is a perfect time to take your mind off the specific technique you were doing. This mental break allows you to refocus and start again with 100% of your attention on the next drill.

Training more frequently for shorter periods of time has been proven to have a positive effect on the subconscious storage of the skills you are training. Frequency and duration may be affected by many factors, including your resources, your goal and how difficult it is, your current skill level, and the time you have or have set to reach your goal. Most experts in the training world agree that training a minimum of three times weekly is required to build skill and at least once per week to maintain it. This does not necessarily mean that all of your session must be live fire training. These three sessions weekly may be live fire, dry fire, or other methods of training. Believe it or not, if you have the self-discipline to do a mental training session (imagine it in your mind), your subconscious doesn't really know the difference. Either way, just remember it's important that you train at least three times a week.

For someone who is really intent upon developing a high level of skill, training four to six times a week may be necessary. It might be very difficult for normal people with normal lives to train four to six times per week, but even so, this frequency of training often leads to burnout. Training this often may also lead to boredom and a lack of attention to detail. If you don't pay attention to the exact details you are trying to train you may train them incorrectly. Once you have ingrained a skill incorrectly, it is actually impossible to completely break that habit. The only way to fix the training error is to write (see myelination from the previous chapter) another, stronger program. Think about this – if it takes one thousand repetitions to develop a skill, it may take two thousand repetitions to write a stronger skill program.

Training Location

Okay, this may be a no-brainer if you are doing just a shooting training program. You're probably going to shoot at one range right? Think about it though, if you have the ability to train in different locations, it might have the effect of preparing you for different environments. From a shooting skills standpoint, the different training locations will hopefully have different backdrops and scenery, so you might notice a change in your ability to see the sights or your optic dot in different lighting conditions or with changes in the background. This may seem simple, yet it will pay dividends if you end up in a situation where you have to perform in a similar environment.

Training Efficiency

I would guess that if you are reading this book, you are likely someone who has a pretty normal life filled with things other than training. If not, and if you are one of the lucky few who have all the time in the world to devote to your goal, congratulations! The rest of us need to understand that there is a way to meet our goal, no matter how busy we are, if our goal is a priority. This section will cover some of my thoughts about how to increase your overall training efficiency through a systematic process that uses your time as efficiently as possible.

Planning and Preparation

I have said this several times throughout this book in different sections and I will say it again here. Planning and preparation for your training sessions will increase your efficiency. Most of your preparation can be conducted the night before, or during the time when you are home and may not have anything else pressing for your time but the T.V. You may have to wait until the kids go to bed or whatever, but this time is important in making your session the next day efficient and timely.

Time Management

When I was developing my skills years ago, I knew that I had to spend a certain number of days at the range training. During that time, I was a full-time police officer working a very busy schedule for a pretty small paycheck. Because of this, I had to work twenty to thirty extra hours each week on overtime shifts or extra jobs just to pay for my shooting habits.

This crazy schedule helped me focus on managing my time well and making sure I was not wasting any of it. I trained alone most of the time, but if you were to transport yourself back in time and watch how I performed my sessions you would see that I was very task focused and did not waste much time. Many of my training sessions had to fit within a certain window of time between my work shift and a side job or overtime, so I had to be ultra-efficient.

The first step in this was the planning and preparation in the manner mentioned above. The second step was ensuring that I did not lose any time to "time vampires" that loomed around the range. Most of the time, "time vampires" were people who wanted to chitchat about this or that, or even those on the range who just wanted to say a quick "hello." While I love this part of the training, and love to talk about it, when I was in "training" mode, I chose not to do much socializing. Anyone who has trained with me in the past will tell you that I like to focus intently on the learning experience rather than the socializing. Effective time management is more of a concept than an actual thing I could teach you. Time can be found anywhere, but can also be lost anywhere. Load your magazines as you walk down range to paste/score your targets. Go through your mental routine while you are driving to the range. Prepare your gear and review your logbook during your lunch break. Just do everything you can to maximize your time efficiency.

> *Practice Tip:* My preparation normally goes like this: I get my training plan/log out of the car and look it over for issues that I may have observed in the last session. I carry those things over to my plan sheet so they are the first thing I read when I get to the range. Next, I get gun, gear, and ammunition checked and ready to strap on and shoot. I actually prepare (load) all of my magazines (as many as I have) during this time just so I can get shooting faster. I should already have all of my drills written into my notes (the ones I am going to do), and I make sure that I have read over the drill sheet and know how I am going to set them up. I get props or anything else I may need to conduct the drills in the vehicle, and get my targets ready to go (possibly painted, etc.).

In the next two major sections I will list all of the drills, both live and dry, that you will need to complete my training program. Before I do so, an overview of the program might be in order so that you might understand, and use it more effectively.

Drills Build Skills

I have heard "drills build skills" before. I am not sure who said it first, but I would say: "Correctly designed and executed drills build skills." Developing this training program was much more of a challenge than it should be to use it. It should be simple to follow as long as you are not afraid of hard work. I had to develop a program that addressed largely varying levels of skill, while still being functional for all users. It also had to be a complete program that developed skills at various ranges that you might find yourself in during a lethal encounter in.

With those goals and others in mind, I have developed a program that addresses each skill I found to be important. I have packaged it into a crawl-walk-run system that will take your skill level and increase it substantially. To do this I have developed training drills that address each one of the skills in the technique section. Some of the skills will be developed during live fire, some during dry fire, and some skills will be worked in both sets of drills. Some skills will be worked more than others since they are more critical skills to have. Some will be worked with smaller drills that do not replicate any lethal encounter situation, but simply focus on the skill itself (or a component of it). The main point is that in order to understand what you are supposed to be working on during a drill, it is critical that you understand why I am having you do it. When you begin the program, make sure you pay attention to the _purpose_ and _critical points_ listed in each drill. Those sections are very important, and I have listed them for a reason. In most of the drills, I will list technique reference pages in the drill sheet itself, so you can refer back to the technique section and the exact page for reference. If you want a visual reference, please consider ordering the DVD that compliments this book (see my website for more information).

Skill Development Concept

The program consists of both live fire and dry fire drills. Each drill is designed to work a specific component(s) of a skill. A complete technique such as rifle reload process is made up of multiple components of skill. When you perform training repetitions of those components, your focus should be on improving the components in that skill. In this program you will use a variety of drills that focus on those important components, within the core techniques that you will need to shoot well. Most of the drills in the dry fire and live fire section are measurable with a combination time/points system. This means that if you can accomplish the same level of accuracy, in a shorter amount of time as you progress through the drills, you are improving. This measurement of skill must be balanced with the correct tactical procedures if required in that drill, but generally you can verify improvement if you track lower times. Certain drills are movement-related drills where the time may vary because you moved either faster or slower during the drill. On these drills I recommend that you measure your success by a greater percentage of combat effective hits. For the dry fire drills, you will be able to measure your improvement by lowering your MTT (Maximum Technical Training) speed on an electronic timer (see the dry fire drill section for more details).

Separation of Skills During Development

Each skill component developed by the drills may be used separately, or in conjunction with other skills developed in the program when you need to perform a technique. The need to reach into your skill "toolbox" and use one will be dictated by the situation.

That being said, I want you to understand that it is not possible to design a set of training drills that all contain specific defensive contexts.

For this reason, you will find that some of the drills do not directly replicate the full set of skills (components) you might use in a fight, but only one or two. The reason is that by focusing on one of two skills, the learner has the ability to place full mental focus into that one key area. This will develop a higher level of mastery of each particular skill over time.

Phased (crawl, walk, run) Approach to Training

The program is designed to develop skills in a "craw, walk, run" format, which will allow you to learn the skills correctly along the way and ensure you do things correctly. One thing that may stand out to some of you with more experience is that in the first phase of the program, all drills are done statically. This may seem counterproductive to the end goal, which is to learn to move during a lethal encounter, as this often increases your chance of survival. I know this and specifically designed the first phase of training to be static because there are so many skill components in each drill, and it is important to focus on key details without getting overloaded. The first phase of the program is the shortest phase, because as soon as possible I want to add drills that add movement. In addition, the dry fire drills that you will be doing during each phase will mimic the live fire drills. This will help build higher levels of skill without the additional expense of shooting more ammunition. Remember, the program as a whole is designed to work well, and this requires a step-by-step approach. Stay the course.

Training Program Overview

Your training program will consist of both dry and live fire drills. This program is different from the handgun programs you will find in my other books, in that it is designed to keep your training sessions relatively short, simple, and 100% accomplishable. My goal was to have you practice with one or two drills per session so you could focus your attention on mastering the skills within that specific drills rather than numerous drills that dilute your attention to detail. The principle of focusing on one thing at a time is critical in skill development, and the saying: "if everything is a priority, nothing is," is a very true statement. This program minimizes overburdening you by limiting the drills done per session.

Additionally, each training week requires only one live-fire range session. Most people cannot shoot three or four times per week, so I require only one live-fire session supplemented with liberal dry-fire sessions. The dry-fire sessions are absolutely critical to your development, and if skipped you will not reap the benefits from this program. Make sure you do them.

The table on the next page shows the entire program broken down into weeks. Simply look at the week you are on and perform the required drills. The specifics of each drill are on the dry-fire and live-fire drill sheets. The technique details used in each drill can be found in the technique section.

The following table is an overview of the training program you will follow.
- Do one live-fire training session per week, using the live-fire drills.
- Do two (or more) dry-fire training sessions per week using the dry-fire drills.
- IF you feel you have learned the technique taught in the drill, move on to the next week and next drill. If NOT, repeat your training week again the next week. DO NOT move to the next week/drill until you have learned what you need from the drill.
- Note: in weeks 9-15 you will pick and use the dry-fire drill of your choice; I suggest you pick your weakest skill area.

Week	Dry Fire Drills [1]	Live Fire Drills [2]
Five Shot Group-Zero Check Precedes each live fire training session.		
One	1. Stationary Mount DF	1. Stationary Mount LF
Two	2. Stationary Transition To Handgun DF 3. Stationary Reload DF	2. Stationary Transition To Handgun LF
Three	4. Phase I Malfunction DF	3. Bilateral Stationary Mount LF
Four	5. Pivoting Mount DF	4. Pivoting Mount LF
Five	6. Movement Offline DF	5. Movement Offline LF
Six	7. Phase II Malfunction DF	6. Failure To Stop LF
Seven	8. One-Handed Reload DF	7. Shooting and Moving, Forward and Backward LF
Eight	9. One-Handed Malfunction Clearance DF	8. Shooting and Moving, Multi-Directional LF
Nine	10. *Shooters Choice	9. Sprinting Offline Mount LF
Ten	11. *Shooters Choice	10. Moving Mount LF
Eleven	12. *Shooters Choice	11. Braced Position LF
Twelve	13. *Shooters Choice	12. Extreme Close Quarters (ECQ) LF
Thirteen	14. *Shooters Choice	13. One Shot X-Drill
Fourteen	15. *Shooters Choice	14. Two Shot X-Drill
Fifteen	16. *Shooters Choice	15. Multi-Port LF
Note: This shows fifteen weeks, but it might take you longer if you repeat a week.		
VIDEO	Each of the drills in this program is shown in video form. I strongly recommend you watch these videos to get the complete picture and key details on technique. You can order the DVD's from my website (shooting-performance.com) or download them to your smart device on Vimeo (vimeo.com/ondemand/defensiverifle).	

The next section will cover dry fire, its uses and benefits, and the program that you will follow in this system. Specifically, I will cover:

1. *Purpose of and skills trained in the dry fire program*
2. *Safety*
3. *Definitions*
4. *Time and location*
5. *Gear and equipment needed*
6. *Dry fire sessions*

Purpose of Dry Fire

Dry fire training will be a huge part of your training program. The reason for this is that dry fire training is where I believe most of a person's manipulation skill training should be. Most of you using this program will probably be training live fire no more than once per week. Therefore, using dry fire training to supplement your skill development and maintenance is the best way to develop and maintain your manipulation skill. The top professional shooters ALL use dry fire extensively, and they would not do this if dry fire were not a big key to their success. I am absolutely convinced that dry fire will be one of the best training tools I can give you to increase your skill in a short amount of time. It is free, can be done almost anywhere and will help you develop 85% of the skills you will need to succeed.

> *Key Tip:* In the competition handgun world, I know of at least one world champion shooter that keeps his skill level up with dry fire exclusively. I maintain most of my own skill with dry fire too, and have found it to be one commonality in the great shooters I have trained with. Dry fire will be one of the BIG keys to your success. Pay attention to this chapter!

Are there downsides to dry fire? Not really. I have heard the belief that dry firing will simulate a dead (malfunctioned) gun and trains bad habits if you don't do a clearance every time the trigger goes "click". I have found absolutely no evidence of this from the many very high-level skilled shooters in the competitive circuit as well as tactical arenas. I can remember spending hours of practice when I was shooting competitively in the Marine Corps "snapping in" (dry firing) at miniature targets painted on a white barrel. The Marine Corps rifle team shooters coached us during the big matches, and they strongly advocated dry firing while working positions.

The only other downside of not having recoil to deal with is actually a positive thing when you look at how the body deals with the noise and sound of live fire. I believe that the biggest problem most new shooters have is anticipating the recoil and moving the gun before the bullet exits the barrel. This is due to the natural reaction that recoil, noise, and overpressure impart on the human body. Doing ample amounts of dry fire will help neutralize this "anticipation" effect.

How to go through your dry fire sessions

Dry Fire Safety: This is number one on the list because it is the most important. Follow these rules, or don't dry fire!

- Separate yourself from live firearms and ammunition (use a separate room if possible).
- Set up small dry fire targets with, if at all possible, a backstop that is bulletproof (an extra layer of safety).
- Go through a process of thoroughly inspecting all firearms and magazines, as well as your own pockets, for any live ammunition before beginning.

- If you use dummy (non-live) training cartridges to simulate the weight in your magazines, make sure they are drilled with holes or painted bright orange or another color that will allow you to identify them as dummy rounds. I recommend having one separate magazine (or two) just for dry fire purposes, so you can keep your dummy ammunition in it.
- When you are dry firing, and you have to leave the area for whatever reason, re-inspect yourself for live ammunition when you return.
- When you are done dry firing, and return to an area where you may have live ammunition and firearms, **do not even think about doing one more repetition**... that is how accidents happen.

Follow all standard safety rules when dry firing:
- *All guns are treated as loaded.*
- *Keep your finger off the trigger until you are ready to shoot.*
- *Never let your muzzle cover anything you are not willing to destroy.*
- *Be sure of your target, backstop, and beyond.*

Definitions: The following are some definitions that will be used in the dry fire module.
- *Technically Correct* - The act of ensuring that all elements of the technique are correct in every possible way.
- *Technical Training Speed (TTS)* - The speed at which you should train when learning a technique. There is no emphasis on going fast here, just performing perfect repetitions.
- *Maximum Technical Training Speed (MTTS)* - The fastest speed you can do any given technique meeting all of the elements of technical correctness.

Time and Location

The best time to go through your dry-fire routine will be up to you. I recommend that you do it during a time when you are mentally fully engaged. I often dry fire early in the mornings, when I have no distractions. Your dry fire sessions should be done during a completely separate time than your live fire sessions. Find a location that meets the safety requirements and will allow you to move aggressively. I suggest that you dry fire with your full defensive gear either before you leave your house or when you return at the end of the day. Training before you leave allows you to ingrain those gun-handling skills that you might need during a fight. If you train before you leave make sure you follow a deliberate process of unloading and following the safety protocols discussed, and then reloading and making sure your firearm is ready to use if it is part of your daily gear. Those that stage the rifle as a home defense tool should ensure to reload and stage it after each dry-fire training session.

Equipment Needed

- *PACT Timer* – You will *need* a PACT or similar timer to perform the dry fire module. This is not optional. A timer is such a valuable training tool that you will not be able to execute this program without one. Even if you have to skip a couple practice sessions in order to buy one, please do so. Get a timer that has a loud beep and an easy PAR time function. PAR time is the ability to enter a time and have your timer deliver two beeps, a start beep and a stop beep at the end of the time entered. Having this function allows you to train your skills and begin to lower the time incrementally.
- *1/3 scale targets* – In my competitive dry fire sessions I use IPSC targets that are about 1/3 the size of a regular IPSC target to simulate aiming at the target area I might see if I had a full size target at the correct distance. I recommend training on targets that mimic human shape, but if you cannot find them in a reduced size, try to find the targets I use. They are shaped like human silhouettes and are invaluable for dry firing in reduced distance settings.
- *Dummy Rounds* – Having dummy rounds for emergency reloads and malfunction clearing drills is important. I strongly recommend that you purchase the dummy rounds that have nickel cases and orange bullets, which will allow you to easily distinguish a dummy round from a live round.
- *Cover (a simulated piece of cover)* – This will allow you to practice using cover during some of your dry fire drills. I use a portable target stand and cardboard stapled to it to simulate the edge of something that could be used as cover.
- *Your Gear*- Practice with the exact same gear/clothing that you will carry with. Don't forget to conceal your handgun if you carry concealed.

Active Visualization

Integrate active visualization with your sets and repetitions. Each time you do a repetition (one draw for example); see yourself doing it before you do it. "See yourself do it, then do it." This will tie your mental and physical execution together. This includes practicing your verbal commands and scan process after you perform the shots. Try to see everything exactly like it might occur in the fight. You can read more about active visualization in the mental section.

Trigger Manipulation "fire 3-5 rounds"

When dry firing, you will normally get one click per repetition with most single action type firearms without having to work the slide for another click. To keep from developing a bad habit of firing one time only each repetition, fire one shot (click) and continue to press the trigger to the rear with enough pressure that the gun would be going off if bolt had been cycled. You will NOT get a click while doing this as the firing pin fell on your first trigger press. While pressing the trigger continue to monitor the sights for movement. Press, press, press and verify nothing is moving.

Sessions

You should perform the dry fire drills in the session that corresponds to the training week you are in. Each dry fire session is designed to mimic the live fire sessions you are doing so that you are repeating the same skills over and over. This will help you focus on improving those specific skills. Remember to keep your dry fire sessions short, interesting, and high quality. You will go through a minimum of two dry fire sessions each week.

Sets and Repetitions

You will conduct all dry fire training sessions pretty much the same way. This method of dry firing was designed for high performance competitive shooting skill development, and relies on a PACT timer set on PAR time function to measure the time required to perform a skill. While quick times alone will not ensure you are ready to survive a gunfight, it is nice to have a measurement metric that will allow you to track and improve your progress. Each skill you work on will be trained with three sets of ten plus repetitions. If you desire to do more, that is fine as long as you maintain a high level of quality and attention to detail during the entire session. Be very careful not to over train and do repetitions without doing them correctly. Your sets and repetitions will be broken down as follows for each skill trained:

- *First Set/10 repetitions* – Executed at your TTS (technical training speed), which does not have a time. Your emphasis will be ingraining the key details of the technique into your subconscious memory. You will do 10+ repetitions at this speed then move on to your second set when you have completed 10+ perfect repetitions. This means that you will not count a repetition if you mess one up. If you make a mistake, stop for a second, and figure out why you made the error. Fix the problem then begin again paying attention to what you just fixed.
- *Second Set/10 repetitions* – Performed at your MTTS (Maximum Technical Training Speed) or 100% of you maximum "correct" speed. You will do these repetitions as fast as you can, correctly. You should have a recorded time from you last session, or if this is your first time, simply guess what time to use during the skill and plug that into your timer. Adjust the timer accordingly until you have found a time that is the maximum correct speed at which you can do the skill. Now perform 10 repetitions (hopefully without a mistake).
- *Third Set/10+ repetitions* – Now begin to drop the PAR time by either .05 or .10 increments or less if necessary. When you do this, you will be below (faster) your MTTS, which is faster than you are used to being able to perform the skill. Try to "catch" this time by pushing harder and finding areas where you can improve your technique. Once you "catch" the time and can repeat that five times, drop the timer another .10, plus or minus if necessary. Once you get to the point you can no longer catch the time while doing the skill correctly, log the time you caught as your new MTTS. This is the time you will use in your next session. Remember, when doing these maximum speed sets, you must be seeing the sights and per-

forming the skill so you would get hits in the correct threat engagement area, no periphery hits. Don't train yourself to miss in dry fire, as this is a possibility if you train incorrectly.

- *Move to the next Skill* – You will now begin the next skill and do your three sets: TTS, MTTS, and Catch the Timer. **Note:** Eventually you will hit a point where you can no longer drop the times when you are trying to catch the timer. We all plateau eventually, and you will too. This means that you have ingrained that manipulation skill to the point where you have no, or very little room to improve.

Dry Fire Program

The next section contains the dry fire drills. They are your reference for the full training program. Pay attention to each section in the drills, and specifically the "critical points."

Stationary Mount Dry Fire Drill

Purpose: To build the manipulation skill of mounting the rifle (see page 105).

Start Position: Empty gun with bolt cycled (hammer cocked), with the rifle at the forty-five degree low ready.

Target Type and Setup: One 1/3 size small target (humanoid shape) set directly in front of the shooter at room distance (5-7 yards).

Prop Setup: N/A

Action(s): On the start signal, mount and fire (click) three to five times, aiming at the center of the appropriate target. Go through a scan process (check around you and behind you) before administratively working the bolt to prepare for the next training repetition.

Critical Points: Make sure to deliberately ride the thumb safety and wipe it off as you mount the rifle to the cheek weld position. Strive to make the mount consistent by finding the proper index points during the mount process during each repetition, such as a specific cheek weld to the stock. This will ensure a consistent sight picture, as the eye will be aligned behind the sights consistently.

Visual Cues: Visual shift from the target aiming area back to the front sight or dot.

Mental Cues: Actively visualize the entire drill. Ensure you visualize the technique components (active visualization), as well as elements of a real scenario (that the target is real).

Stationary Transition to Handgun Dry Fire Drill

Purpose: To build the manipulation skill of transitioning (see page 114) due to an empty gun.

Start Position: Aimed in at the target with an empty gun, with an empty magazine inserted into the magazine well and the bolt locked to the rear.

Target Type and Setup: One 1/3 size small target (humanoid shape) set directly in front of the shooter at room distance (5-7 yards).

Prop Setup: N/A

Action(s): Ensure that you have a magazine with 10+ dummy (double check!) rounds loaded into the magazine in the same location where you carry your spare ammunition. In addition, you should have a completely unloaded handgun on and holstered wherever you carry your handgun. On the start signal, attempt to press the trigger to no avail, then perform an transition to the handgun and fire (click) three to five times aiming at the center of the appropriate target. After the transition to the handgun, administratively work the slide and re-holster it. Once the handgun is in the holster, re-acquire the rifle for the next repetition of the drill. Note: In the live fire version of this drill you will practice the steps to reload the rifle.

Critical Points: Effectively getting the rifle out of the way (sweeping it aside) during the transition. Building a proper grip on the handgun after the transition.

Visual Cues: Keep the head and eyes on the threat during this reload and ensure you do not get task fixated on the gun and magazine.

Mental Cues: Actively visualize the entire drill. Ensure you visualize the technique components (active visualization), as well as elements of a real scenario (that the target is real).

Stationary Reload Dry Fire Drill

Purpose: To build the manipulation skill of reloading (see page 116) an empty gun.

Start Position: Aimed in at the target with an empty gun, with an empty magazine inserted into the magazine well and the bolt locked to the rear (if possible).

Target Type and Setup: One 1/3 size small target (humanoid shape) set directly in front of the shooter at room distance (5-7 yards).

Prop Setup: N/A

Action(s): Ensure that you have a magazine with 10+ dummy (double check!) rounds loaded into the magazine in the same location where you carry your spare ammunition. On the start signal, attempt to press the trigger to no avail, then perform an emergency reload and fire (click) three to five times aiming at the center of the appropriate target. Go through a scan process before administratively setting up for the next training repetition. To set up for the next repetition, grab the empty grounded magazine and perform a "tactical reload" placing the full magazine back into your magazine pouch. Pull the bolt to the rear (locking it), and you will now be set up for the next repetition.

Critical Points: Consistency in the position of the rifle when reloading. Make sure that the reload is done behind cover. Work to find an index point that will allow the magazine to be seated into the magazine well consistently (see the technique section).

Visual Cues: Keep the head and eyes on the threat during this reload and ensure you do not get task fixated on the gun and magazine.

Mental Cues: Actively visualize the entire drill. Ensure you visualize the technique components (active visualization), as well as elements of a real scenario (that the target is real).

Stationary Phase I Malfunction Dry Fire Drill

Purpose: To build the manipulation skill of clearing a Phase I malfunction (see page 119).

Start Position: Loaded gun with a magazine loaded with at least ten rounds (DUMMY ROUNDS ONLY) with the bolt cycled and hammer cocked, at the forty-five degree low ready position.

Target Type and Setup: One 1/3 size small target (humanoid shape) set directly in front of the shooter at room distance (5-7 yards).

Prop Setup: N/A

Action(s): On the start signal, mount and fire a dry fire shot (click), perform a phase I (tap, rack, ready) malfunction clearance and then fire again. Because the magazine is set up with ten dummy rounds, you will continue to get clicks after clearing the malfunction. Each clearance of the malfunction is counted as an individual repetition. Continue to clear and engage through all ten dummy rounds until the magazine is empty, which should be a total of ten total repetitions. Set the gun up the same way and repeat.

Critical Points: This repetitive drill will allow you to focus on manipulating through a malfunction while keeping your head and eyes on the threat. Ensure that the finger is off the trigger while manipulating the gun. Pay attention to rebuilding the proper mount on the rifle for each repetition of the clearance.

Visual Cues: Maintain focus on the threat, versus getting fixated on the gun.

Mental Cues: Actively visualize the entire drill. Ensure you visualize the technique components (active visualization), as well as elements of a real scenario (that the target is real).

Stationary Phase II Malfunction Dry Fire Drill

Purpose: To build the manipulation skill of clearing a Phase II malfunction (see page 120).

Start Position: With the gun set up with a phase II malfunction and aimed in on target:
- Lock the bolt to the rear.
- Drop a dummy round in the chamber.
- Insert a magazine with at least one dummy round loaded into it.
- Let the bolt go forward (letting the dummy round from the magazine press into the one stuck in the chamber).
- The bolt will look like it is locked to the rear if set up properly.

Target Type and Setup: One 1/3 size small target (human shape) set directly in front of the shooter at room distance (5-7 yards).

Prop Setup: Note: this drill can be done with or without a simulated piece of cover.

Action(s): On the start signal, attempt to fire. Attempt to perform a Phase I malfunction clearance (which should not work), then fix the gun by going through the Phase II malfunction clearance (lock, rip and sweep, work, tap, rack, ready) and fire (click) three to five times at the threat targets. Go through a scan process before administratively setting up the rifle to prepare for the next training repetition.

Critical Points: Review all steps to the phase II malfunction and ensure you do each one deliberately.

Visual Cues: Due to the length of time this malfunction clearance takes, ensure you do not get task fixated on the gun, instead keep scanning the threat area.

Mental Cues: Actively visualize the entire drill. Ensure you visualize the technique components (active visualization), as well as elements of a real scenario (that the target is real).

Pivoting Mount Dry Fire Drill

Purpose: To build the manipulation skill of mounting the rifle while pivoting (see page 122) toward the threat.

Start Position: Empty gun with bolt cycled (hammer cocked), with the rifle at the forty-five degree low ready.

Target Type and Setup: One small target (human shape) set at room distance, directly in front of the shooter.

Prop Setup: N/A

Action(s): Imagine yourself in the center of a clock, with your threat target at the 12 o'clock position. Begin by facing 2 o'clock and on the start signal, mount *while* pivoting to face the threat and fire three to five times aiming at the center of the appropriate target. Now begin by facing 3 o'clock and repeat this drill. Work your way around the clock by standing in the center of it and using the different numbers to dictate where you start facing. This will force you to work on every possible pivot direction. Work all the way around the clock, and the last number faced should be 10 o'clock. During each repetition, don't forget to go through a scan process before administratively working the bolt to prepare for the next training repetition.

Critical Points: The head and eyes must find the threat first, so snap them to the target as fast as possible. Strive to make the mount consistent by finding the proper index points and cheek weld during each repetition.

Visual Cues: Visual shift from the target aiming area back to the front sight.

Mental Cues: Actively visualize the entire drill. Ensure you visualize the technique components (active visualization), as well as elements of a real scenario (that the target is real).

Movement Offline Dry fire Drill

Purpose: To build the manipulation skill of mounting the gun while stepping offline (see page 123) or to cover.

Start Position: Empty gun with bolt cycled (hammer cocked), with the rifle at the forty-five degree low ready.

Target Type and Setup: One small target (human shape) set at room distance, directly in front of the shooter.

Prop Setup: A simple barricade, or corner of a wall or something similar can be used during this drill to simulate cover.

Action(s): On the start signal, mount *while* moving offline toward cover (large aggressive step) left or right and fire (click) three to five times aiming at the center of the appropriate target. The start position for this drill will be one large step to the left or right of your piece of cover. Practice stepping toward cover while mounting the rifle. Go through a scan process before administratively working the bolt to prepare for the next training repetition.

Critical Points: Strive to make the mount consistent by finding the proper index points during the mount process during each repetition. Ensure that you are paying attention to the proper use of cover.

Visual Cues: Visual shift from the target aiming area back to the front sight.

Mental Cues: Actively visualize the entire drill. Ensure you visualize the technique components (active visualization), as well as elements of a real scenario (that the target is real).

One-Handed Reload Dry Fire Drill

Purpose:	To build the manipulation skill of reloading the rifle with one hand only (see page 126).
Start Position:	Set the gun up so it is empty, bolt locked to the rear and an empty magazine in the magazine well.
Target Type and Setup:	One small target (human shape) set at room distance, directly in front of the shooter.
Prop Setup:	N/A
Action(s):	On the start signal, attempt to fire. Use proper one-handed and fire (click) three to five times at the threat targets. Alternate between each hand (strong and support for every other repetition). Go through a scan process before administratively emptying the gun to prepare for the next training repetition. Rotate through five repetitions of each hand practicing: • With the right hand only • With the left hand only
Critical Points:	Follow one-handed survival shooting shooting techniques and safety points.
Visual Cues:	Keep the head and eyes up as much as possible, do not get task fixated on the gun.
Mental Cues:	Actively visualize the entire drill. Ensure you visualize the technique components (active visualization), as well as elements of a real scenario (that the target is real).

One-Handed Malfunction Clearance Dry Fire Drill

Purpose: To build the manipulation skill of clearing a Phase I and II malfunctions with one hand only (see page 127).

Start Position: Set the gun up for either a Phase I or II malfunction (you will work both).

Target Type and Setup: One 1/3 size small target (human shape) set directly in front of the shooter at room distance (5-7 yards).

Prop Setup: N/A

Action(s): On the start signal, attempt to fire. Use either a Phase I malfunction clearance or Phase II malfunction clearance and fire (click) three to five times at the threat targets. Alternate between each hand (strong and support for every other repetition). Go through a scan process before administratively working the bolt to prepare for the next training repetition.

Rotate through five repetitions of each hand practicing:
- Phase I clearance
- Phase II clearance

Critical Points: Follow all one-handed survival shooting techniques and safety points.

Visual Cues: For combative purposes, focus on keeping head and eyes on the threat - do not get fixated on the gun.

Mental Cues: Actively visualize the entire drill. Ensure you visualize the technique components (active visualization), as well as elements of a real scenario (that the target is real).

Live Fire Drills

This section will contain the live fire drills you will use in this system. Remember, live fire is specifically designed to allow you to work through the firing cycle and improve your ability to manage three things: 1) sights (gun direction); 2) trigger; and 3) recoil control. Specifically covered:

1. *Skills trained in the live fire program*
2. *Live fire training schedule*
3. *Execution of live fire training sessions (pre, during and post session)*
4. *Live fire training drills*
5. *Live fire training phases*
6. *Procedures for performing the drills*

Skills Trained

The live-fire training module will improve your ability to shoot better and integrate smart procedures such as performing an after-action scan process. Remember, the firing cycle is the trigger, sight, and recoil management that you must master in order to shoot fast and hit your target. You will primarily develop your manipulation skills in dry fire, so the focus will be on improving elements of the firing cycle during your live fire sessions, integrating the mental visualization techniques mentioned in the mental section, and performing correct tactics. Generally speaking, your live fire training time is better spent if you are focusing on the concepts of improving your ability to hit the target faster and more accurately. Always focus intently on what the rifle is doing during recoil and attempt to improve your ability to put rounds on target faster. Remember, you will work on your manipulation skills primarily in dry fire sessions.

Live Fire Training Schedule

You will be doing one live fire sessions on the range each week. You will be using one live fire drill that will focus on your session on specific skills. If you feel you have developed enough skill to move to the next week's drills, move on. Remember, this program is about skill development, and while you do not have to completely master the skill the drill teaches, moving on before gaining a solid grasp on it will hamper your improvement. So at the end of each week, assess your performance on the skills you worked on and either, a) move on the next week, or b) repeat the week's drill the next week. On another note, while the minimum is one live fire session per week, if you have the means and time to do more, do so! Repeat the same live fire drill during that extra session.

Two Separate Training Phases

The base training program will all be done in around fifteen weeks. At the end of your training program, there is an additional maintenance routine that will help you maintain your skills with a simple practice routine. There is no end to this program, and once you begin to follow the maintenance program, you should follow the training design cycle principles to help you continually modify your training drills to build better skills. The below chart shows a sample week of training.

Sun	Mon	Tue	Wed	Thu	Fri	Sat
Off	Dry Fire Session	Live Fire Session	Off	Optional Live Fire Session 2	Dry Fire Session	Off

The actual days you do these sessions could vary, but this is an example of a great split that allows you to train two days in a row with several days off. Remember, the dry fire drills you will be performing mimic to an extent, the live fire training. Another important thing to remember: if you miss a training session pick it up the next time you train, don't skip over it. An overview of the full training program drills done during each session during the skills development phase follows:

Week	Live Fire Drills [1]
Five Shot Group/Zero Check Precedes each live fire training session.	
One	Stationary Mount LF
Two	Stationary Transition To Handgun LF
Three	Bilateral Stationary Mount LF
Four	Pivoting Mount LF
Five	Movement Offline LF
Six	Fail To Stop LF
Seven	Shooting and Moving LF
Eight	Shooting and Moving, Multi-Directional LF
Nine	Sprinting Offline LF
Ten	Moving Mount LF
Eleven	Multi-Position Braced LF
Twelve	Extreme Close Quarters (ECQ) LF
Thirteen	One Shot X-Drill
Fourteen	Two Shot X-Drill
Fifteen	Multi-Port LF

The following chart shows a suggested maintenance routine.

Maintenance Routine Drills	Live Fire Drills [1]
Practice Routine #1	
Stationary Mount LF	
Stationary Transition To Handgun LF	
Bilateral Stationary Mount LF	
Practice Routine #2	
Pivoting Mount LF	
Movement Offline LF	
Fail To Stop LF	
Practice Routine #3	
Shooting and Moving LF	
Shooting and Moving, Multi-Directional LF	
Moving Mount LF	
Practice Routine #4	
Sprinting Offline LF	
Multi-Position Braced LF	
Extreme Close Quarters (ECQ) LF	
Practice Routine #5	
One Shot X-Drill (for time, beat your last time)	
Two Shot X-Drill (for time, beat your last time)	
Multi-Port LF (for time, beat your last time)	

Skills Testing

For those of you that want to measure your skills regularly, I am going to provide a rifle skills test (RST) in Chapter 10. It is a simple, yet effective way to measure your progress on a regular basis. I recommend you go through the testing process before you begin your training program

if you currently possess the skill to do so. If you are a very new beginner however, begin the training program and test after you are through it as your first baseline. Remember, even after you go through all of the drills, you are going to continue to practice and improve. Make sure to test yourself along the way.

If you run this test alone, certain portions of it require the correct use of tactical procedures such as scanning. Score yourself honestly if you do the test. Maintaining your skills once you have gone through the program can also be done by simply shooting the RST for score. I alternate between the RST and Maintenance routine above for most of my practice sessions. *Keep in mind that the RST is the key to identifying your weaknesses. If you are performing poorly on one of the stages in the RST, then select the dry and live fire drills that will help you fix that skill and work on them for a few weeks before re-testing.*

Live Fire Training Drills

The majority of the training drills in this program are simple and allow you to focus on a specific areas of skill. These are in addition to the correct tactics that might be used in a fight. Additionally you should be integrating the mental side of the game through visualization. When you reflect upon your notes from training, the mistakes you find will usually be small things that you must focus all of your mental attention on when correcting. The drills are designed to increase your skill with the rifle dramatically. They don't all directly simulate a defensive situation you might be in, but instead focus on just one or two skill areas that could be applied in that situation. That's okay as long as you realize that during these drills you are developing skill only, and not tactics or applications other than shooting skills that will be used in the fight. Good tactics are a separate subject and I suggest you seek out training from a qualified instructor.

That said, some drills are progressive in that they will require you to vary the round count and apply tactical considerations like scanning. To refine technique to the level of mastery, you will have to review every detail of every skill and constantly train those areas, moving toward perfection of your technique. Stay mentally connected and try to envision that you are engaging a threatening person that is intent on doing you harm, rather than a paper target.

One last thing – each training session will begin with the five shot zero/warm-up drill. This will ensure that your gun is zeroed and the ammunition that you are shooting is performing as expected. Shooting these groups tests both your fundamentals and removes any excuses for shooting errors during the drill. Perform this warm-up drill with both your practice ammunition and your defensive ammunition, if they are different. This will give you the confidence in your weapon and ammunition should the need for pinpoint accuracy arise at any time in the future.

Training Drills Sheets and Instructions

The next section lists the Training Drill Sheets and general instructions that will help you use them properly. Remember, these drills are all designed to work certain key skills and they have a specific design, so follow them exactly as they are written. If you start to modify the drills, then the next time you train you will have NOTHING to compare to because the drill was done differently each time you trained. I strongly suggest you consider purchasing the DVD set that was filmed to compliment this book, or view the drills on your mobile/smart device by visiting my Vimeo page (you can rent or purchase the drills and watch them on the range!) You can find the DVD's on my website and or visit: vimeo.com/ondemand/defensiverifle

Required Equipment

The training drills are designed to be very simple in nature, and require very little to actually perform them. I designed them so the average shooter, with little range gear could use them without having to buy expensive steel targets, or specialized equipment. You will need, at a minimum, the following:

- Targets (I like the ANT-7UT sold by L.E. Target), or something similar that replicates the human torso and has combat effective areas marked.
- Pasters (find tape or pasters that re the same color as the targets you are practicing on)
- Paint (white)
- (5) Target stands (I have used the folding ones made by GT and they work fine, but any design will work)
- Target sticks (lath) to staple targets to
- Stapler and staples
- (13) Small orange cones or small marking disks (the small disks that you can press into the ground are great)
- (2) Barrels (the large plastic ones are preferred), these can be substituted with 5-10 gallon buckets or anything similar, or even orange traffic cones.

Starting Distance

Each drill has a starting distance in the main body. I recommend that all shooters start using this distance, and work on "advanced skill" by trying to perform the drill faster and more accurately. Having said this, the distance in the drill is for shooters that are beginners. Those who begin the program at a more advanced level may use the alternate "advanced distances" by simply moving farther away from the target. Remember, if you vary the distance used in the drill, document that for later reference in your logbook.

Alternating Target Area

Several of the drills require the shooter to alternate between target areas (head and body hit zones). This is to work the skill at two different paces. When doing the drills, shooters MUST accept that there will be a significant difference in the pace they can hit the head and the body. Understand that this concept does not imply that you are shooting the head target due to a failure to stop (although that concept is addressed in the technique section), but simply allows you to train two distinctly different target sizes with the use of one target at one distance.

Technique

You will notice *(See page XX)* in multiple sections of each drill. The page numbers are listed so you can refer back to a detailed description of the technique quickly and efficiently. Each key point in the drill that has a technique reference is listed with the page number so you can reference it if necessary. Please reference back to that technique if you do not remember how to perform it correctly.

Varying Round Count and Progression Sequence

During most of the drills I assign you to shoot either a specific round count, or a progression sequence instead of XX number of shots during repetitions of the drills. This sequence will allow you to work the drill without always firing XX number of shots and developing a habit of just firing that number. On some drills it will also cause you to run out of ammunition at unknown times, allowing you to work your transition to handgun or emergency reload. Manually operated rifle shooters will have to modify the sequence a bit just because you are limited on ammunition. In the drill, I will give you the number of shots you will progress to. The sequence is as follows for a progression of four (4).

Progression of four (4)
Initiate the drill (whatever is described in the actions section) and:
1st Repetition: Fire one shot (this may be one shot to a target area, or just one shot depending on the drill.)
2nd Repetition: Fire two shots
3rd Repetition: Fire three shots
4th Repetition: Fire four shots
5th Repetition: Fire three shots
6th Repetition: Fire two shots
7th Repetition: Fire one shot
Total Rounds: 16

Note: If you are doing a drill that has multiple targets, then you can multiply the number of targets by the total number in the sequence to find out how many rounds the drill contains.

Sections

Each drill is broken down into different sections. These sections will give you all of the information you will need to successfully execute the drills.

Targets

Unless otherwise noted, all targets for drills are 5' high at the shoulder or set so they mimic a real human in height.

Equipment

Use the exact gear you carry your firearm with, in the manner that you carry it so that your training reflects real life skill.

Consistency

It is incredibly important that you keep things consistent when doing these drills. Failures to do so will result in times and hits that are not trackable or measurable. The goal is to measure the metrics of the drills as you evolve so you can watch your progress, always driving your skill to the next level.

Scoring/Tracking

Shooting to an effective target area is something that will make a big difference in stopping a potential threat. Massad Ayoob confirms "placement of the shot is more important than any other factor in stopping the threat posed by the homicidal human" in his great book "Combat Shooting." Your training drills will be flawed if you do not train yourself to hit areas on the target that will stop the threat. I call these areas *"combat effective"* (C.E.) hits.

Hits should primarily be in the Combat Effective zones, defined as the two zones of the body (head and torso) that are the most likely to incapacitate the threat quickly. These areas are:

- A six-inch circle in the high center chest, directly in the center of the body with the heart directly in the center.
- A three-inch circle in the head area with the nose high in the circle. This will keep the bullet from hitting too high, which in some cases can cause a spasmodic reflex of the muscles, possibly causing the person to pull the trigger if they are armed. A perfect headshot would be one where with the head erect, the bullet travels through the soft tissue of the nasal area into the brain. Ayoob notes that if the person is facing another direction, "picture a headband pulled down over the ears, and now wrapped around those ears, and the nose, and in the back, the occipital protuberance, that bump you can reach up now and feel in the back at the base of your skull."[15] A shot anywhere in that "headband" will have the proper affect on the threat.

Note: You can consider where these areas are if the body was turned sideways by envisioning the person in 3-D.

During the repetitions, document the times for each drill repetition, and anything noteworthy.

- After the prescribed number of repetitions has taken place, look at the hits on the target, hits in the combat effective zone, and any hits off the target.
- Your goal should be to have the majority (90% +) of the hits in the *combat effective* area, and no misses off the target.
- Paste hits outside the *combat effective* area and get set up for the next drill. The reason I just paste non-*combat effective* hits and leave the holes in the center of the target is to save time. A side benefit is that having holes in the target forces you to call bad shots from the sight picture you see (sight alignment), versus looking for hits on the target as you are shooting.

---

[15] Masaad Ayoob, Combat Shooting, Vol. 1 (Iola: Gun Digest Books, of F+W Media, 2011) 1 vols.

Pay attention to your overall shot grouping on the target when you are done training. The pasters and holes can be viewed from several steps back and assessed for technique mistakes. Try to assess where the majority of non-*combat effective* hits are, and do your best to figure out why you are hitting that area.

Rifle Zero Theory

Before you begin your drills it is incredibly important to both understand and apply the principles of zeroing your gun. There are numerous theories on what distance to zero a rifle for maximum performance. If you do any research, the first thing you will find is that opinions on this subject are strong, and there is not one standard answer. The U.S. Military differs in its opinion on zeroing an M-16 variant rifle depending on which service you research, and if you get deeper in the weeds, there are some special operations units that opt for unique zeros that meet their needs.

So how do we decide on our own personal zero? Let's simplify. Let's set some goals:
- Our zero must meet our own needs, and more specifically our engagement potential distances.
- Our zero should give us the most flexibility in hitting targets at different distances, without having to do mental math of any significant amount of hold over or under.

So given the above goals, what distance should we zero our rifle? Let's consider three choices and look at the potential of each choice: 25-, 50-, and 100-yard initial zero. Keep in mind that the initial zero on your rifle is the first point at which your line of sight intersects with the bullets path. Depending on your zero, there will be a secondary point where the bullet once again intersects with your line of sight. The closer (range) the initial zero is, the more the bullet travels in an arc pattern. The key is to find a zero that allows you to hit at the ranges you want to, and offers the flattest possible trajectory.

I personally prefer a 50/200-yard initial and secondary intersecting point zero due to the fact that the bullet travels at a predictable arc that allows me to engage targets to 200 yards without worrying about hold overs (holding the rifle sights over or under the desired point of impact). The maximum the bullet travels over my line of sight between the 50 and 200-yard distances is around two inches. Since the combat effective area on a human's chest is a six-inch circle, if I have a two inch variable, I am still going to hit within that six inch area if I do my job of steadying the rifle and managing the trigger.

Compare that to a 25/300+ yard zero. With that zero, the bullet would find it's initial intersection at 25 yards, but by 100 yards the bullet would be close to 6 inches high. That means that if you were to hold center of that six inch combat effective area, you would have the round impact three or more inches outside of it (high). This zero would require some serious mental math to get hits.

Now lets look at a very popular 100 yard zero with no secondary intersection. This zero is a viable zero for most uses including hunting where the typical animal distance is around 100 yards. The problem is that the bullet drop increases considerably after that intersecting point at 100 yards. At 200 or more yards the round is going to be three or more inches low, which once again nearly puts the impact outside of the six-inch combat effective area if you held the dot in the center of that aiming area. The good news is that most of us would not be likely to engage at distances beyond that 100-yard range.

Keep in mind a few last thoughts when it comes to zeroing. *Everything* affects it! Ammunition velocity and type, barrel length, height of the scope over the bore, and environmental factors all change where the bullet actually hits. It is imperative to check your zeros at different distances. My suggestions:

- Zero your rifle at 50 yards.
- Refine your zero at 100, 150, and 200 yards. Adjust for windage and learn exactly where your ammunition hits in terms of elevation at those distances. Impacts should not exceed 2-3 inches above or below your aiming point from 50-200 yards.

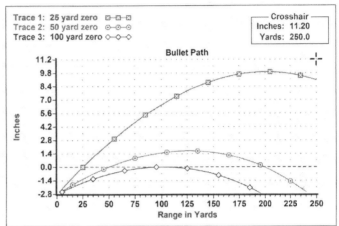

Figure 62 This chart shows the ballistic path of the three zeros discussed.

Once you have refined your zero, the only thing you will have to consider when taking a precision shot is your mechanical offset at extremely close distances. No matter what zero you choose, the mechanical distance between the bore and optic causes an offset of 1.5-2 inches when shooting at closer ranges. This is important to know as well, because you might have to take a shot at short room distances, which might be 5 yards. To hit a shot at that close range, the dot/crosshairs will have to be held slightly high.

Other than this mechanical offset, a good zero will give you the ability to place the dot in the same aiming area from distances of 10 yards to 200, without having to worry about doing any mental math before pulling the trigger. And that is the goal!

Safety Rules

Without Safety, my goal in writing this book will never be met! Here is your warning: <u>Firearms training is risky business even for an experienced person</u>! We must always be very aware of the fact that we are using extremely dangerous tools that could harm others or us at any time. For these reasons, I require that you follow these safety rules anytime you are around firearms. If you do not understand, or if you may be new to shooting, then I HIGHLY recommend that you find a competent instructor or training academy to assist you in your initial training. Please read each of the following rules in detail:

- **Always** treat every firearm as if it were loaded all the time.
- **Always** keep the firearm pointed in a safe direction – a direction where a negligent discharge would cause minimal property damage and zero physical injury.
- **Always** keep your trigger finger off the trigger and outside of the trigger guard until you have made a conscious decision to shoot.
- **Always** be sure of your target, backstop, and beyond, as well as items in the foreground that may deflect bullets causing injury.
- **Always** have an emergency plan, communication device, and first aid kit available in case of a range accident.

> *__Reminder-__ please consider visiting my Vimeo page or purchasing the DVD's that were filmed to compliment this book. The Vimeo page has several free videos and also videos for rent or purchase. They are the ultimate tool in watching the techniques and drills while on the range! You can find the DVD's on my website and the Vimeo page at vimeo.com/ondemand/defensiverifle*

Five Shot Group / Zero Check

ROUNDS PER REPETITION: 5   **REPETITIONS:** 3+   **TOTAL ROUNDS:** 15+

Purpose:	To verify gun and ammunition combination is shooting point-of-aim (POA) to point-of-impact (POI), by shooting a group on a specific spot. To verify basic mechanics on the process of sight and trigger management. Once you verify the gun is zeroed with the ammunition you are training with, analysis of other training factors is easier (i.e., you don't blame the gun for a bad shot). This five shot group should also be shot with your defensive ammunition on a regular basis.
Start Position:	Prone and standing position.
Target Type and Setup:	One (1) threat target, set at seven (7), twenty five (25), and fifty (50) yards directly in front of the shooter with a 2" x 2" piece of black tape, or marker in the center of the combat effective zone.
Prop Setup:	N/A
Action(s):	With no time limitations, shoot 3 groups, using the following guidelines: • First group of five shots, fire as slowly and accurately as possible from 50 yards in a prone position. Assess group for size, and position and adjust sights if necessary. Repeat if necessary. Any shots that are bad shots, i.e. fliers should be noted and called when shot. • Second group of five shots, fire at controlled speed from 25 yards in a standing position. Aim directly at the marker and fire as fast as you can hit it but no faster. Look for a group significant group shift in windage and elevation from the 50 yard zero group. • Third group of five shots, fire at controlled speed from 7 yards in a standing position. Aim directly at the marker and fire as fast as you can hit it but no faster. Look for a group significant group shift in windage and from the 25 yard zero group. ***End goals***: A solid zero and direct hits at 50 yards, a slight elevation shift and neutral windage at the 25 and 7 yards distances. This drill will also teach you exactly what your mechanical offset is.
Critical Points:	Fundamental sight and trigger management.
Visual Cues:	Use a perfect sight picture and alignment for this drill.
Mental Cues:	N/A

Stationary Mount Live Fire Drill

ROUNDS PER REPETITION: *1-4* **REPETITIONS:** *20+* **TOTAL ROUNDS:** *150+-*

Purpose: To work on the static mount (see page 105) and firing cycle components while firing to both the body and head combat effective areas.

Start Position: Loaded gun with the rifle at the forty-five degree low ready.

Target Type and Setup: One (1) threat target, set at seven (7), ten (10), and fifteen (15) yards directly in front of the shooter.

Prop Setup: N/A

Action(s):
1. On the start signal, mount and fire the prescribed number of rounds while shooting through a progression of four (4), scan, and re-set for the next repetition.
2. When the gun runs empty, reload and repeat the drill with your second magazine from ten (10) yards.
3. When the gun runs empty, reload and repeat the drill with your third magazine from fifteen (15) yards.
4. When the gun runs empty, reload and repeat the drill with your third magazine from twenty-five (25) yards.
5. Reload magazines and repeat this drill with headshots only.

Critical Points: Acquire index points while gripping the gun in the holster. Manage the sights and trigger during the shots. Ensure proper follow through and scan process.

Visual Cues: Focal point should be exactly where you want to hit, and the focus should shift from that point to the front sight as the front sight comes into view during extension.

Mental Cues: Visualize the mechanics of the drill, as well as the reality of the target. Imagine that the target is a real person rather that a range prop.

Stationary Transition To Handgun Live Fire Drill
ROUNDS PER REPETITION: 1-4   REPETITIONS: 20+   TOTAL ROUNDS: 150+-

Purpose: To work on transitioning to a handgun, reloading and dealing with Phase one malfunctions (see page 116 and 119). After this drill, if the situation dictates, you will use the transition skill in any case where you have a non-firing weapon.

Start Position: Rifle set up as explained below, at the forty-five degree low ready. Loaded handgun holstered in your carry position.

Target Type and Setup: One (1) threat target, set at seven (7) yards directly in front of the shooter.

Prop Setup: N/A

Action(s): Note, if you would NOT be armed with a handgun along with a rifle, skip to the **Stationary Reload Drill** (next).

Set the gun by preparing your magazines with a combination of live ammunition and dummy rounds. Place five (5) dummy rounds in each magazine (if using a 30 round magazine). On the start signal, mount and fire through a progression of four. When the rifle malfunctions or runs out of ammunition (bolt locks to the rear), transition to the handgun and finish firing the remaining rounds with the handgun. Here is an example of how your repetitions would go:

Don't forget about the sequence of checking and fixing the rifle to get it back into the fight.

Critical Points: Effectively getting the rifle out of the way (sweeping it aside) during the transition. Building a proper grip on the handgun after the transition.

Visual Cues: Keep the head and eyes on the threat while getting the rifle back into action.

Mental Cues: Actively visualize the entire drill.

Bilateral Stationary Mount Live Fire Drill
ROUNDS PER REPETITION: *1-4*   **REPETITIONS:** *20+*   **TOTAL ROUNDS:** *150+-*

Purpose: To work on the stationary mount (see page 144) and firing cycle components while shooting off both the strong and support side shoulders.

Start Position: Loaded gun with the rifle at the forty-five degree low ready.

Target Type and Setup: One (1) threat target, set at seven (7) yards directly in front of the shooter.

Prop Setup: N/A

Action(s): Prepare three full magazines. On the start signal, mount and fire the prescribed number of rounds while shooting through a progression of four, re-engage the safety, transfer to the other shoulder and fire the prescribed number of rounds on that shoulder. The next repetition should be done by starting on the shoulder that the last drill ended on. When the rifle malfunctions or runs out of ammunition (bolt locks to the rear), transition to the handgun and finish firing the remaining rounds with the handgun, reload or clear the malfunction, and continue the drill.

Reload magazines and repeat this drill, headshots only.

Critical Points: Acquire index points while gripping the gun in the holster. Manage the sights and trigger during the shots. Ensure proper follow through and scan process.

Visual Cues: Focal point should be exactly where you want to hit, and the focus should shift from that point to the front sight as the front sight comes into view during extension.

Mental Cues: Visualize the mechanics of the drill, as well as the reality of the target. Imagine that the target is a real person rather that a range prop.

Use Of Cover Live Fire Drill

ROUNDS PER REPETITION: *1-4*   **REPETITIONS:** *20+*   **TOTAL ROUNDS:** *120+-*

Purpose:	To work on shooting the rifle from behind a piece of cover by mounting and firing with both shoulders (see page 140).
Start Position:	Rifle set up as explained below, at the forty-five degree low ready.
Target Type and Setup:	One (1) threat target, set at seven (7) yards directly in front of the shooter.
Prop Setup:	A barricade or simulated piece of cover placed one yard in front of the shooting position.
Action(s):	Note, you may or may NOT be armed with a handgun during this drill and you will NOT transition to the handgun because cover is available.
	Prepare three magazines with a combination of live ammunition and five (5) dummy round per magazine (if using 30 round magazines). On the start signal, mount and fire the prescribed number of rounds while shooting through a progression of four, from the strong shoulder from the strong side of cover. Clear malfunctions from behind cover as they arise. Practice with two (2) magazines on the strong side, off the strong shoulder, and repeat the drill by using the support shoulder and support side of cover for the last two. Ensure that any reloading and malfunction clearing occurs behind cover.
	Reload magazines and repeat this drill, headshots only.
Critical Points:	Proper index points while reloading the rifle. Re-acquiring a proper mount on the rifle after the reload. Pick a consistent spot to do the reload (tuck rifle under the arm or keep mounted on the shoulder).
Visual Cues:	Keep the head and eyes on the threat while getting the rifle back into action.
Mental Cues:	Actively visualize the entire drill.

Pivoting Mount Live Fire Drill

ROUNDS PER REPETITION: 1-4   **REPETITIONS:** 20+   **TOTAL ROUNDS:** 150+-

Purpose:	To work on the pivoting mount (see page 122) and firing cycle components.
Start Position:	Loaded gun with the rifle at the forty-five degree low ready.
Target Type and Setup:	One (1) threat target, set at seven (7) yards directly in front of the shooter.
Prop Setup:	N/A
Action(s):	Start by facing an imaginary 2 o'clock if you were standing in the middle of the clock (your head and eyes should face whatever clock position each time). On the start signal, mount and fire the prescribed number of rounds while shooting through a progression of four (4) scan and re-set for the next repetition. On the next repetition, start by facing 3 o'clock. Continue to work your way around the clock. When you get to 6 o'clock, practice one pivot turning counter-clockwise and one pivot turning clockwise. Your last pivot will be the one done while facing 10 o'clock. When the rifle malfunctions or runs out of ammunition (bolt locks to the rear), transition to the handgun and finish firing the remaining rounds with the handgun, reload or clear the malfunction, and continue the drill.
Critical Points:	Remember that getting your eyes on the threat faster will allow you to make a lethal force decision faster, as well as increase the speed of your pivot. Keep the toe of the stock of the rifle in the same position allowing for a faster mount during each repetition. Pivot on the balls of the feet.
Visual Cues:	Focal point should be exactly where you want to hit, and the focus should shift from that point to sight as it comes into view during the mount process.
Mental Cues:	Actively visualize the entire drill.

Moving (Offline) Mount Live Fire Drill
ROUNDS PER REPETITION: *1-4*   **REPETITIONS:** *20+*   **TOTAL ROUNDS:** *150+-*

Purpose: To work on mounting the gun and applying proper firing cycle components while moving offline (see page 124). This may be to cover or in the open if none is available.

Start Position: Loaded gun with the rifle at the forty-five degree low ready.

Target Type and Setup: One (1) threat target, set at seven (7) yards directly in front of the shooter.

Prop Setup: A barricade or something similar set at 6 yards from the target that will allow you to move to a simulated piece of cover. Be sure this piece of cover is not metal to prevent ricochets if shot accidentally.

Action(s): Alternate your start position so that you are either one large step left or right of the simulated piece of cover. You will also be one yard away from the cover because the prop is set at six yards from the target, while you will be shooting from seven yards. Feel free to vary this start position so that you can work multiple angles while stepping to cover. On the start signal, mount while moving offline toward cover and fire through a progression of four, scanning and resetting for the next repetition. Malfunctions and reloads will be handled from behind cover.

Critical Points: Explode offline aggressively while mounting the rifle. Movement is the key. Try to stabilize and build a good shooting position as soon as possible once in the position. Enter low and stay low and aggressive, don't stand up while shooting. Remember to try not to cross the feet to keep from tripping. Keep as much of the body behind cover as possible.

Visual Cues: Visual shift from the target aiming area back to the front sight.

Mental Cues: Actively visualize the entire drill.

Fail To Stop Live Fire Drill

ROUNDS PER REPETITION: *6-9* **REPETITIONS:** *20+* **TOTAL ROUNDS:** *150+-*

Purpose:	To work on the skill of transitioning to an alternate target area of the body, due to a failure to stop on the primary combat effective area (high center chest).
Start Position:	Loaded gun with the rifle at the forty-five degree low ready.
Target Type and Setup:	One (1) threat target, set at seven (7) yards directly in front of the shooter.
Prop Setup:	N/A
Action(s):	On the start signal, mount and fire four rounds to the high chest target area and while continuing to fire transition to either the head or pelvic girdle target area. The total number of shots may be varied in this drill between six and nine total. The key is to ensure you transition to the alternate target area and get hits in that area. Perform your repetitions, alternating between transitioning to the head and pelvic girdle every other repetition.
Critical Points:	Transition quickly to an alternate target area. Maintaining a strong mount on the rifle as it moves to an alternate area. Learning the speed with which you can hit the alternate target area when transitioning to the head.
Visual Cues:	Focus and visual awareness on the sights and where the gun is pointed while moving the gun to an alternate area is critical during this drill.
Mental Cues:	Visualize the mechanics of the drill, as well as the reality of the target. Imagine that the threat is failing to stop as you fire to the high center chest, causing you to transition to the alternate target area.

Shooting And Moving Live Fire Drill
ROUNDS PER REPETITION: *1-4*   **REPETITIONS:** *20+*   **TOTAL ROUNDS:** *150+-*

Purpose:	To learn how to correctly manage the sights and trigger while on the move, stabilizing the gun and calling good shots (See page 124).
Start Position:	Loaded gun with the rifle at the forty-five degree low ready.
Target Type and Setup:	One (1) threat target, set at ten (10) yards directly in front of the shooter.
Prop Setup:	N/A
Action(s):	Begin moving from the forward starting position at the ten (10) yard cone. Mount the gun and fire one shot while continuing to move. Stop at the three (3) yard cone. Now begin moving to the rear, mounting the gun and firing one round while on the move to the rear cone. Now repeat the drill firing through a progression of four (4) in each direction. Here is a sample of how your repetitions will look:

- Moving forward, mount and fire one
- Moving to the rear, mount and fire one
- Moving forward, mount and fire two
- Moving to the rear, mount and fire two
- Moving forward, mount and fire three
- Moving to the rear, mount and fire three..etc.

Critical Points:	Take short steps using heel-to-toe and toe-to-heel movement, short steps (see the technique section). Stabilize the gun and press through the trigger when the sights settle (accept some wobble/movement).
Visual Cues:	You should have a very hard focus on the front sight or dot, it is critical to call the shot by looking at the front sight/dot placement on the target when the rifle goes off.
Mental Cues:	Actively visualize the entire drill.

Shooting And Moving, Multi-Directional Live Fire Drill
ROUNDS PER REPETITION: *Varied* **REPETITIONS:** 5 **TOTAL ROUNDS:** *150+-*

Purpose: This is an advanced skill building drill due to the difficulty of the movement. This drill will help you work on shooting during multi-directional movement.

Start Position: Variable (see start position instructions) one yard behind either barrel.

Target Type and Setup: One (1) threat target, set at seven (7) yards directly in front of the shooter.

Prop Setup: Two barrels (or something similar) set at seven (7) yards (measured from the front edge) yards from the targets, spaced one yard apart.

Action(s): Prepare your magazines to full capacity with no more than thirty (30) rounds total. On the start signal, mount and fire all ammunition in your magazines while continuing to move in a sideways figure-eight pattern through the barrels. This movement will force every conceivable angle of movement. Transition when the gun runs dry or a malfunction occurs.

Critical Points: Keep your weight low, and float the gun in front of the face, keeping a solid mount on the gun. Stabilize and fire the shots only when the sight settles in the target area.

Visual Cues: You must have a very hard focus on the front sight or dot, and should always know where the gun is pointed while moving. A key point is to watch for and call the shot when the sight or dot lifts.

Mental Cues: Actively visualize the entire drill.

Moving Mount Live Fire Drill

ROUNDS PER REPETITION: 3   **REPETITIONS:** 20+   **TOTAL ROUNDS:** 150+

Purpose:	To build the manipulation skill of mounting the rifle while sprinting from position to position.
Start Position:	Loaded gun with the rifle at the forty-five degree low ready.
Target Type and Setup:	One (1) threat target, set at seventy five (75) yards directly in front of the shooter.
Prop Setup:	N/A
Action(s):	Prepare your magazines to full capacity with no more than thirty (30) rounds total. On the start signal, immediately sprint four paces, mount and fire three rounds on target. Do whatever necessary to stabilize the gun for the shots. Repeat and sprint three paces and stop and fire four shots. Continue repeating the moving mount drill until the rifle is empty, at which time you may perform a transition, or reload (see the technique section for explanation on when/why). Note that at a certain distance and closer you will NOT have to come to a complete stop to hit the shots. If a malfunction occurs take your choice of transitioning or clearing the malfunction. Reload the rifle and move back to the seventy-five yard line and repeat.
Critical Points:	Stabilize and fire the shots only when the sight settles in the target area.
Visual Cues:	You must have a very hard focus on the front sight or dot, and should always know where the gun is pointed while moving. A key point is to watch for and call the shot when the sight or dot lifts.
Mental Cues:	Actively visualize the entire drill.

Sprinting Offline Live Fire Drill

ROUNDS PER REPETITION: 1-4   **REPETITIONS:** 20+   **TOTAL ROUNDS:** 150+-

Purpose: To build the manipulation skill of mounting the rifle while sprinting offline to the left and right.

Start Position: Loaded gun with the rifle at the forty-five degree low ready.

Target Type and Setup: One (1) threat target, set ten (10) yards directly in front of the shooter.

Prop Setup: N/A

Action(s): Prepare your magazines to full capacity (minimum of two magazines) with no more than thirty (30) rounds total. On the start signal, immediately sprint three-four to your right (moving left to right), remount the rifle and fire through a progression of four. Now repeat the drill, but sprint right to left. Do whatever necessary to stabilize the gun for the shots. Continue repeating the drill until the rifle is empty, at which time you will transition to your handgun, or reload (see the technique section for explanation on when/why).

Critical Points: Stabilize and fire the shots only when the sight settles in the target area.

Visual Cues: You must have a very hard focus on the front sight or dot, and should always know where the gun is pointed while moving into position. A key point is to watch for and call the shot when the sight or dot lifts.

Mental Cues: Actively visualize the entire drill.

Multi-Position Braced Live Fire Drill
ROUNDS PER REPETITION: 1-4   **REPETITIONS:** 20+   **TOTAL ROUNDS:** 150+-

Purpose:	To build the skill of bracing the gun against a solid obstacle, using it for stability.
Start Position:	Loaded gun with the rifle at the forty-five degree low ready.
Target Type and Setup:	One (1) threat target, set at fifty (50) yards directly in front of the shooter.
Prop Setup:	A barricade, study pole, or solid position of some sort that the rifle can be braced against.
Action(s):	Prepare your magazines to full capacity with no more than thirty (30) rounds total. On the start signal, mount while bracing on the right side of the barricade, and fire through a progression of four, scanning and resetting each time. Work through two (2) magazines, then transfer the rifle to the support side shoulder and repeat from a braced position from the support side shoulder. Use your fifth magazine to work on whichever side you like. Do whatever necessary to stabilize the gun for the shots. See the technique section page 146 for details on the gun position while bracing.
Critical Points:	Drive the gun into the braced position to stabilize it. Make sure to hold the front end of the gun up with the lead hand. DO NOT let the barrel of the rifle touch the brace position.
Visual Cues:	You must have a very hard focus on the front sight or dot, and should always know where the gun is pointed while moving. A key point is to watch for and call the shot when the sight or dot lifts.
Mental Cues:	Actively visualize the entire drill.

Extreme Close Quarters (ECQ) Live Fire Drill
ROUNDS PER REPETITION: *1-4*   **REPETITIONS:** *20+*   **TOTAL ROUNDS:** *150+-*

Purpose:	To build the skill of firing from the high ready position (close quarters).
Start Position:	Loaded gun with the rifle at the forty-five degree low ready.
Target Type and Setup:	One (1) threat target, set at one foot (1) to three (3) yards directly in front of the shooter. Note: The target must be a strong, cardboard target that is mounted securely or it will get blown off the target stand when shooting.
Prop Setup:	N/A
Action(s):	Part 1 – **Under the Arm**. Stand in front of the threat target close enough so that when at the forty-five degree low ready, the muzzle touches the target. On the start signal, retract the rifle and tuck it under the arm while taking one big step to the rear. Fire through a progression of four (4) starting each time with the rifle touching the target. Part 2 – **Over the Shoulder**. Stand in front of the threat target close enough so that when at the forty-five degree low ready, the muzzle touches the target. On the start signal, retract the rifle and pull it over the shoulder while taking one big step to the rear. Fire through a progression of four (4) starting with the rifle touching the target. Note: After the shots move two more steps to the rear each time and perform a scan process to practice the habit of creating distance after the shooting.
Critical Points:	**Safety Points:** Pay specific attention to the muzzle position during these drills. Do not use a metal target frame unless you ensure that there will be no ricochet hazard. If you have a gun with an exposed charging handle, ensure that during the second part of the drill the bolt is not touching the chest area, causing a malfunction. If you transition to your handgun during this drill, consider using a close quarters position with it (see vimeo.com/ondemand/defensivehandgun)

Visual Cues: Awareness of where the gun is pointed is the only visual stimulus the shooter will receive on this drill since the gun is not in front of the face.

Mental Cues: Actively visualize the entire drill.

Advanced Skill Developing Bonus Drills

This section contains drills that I use in practice that will help you develop a really high level of skill. While I am not sure they are necessary for a defensive shooter's program, they will add a challenge and force a level of skill development that is similar to the best shooters in the world. I recommend using them as bonus training drills, or maybe even using them to push yourself to the next level. What I did not want to do was label them as defensive drills that you have to use each training session. Time is valuable to me as well as you, so the previous program contains the drills you need to take you to a great skill level - but if you want to go farther, try out these bonus drills.

Suggested Use - Once you have finished your three phase training program, begin your maintenance routine. On off days, use the bonus drills to test your skill. Each has a specific set up, round count, and purpose so they can be tracked easily with your logbook. This will allow you to compare results at a later date. You may also consider going through your practice routine, and then adding one bonus drill at the end of the session if you have time. Rotate through them and always try to push to the next level. Experiment with different distances and target set-ups.

One Shot X-Drill (Live Fire)

ROUNDS PER REPETITION: 8   **REPETITIONS:** 20+   **TOTAL ROUNDS:** 150+

Purpose: This is a skill building drill that teaches recognition of the correct sight picture (faster), and target acquisitions of varying size targets.

Start Position: Loaded gun with the rifle at the forty-five degree low ready.

Target Type and Setup: Two (2) threat targets five feet high at the shoulder, seven yards directly in front of the shooter three yards apart.

Prop Setup: N/A

Action(s): Mount and fire one round to each of these target areas and repeat the sequence (for a total of 8 rounds per repetition). Alternate your starting point and follow the sequences below.

1. T1 body, T2 upper, T1 upper, T2 body
2. T1 upper, T2 body, T1, body, T2 upper

Critical Points: Focus on seeing what you need to see to hit the C.E. zone shot on the two different target areas. You must have more visual patience for the headshot. Prep the trigger as the gun is driven to the next target and enters the target area (not before). Stop the gun as much as needed to fire the shot. Drive the gun hard to the next target. Maintain the cheek weld on the stock during the gun movement.

Visual Cues: Look at the spot we are driving the gun toward. When the front sight/dot touches the target we should be verifying alignment and placement of the sights.

Two Shot X-Drill (Live Fire)

ROUNDS PER REPETITION: 16   **REPETITIONS:** 10   **TOTAL ROUNDS:** 160+

Purpose: This is a skill building drill that teaches you how to manage the sights and trigger during target acquisitions of varying size targets. This drill is designed to allow you to work the different paces you can shoot at and hit varying target sizes (head versus body simulates the different sizes).

Start Position: Facing up range, loaded gun with the rifle at the forty-five degree low ready position.

Target Type and Setup: Two (2) threat targets five high at the shoulder, seven yards directly in front of the shooter two yards apart.

Prop Setup: N/A

Action(s): You may choose between the reload or transition option below (depending on your gear set up). Set the gun up with eight (8) rounds total during the initial load (this will force an emergency reload). On the start signal, turn, mount, and fire two rounds to:

- T1 body, T2 head, T1 head, T2 body.

Option A: **Reload** – Perform a reload, and repeat the sequence.

Option B: **Transition** – Transition to the handgun and finish the sequence with the handgun.

Critical Points: Make sure you are seeing what you need to see to get hits on the two different target areas. The pace should be completely different between the body and headshots. Drive the gun hard to the next target. Pay attention to the mechanics of the firing cycle during the shooting.

Visual Cues: When the front sight/dot touches the target you should be verifying alignment and placement of the sights.

Multi-Port Drill

ROUNDS PER REPETITION: 8   **REPETITIONS:** 20   **TOTAL ROUNDS:** 160+

Purpose: This is a skill building drill that will really teach you how to move around and use different positions and angles to maximize use of cover. This drill builds an incredible awareness of the relationship of the gun and pieces of cover or obstacles.

Start Position: Loaded gun with the rifle at the forty-five degree low ready position.

Target Type and Setup: Two (2) threat targets, set at seven yards directly in front of the shooter three yards apart and five feet high at the shoulder.

Prop Setup: A small piece of stiff cardboard or a plastic target backer (I use an IPSC target stapled upside down) with a small port 6" wide by 12" high cut in the center. Position the top of the port at about mid chest level. Depending on your muzzle break, and cardboard IPSC may work. To set this up with an IPSC target, cut the center A-zone and head off the target and staple it upside down with the bottom of the target at shoulder height. You now have four different shooting positions: a) left side of the prop, b) middle port (medium squatting), c) right side of the prop, and d) below the bottom of the prop (low squatting/kneeling). This prop should be placed directly in front of you far enough away so that it is a couple inches away from the muzzle of your gun when it is fully extended.

Action(s): Starting directly behind the prop, engage each target firing two rounds on each shooting the left target first and then right target from each firing position in this order: a, b, c, and d. Reload as necessary when you run out of ammunition.

Critical Points: The head and eyes must find the threat first, so snap them to the target as fast as possible. Strive to make the mount consistent by finding the proper index points and cheek weld during each repetition.

Visual Cues: Wait for the sights to be in the target area before shooting. Be patient on the sights when in low or off balance positions.

CHAPTER 8

Alternate Methods Of Training

Some of you might have difficulty shooting as much as recommended in the full training program. This chapter breaks down the details behind using airsoft and .22 conversion kits to enhance your learning.

Covered in this chapter:

1. Alternate Methods of Training
2. Airsoft Training
3. .22 Caliber Training

Purpose

In this chapter we will discuss alternate methods of skill development like airsoft and .22 conversion kits in detail, including their uses and practicality. I hope you have realized by now, there is much more to training for a firearm-related goal than just practicing at the range. This section was written as a solution for those of you that really want to develop your skills to the highest level, but have reduced means to do so. For some of you it might be a shortage of ammunition, and for some, inadequate access to a range. Either way, this section will help you understand some of the training solutions out there, and how they will help you reach your self-defense goal.

Alternate Methods of Training

Alternate methods of training include any other method of training that is not standard live fire training with your primary gun and caliber. This includes dry fire, live fire .22-caliber training, airsoft training, and anything else you might be able to use to develop your skills. In this day and age ammunition is getting very expensive. For some of you it is important to find other methods with which you can train your skills. How valuable are these alternate methods of training? In my opinion, critical, especially for those of you with limited resources. I personally use extensive dry fire (non-live) and .22-caliber training in my own training sessions, and have also used airsoft guns to enhance my training.

Air Soft Training

If there is a gun made today, there is probably an air soft version of that same gun. Air soft

Figure 63 The top gun is an airsoft gun that looks, feels, and operates identical to the live fire gun below. A great tool to use for a variety of drills. Recoil control must still be practiced with a full power rifle in live fire drills though.

guns made today have come a long way compared to the airsoft guns made ten years ago. Airsoft guns today are realistic in weight, size, and function. Most airsoft rifles you can buy on the market today use some sort of compressed gas or battery operated mechanics to cycle the bolt. I strongly recommend that you purchase a higher-quality gas airsoft gun, rather than a lower quality spring-operated gun. When selecting your airsoft gun, try to find a model that closely replicates the weight of your real firearm. All manipulation devices, including the magazine release, slide release, and trigger should be very closely designed to replicate your actual firearm. If you can, choose one that allows you to switch out the sights and mount optics or equipment onto pre-existing rails. You will want to set up your airsoft gun with a set of sights that is exactly the same as your real gun. The whole idea is to train your visual system to see what you need to see to make a good shot with the same equipment you will use on your actual firearm.

Airsoft rifles I have used look and feel exactly like the real thing. Once again, with an airsoft rifle you'll want to take the time to set it up exactly like your real gun.

Training with an airsoft firearm will require that you go to an area inside your house or possibly in your yard where you can safely contain the projectiles that will be shot from the firearm. There are many manufacturers that are making very high quality bullet traps with special netting that will catch the BB's fired from the airsoft firearm. When doing this type of training, all applicable safety rules should be followed. The BB's are fired at high velocities and could easily damage your eyes or body parts if you violate safety rules that we follow when we are firing with live fire ammunition.

.22-Caliber Conversion Kit Training

Training with a .22-caliber conversion kit or full-time rifle is an awesome way to increase your skill level and save money doing it. Most kits are either a replacement bolt that fires out of the existing barrel, or complete upper's that can be used with an existing rifle. There are also several manufacturers who make .22 caliber rifles that look and feel like their big brothers, with the Smith and Wesson .22 being a great example.

Figure 64 The top gun is the .223 (Smith and Wesson M&P 15) and the bottom is the .22 caliber rifle. The .22 offers the exact same controls and feel as the live fire rifle except for weight.

Ammunition prices today are as high as they have ever been and the forecast is that ammunition prices will continue to rise. This will make training on a regular basis, two to three times a week for some of us, very difficult to afford. A .22 caliber conversion kit may be the solution that you have been looking for to increase your skill while saving money.

With replacement uppers your grip area, trigger pull, and everything you need manipulate your firearm, will feel the same because you will actually be using your own lower receiver. The main thing you will want to look for when purchasing a 22-caliber conversion kit is reliability. There are some kits on the market that don't run well. Most kits sold today will feed several types of ammunition very well, and other ammunition poorly. The last thing that you want is to buy a .22-caliber conversion kit and have to fight it every time you try to train with it. Just like any firearm, a gun that doesn't run will hamper performance and impede your training. I strongly suggest purchasing a high quality conversion kit from a reputable dealer.

Some other things to be aware of when purchasing and training with a conversion kit:

Lack of recoil. A .22 conversion kit, when fired, has virtually no recoil. This lack of recoil can be a pro and sometimes a con. For example, when firing full power ammunition, sometimes you will not see all of the movement of the gun before it goes off. When you switch to a .22-conversion kit, you will normally see more of these subtle details like gun movement during trigger manipulation. As discussed, above the lack of recoil when firing a .22-conversion kit is a pro, but it can also be a con. The problem you will find when training without recoil, is that it does not allow you the opportunity to truly go through the firing cycle as you normally would. When firing full power center fire ammunition you may manipulate the trigger a little differently than you would with the .22-conversion kit. The recoil of a full power handgun, for example, allows you to reset and manage the trigger during the guns rearward movement. With the .22-conversion kit, you will not experience this because there is no significant recoil. Due to these limitations, I suggest that each training session should involve some live fire training with your full power firearm. At a minimum, if you can't train every session with your full power firearm, try to shoot it at least every other training session. In cases where you shoot a .22 conversion kit and your full power gun, I suggest that you end your training sessions with the full power ammunition.

Firearm Manipulation. Manipulating the trigger and other devices should be exactly the same as when you are training with your standard firearm. The only problem you may have when training with the .22 conversion kit is when you perform your reloads, you will find that most conversion kits do not offer a magazine that is exactly the same size and weight as your live fire magazines. Since conversion kits are normally just the replacement of the slide on your handgun, or upper assembly on a rifle, you should be able to perform your draw processes or mount processes with a rifle exactly the same. If you were working on transferring the firearm to the support hand or firing the rifle bilaterally, then working with a .22 conversion kit will be duplicative of your standard firearm.

Low Power. A .22 conversion kit that fires standard .22-rimfire rounds will not have nearly as much power as even a very low velocity 9mm round. This means that if you're training on steel targets that fall over when shot, a .22 conversion kit may not make that target fall. If steel targets are freshly painted, allowing you to see the hits while you're shooting, this will not be a problem. I have used Stinger bullets, which are very high velocity .22 rounds to compensate for this problem, however, but with heavy steel targets they may still fail to fall.

Summary

In this chapter I have discussed the shooting skills training program. I have given you a set of live and dry fire drills, as well as alternate methods of training. You should have a clear understanding of how your brain learns, and how you improve your ability to process information and store information in both conscious and subconscious minds. You should once again, clearly understand that correct training design and perfect training execution is the key to your success. By this point, you should have a good understanding of the fact that your shooting skills training program must always evolve, it must never stagnate and must continue to improve your skills. While I have given you the drills in this book and a training program to follow, once you have used them don't be afraid to adjust as necessary to meet your goals. The only way you can do this is by changing your program as needed. Once again if you understood the steps of the training design cycle, you realize that you will modify your training program based on the results your program is giving you.

Summary and Action Steps:

1. Cost of training ammunition and access to shooting ranges is often the limiting factor in training. Consider using airsoft and .22 caliber conversion kits (or guns) to remedy this limitation.
2. There are some limitations when using alternate methods of training to be aware of:
    a. Lack of significant recoil.
    b. Slight differences in weight.
    c. Lack of power to shoot longer ranges or knock down steel targets.
3. Remedy this limitation by using a combination of the airsoft and .22 caliber guns with live fire training sessions with the full power firearm and ammunition.
4. Consider using airsoft and .22 caliber conversion kits to practice:
    a. Weapon manipulation.
    b. Building shooting positions.
    c. Target acquisition.
    d. Trigger control.
    e. Proper use of cover.
    f. Movement skills.

CHAPTER 9

Documenting Your Training Sessions

Documenting your training sessions and any real or simulated events that may have tested your skill is critical. This chapter will introduce you to multiple methods of documentation and discuss each of them, and teach you how to integrate the results of those different documenting methods.

The topics I will cover in this chapter:

1. *Purpose of Documentation*
2. *Types of Documentation*
3. *Analysis of Documentation*
4. *Program Analysis*
5. *Program Modification*
6. *Live Fire logs*
7. *Dry Fire logs*

Purpose of Documentation

Documentation of training sessions is probably the single most important thing you can do to increase the effectiveness of your training program. I have made the error of failing to do this in the past and have regretted not having the ability to look back at my notes and use them to increase the effectiveness of my training program. One thing that really stood out was that I really had no way of knowing if I was improving when I failed to document my training sessions and match results. I thought my training sessions were effective, but did I have the proof? I have since started logging all training sessions and matches just like I am outlining in this section and I have found it to be extremely valuable.

Types of Documentation

When documenting your training sessions you will have a couple options. The first is good 'ole fashioned pen and paper. This is the primary method I use to document. The second is video and/or audio documentation of training sessions. I strongly recommend both when you are documenting, because each has its benefits when reviewing data and improving your training processes. If you happen to be a trainer that trains large groups, I recommend that you issue training logs to all of your students and mandate that they use them. Make them document their training so they have a reference later on. In the Marine Corps, we had rifle logbooks issued in boot camp and we used them to log every range session we attended. The Marine Corps was on to something; they knew the importance of being able to reference previous data from training sessions.

Written Logs - Written training and event logs are the simplest and easiest way to document your training sessions. Your written logs should capture everything that is important during your training session. I used to log my data on pre-printed pages that I had in a three ring binder until I developed the logbook "Your Performance Logbook" so that I could capture an entire years worth of training and events in a bound format. (For more information visit my website.)

Some of the things that you will find in the log pages:
- **Date:** Nothing to explain with this one.
- **Weather Factors:** Capture everything you might want to refer back to, such as temperature, conditions, etc. Weather effects how you shoot!
- **Gun:** I practice with several different guns, and I always make sure to capture the gun/serial number (I have two of most guns, so if I don't write serial numbers down I will not know which one I shot). This section is important if you have a gun that is failing you in some way (so you know which one to get rid of).
- **Gear:** I train for several different purposes, and depending on what I am training for, I will use different gear. I capture that here.
- **Ammunition:** Always document what ammunition you were using in your session or event. This is important for future reference.
- **Emotional Control Zone:** This is more of a reminder section for me, but I actually have a block I check off that documents and reminds me of where I need to be in terms of control.
- **Active Visualization:** Another reminder block for me, but I check the box here too (if I did it). I should actively visualize for each drill every session.
- **How I felt:** I like to write down if I am feeling well or not (because it affects my performance).
- **Drill Factors:** In this section I capture the actual information I will analyze later. Write each drill down and then document your performance metrics (times, points, etc.) as well as any notes you may have on that particular drill. I ALWAYS note if I did something well here, and try to capture why I did it well.

- **Solution Analysis**: I write down overall solutions I found or need to find in future session here. This is a key area I will review before the next session (usually as I am loading my magazines).
- **Success Analysis**: I always take the time to write down something positive here. Even if I am shooting poorly, I find something that went well and emphasize it by writing it down.

Video - There is nothing comparable to video in terms of having true documentation of what you actually did during a drill or event. In your written documentation you can capture your metrics and how you felt during the performance of your drills, but you don't always get the whole picture. I can't tell you how many times I have seen myself on video and noticed something that I had no idea I was doing. I have also used video to show countless students small things that they are doing wrong, especially when they don't believe they are doing it. I use a tripod and a small, cheap camera to capture my training session drills. You may also set up a camera and then start and stop it with the remote (if you can find one with this feature). I set my camera up in a position so I can see as much as possible during the drill. I normally set my gear bag up near the camera so I can get my gun ready and prepare my magazines with ammunition, and then I start the camera and walk out to my shooting spot where I am going to do the drill. You will probably want to mark the spot you are shooting from (or set up a shooting box) so you know you will be centered in the video when you are doing your drill. I don't video my entire sessions, but I do video critical drills that I might be having trouble with.

Analysis of Documentation

Okay, so you are documenting your training with written and video logs. You're done with the hard part right? Not so fast. Now we have to use the information that we painstakingly recorded during our training sessions and events. When you review your logs it is important that you analyze them correctly, and in a very specific order. I will break this down by timeline.

- *Post-session review* - This review and analysis is done right after the session, or as soon as possible. If you can, review your video first, because what you see may need to be logged into your session or event notes. If you see yourself doing something wrong on the video, enter it in your "solution analysis" written log section. Now review all other notes, and take a moment to transfer key items to the next log you will use, as a reminder for your next training session. Your future session will already be planned, but your notes from this session will affect some of the things you will focus on. If you write down notes on your future log reminding you of some things you want to work or focus on, this will make your next session more effective. Each training log should affect your next session, even if just to validate what you are doing (because it is working).
- *Pre-session review* - This review will be done right before you begin your training session. Look at the last session notes, and also at what you carried over from your last ses-

sion. You might look at some of your key metrics (times and points) from drills you did, so you have some idea of where your metrics should be during this session.
- *Monthly review* - I like to take my training session notes out and review them to look for trends on a monthly basis. This will only take a moment, but is really a great way to see if you have some good or bad trends happening. You will also be able to compare your metrics and hopefully see them improving across a month's time. Seeing improvement is a big key to your success! Look for gear and gun issues that seem to be recurring, and any other things that stand out when you look at a month's worth of data. Make sure to take a couple notes on your monthly review and what you found so you can take action into future sessions. I don't normally recommend changing your program with just one month's data, but I do recommend slight changes or increased focus on areas that you notice as problematic.
- *Cycle or Yearly review* - I tend to train in 6-12 week cycles. This data review is where you will look for trends that will influence your decision to change your training program. Once again, examine all of your data and take notes on good or bad trends, along with your performance metrics. You should see some distinct improvement in them after you have been through a complete training cycle. If not, you will want to look hard at your drills and how you are training. No improvement can be a result of many different things, like poor drill design, lack of frequency (you're not training enough), lack of duration (you're not training long enough), etc. The notes from this review will be what you use to modify your program.

Program Measurement

How do we measure whether or not our training program is working? Actually it's quite simple; we simply look at the results of some type of objective measurement, or possibly a real world event to assess our performance. As stated in a previous chapter, "game day" is the event for which you are training, so hopefully most of you will not have the ability to assess your training program and modify it after multiple gunfights (I hope you avoid those!). For most of us, the objective test we submit ourselves to will probably be a something like a qualification test (a good one), some high intensity training/testing with N.L.T.A. (Non-lethal training ammunition), or maybe against our own standards of performance from logged training drills. If you are improving, your results will show it – if not, you will see that too.

The following section contains some reference to failure and how one could use them for positive change. It is written from the viewpoint of competitive shooting and how to use failure at a match to improve performance. While I hope you are not "failing" in gunfights, there are some learning points; therefore I left the text intact. Hopefully you can use it to reflect on training failures and bumps in the road during your preparation.

Failures Reflected Upon

Don't get caught in the trap of measuring your success or failures based on how you felt you did during an event. ALL issues that happen to you during your performances are a result of how you train. If you tank, and mentally crash in certain areas, then you trained yourself to do exactly that. If your physical skills are not where they should be, and you have mistakes or failures because of them, then your training program caused that. Don't get in the habit of just thinking you had a bad day because your preparation should be thorough enough to get you through any "bad day" without any huge problems.

We *prepare* ourselves to perform on a "bad day" by minimizing or eliminating them. You might be thinking that I am saying that if you have developed your training program correctly and executed it perfectly, you will be mistake free. Not so, I am simply saying that you will make errors on the scale that you allowed them to happen during your training. You can make errors and still succeed in your shooting goal, but they have to be minimal, and you have to be able to react and flow through them. Big errors should not happen often, if at all, if you trained correctly. Now, I am not saying that you will reach this well-trained state overnight. It may take ten years of hard training to get to the level where you are performing relatively mistake free. As much as I have not wanted to take responsibility in the past for my own mistakes on game day, when I reflected back and analyzed my training program, I always found the flaw. No problem. Because the training design cycle is a *cycle*. The concept is that you are in a never-ending loop of perfecting your performance by perfecting your training program and its efficiency.

Program Evaluation

All training programs should be evaluated and modified at some point. In this particular program, some of you might be advanced enough to modify certain things right away, but I strongly caution you against this until you have gone through my program it in its entirety. Here is a visual of the program learning and modification cycle:

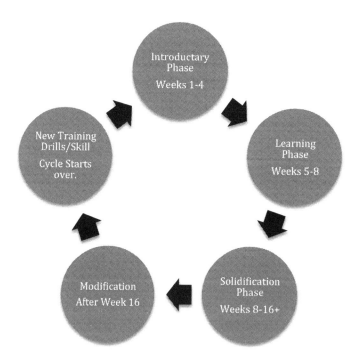

If you look at the cycle above, it demonstrates how a new skill is learned. Each phase is different and this cycle shows why it takes time to learn a skill well enough to consider modifying it. You can see that the introductory phase is up to four weeks long, and this means that when a new skill is introduced, it takes weeks to begin to process and learn it. After that, the programs are beginning to become written into your subconscious memory during the learning phase, and this is where you will see the most improvement. During the solidification phase, the skills are hardwired in and become habits (automatic responses). After that, it is time to consider adding new skills, or possibly modifying the program to push the current skills to new levels. The main point is that modification of a training program should occur after you have gone through this cycle, as it takes time to ingrain new skills. Modifying too early may just cause confusion and be counterproductive.

Objective Assessment

I am a firm believer that doing an objective assessment of your performance is the only way to consistently improve. We've established that measuring your performance will happen in one of three ways. Either you will look at your game day performances which may consist of a valid qualification skills test, some sort of scenario evaluation, or possibly a real world event (maybe an actual operation/gunfight). Unless you are on some high-risk stake out squad or special operations team, its unlikely that you will be able to measure this program's success in real gunfights (for most of you, I hope you aren't "gunfighting" very often, if at all!). This is one reason why I suggest some sort of scenario-based testing/training that can be used to increase your stress levels and test your skills. Professional trainers often use N.L.T.A. (non-lethal training ammunition) or airsoft at the end of an advanced course to allow the students to learn from what we call "stress inoculation." I suggest you find a place that does the same. Once we've gone through either of these types of tests, it's incredibly important that you look at the results objectively and have the ability to take those results and modify your training program. By objectively, I mean that you look at results and compare them to some sort of documented metrics or rely on video review to ensure that you are looking at what is actually happening, rather than how you "feel" you are doing. In order to have these metrics, you will have to be disciplined in how you set up your training drills and how you document the results.

Modification of the Program

Okay, you have completed the majority or all of a XX-week cycle and you have documented your training sessions. You have taken some game day "tests" along the way and documented them too. Now what? It's time to look at that critical data and begin the process of modification. One great thing about this step is that it will both increase your program's efficiency and give you a fresh new set of objectives and training drills. Even if you have just modified your initial drills they will still be different and possibly more challenging, which will stimulate a new learning curve. There are some logical steps in analyzing your results and modifying your program.

It doesn't matter if you met your goal or not – you will still want to go through these steps and modify your program where it needs to be modified. This will allow you to continually push to meet your goal or reach for the next level. There is always a next level.

- *Step one*. Review your training logs. Don't have any? You're stuck. Seriously, that is why you must log your training sessions. If not, you are on a deadend training road. Okay, so what are you looking for? Trends? Solutions to statements? What you did really well? Lack of improvements in your numbers from one session to the next? If you took good notes, it will all be right there for you to act on and use to modify your training program for the better. Write all of these trends and statements down on one sheet, if possible, so you can view it all at a glance.
- *Step two*. Take your notes and separate them into different areas. Each area will affect what you modify in your program. For example, if you find that you consistently documented that you did a certain skill really well, you might want to work less on that skill in future training sessions. You might take the drill that trains that skill and remove it or lessen the frequency that you do it. I would rather spend the time working on something I noted as something I needed to find a solution for, than waste my time working on something I am already good at. By the way, this is not human nature. We would

much rather work on things we like than things that are not fun for us. Make sure to categorize drills for which you lack improvement. This indicates that something is not working with the drill, or maybe it is possible that you are "maxed" out on that skill and have no room to grow (this is very rare). Either way, you may need to look at those specific drills and modify them.

- *Step three.* Modify your program based on what you noted above. The key areas that will likely need to be modified are: training drill specifics (not meeting their goal of improving your metrics) and training session layouts (frequency, duration, drills used). Modification will require some common sense and time, since you are reworking your training program. Modify drills to better suit your needs, and modify your training session layouts so that it does what you need it to as reflected in your notes. This may be more of one drill and less of another, and possibly even the design and addition of a completely new drill. If you have done your job in documenting, you will simply follow your notes.
- *Step four.* You must validate. Before you go to the trouble of printing out your new training plan in its final version, with your modified drills and sessions, go to the range and use them once. You will catch things that are not working out as well as you might have thought. Note your changes, make them, and then finalize the drills and begin another training cycle.

Modification of your training program should be ongoing and never ending. As your skills continually evolve and improve, so will your training program. Modify your drills so that they continue to challenge you and keep you on your performance edge. The better your training program is, the more you will increase your skill because you will become more efficient at training. This will lead to superior skills in the long run.

Training Log Pages

Please see the next pages for some shortened sample live fire, dry fire, and event (match) logs. These pages were designed for my competition book "Your Competition Handgun Training Program," but you will get the idea of how I design my pre-printed logs.

Live Fire Training Log - General Details

DID YOU REVIEW YOUR LAST TRAINING LOG FOR KEY INFORMATION BEFORE BEGINNING??

Session: _____ Date: _____

Weather: Sunny Cloudy Rain Snow Windy Temp:_____

Gun: _____ Problems: Y N Ammo: _____

Holster/Rig: IPSC - IDPA – Carry

Video Taken: Y N   Emotional Control Zone (overall): 1 - 2 - 3   Did Active Visualization? Yes - No

Today I felt: Great Good Mediocre Sick

Drill:											Totals
Times											
Points											
Key Notes											

Drill:											Totals
Times											
Points											
Key Notes											

Success Analysis: (What I did really well)

_____
_____
_____

Solution Analysis: (What I figured out or need to figure out)

_____
_____
_____

General Notes: (Any additional notes on the training session)

_____
_____

Dry Fire Log

Session (A, B, C, D, Other): _____ Date: _____

MTTS: Maximum Technical Training Speed (100% of your potential speed doing the technique correctly).

Before you begin:

- ➢ Focus Breath (key touch point and 6-2-6)
- ➢ Run your visualization video (passive, personal success video)
- ➢ Use Active visualization in between your drills, see yourself do it and then do it.
- ➢ Use your *performance statement* and read your *self image booster* (should be on a 3x5 index card in your shooting bag)

Preparing for:	
Gun/Gear (IDPA, USPSA, Etc.):	

Dry Fire Drill	*Beginning MTTS PAR Time*	*Ending MTTS PAR Time*

Today's goal statement: (Where I want to go)

_____
_____
_____

Notes: (Anything else)

_____
_____

Chapter Summary and Action steps:

1. Logging your training sessions and keeping track of your results is important and must be done in order to modify and improve in the future. Start now!
2. Consider using pre-formatted log pages or a logbook to capture the data you will need in the future. Preformatted sheets are important because they save time.
3. Consider videoing sessions and other events so you have some sort of after-action review you can do objectively. Often times you will find things you did not realize you were doing.
4. When considering modifying your training program, ensure you have trained the skill(s) for a period of time (remember the cycle) so that you do not modify too early (before the actual learning has begun.

CHAPTER 10

Testing Your Skills With The Rifle Skills Test (RST)

The key to reaching new levels is metrics. You must be able to track your improvements, which requires that you measure where your current skill is, then re-measure sometime in the future and compare the results. This chapter contains the skills test that will both challenge you and allow you to drive yourself to your very best.

The topics I will cover in this chapter:

1. *Introduction to the Rifle Skills Test*
2. *Rifle Skills Test Stages*

The rifle skills test (RST) is a unique test in that it is different from most scored qualifications. Additionally, the RST does not have a pass or fail score, or even a perfect score. Rather, it is a test that simulates the context of what you are training for as closely as possibly, while keeping the testing simple. It was developed by myself and my friend Brian Hill as a way to test skills, and it closely resembles the handgun skills test I use in my handgun program *Your Defensive Handgun Training Program*.

General Information:

Purpose: To test core handling and shooting skills.
Developed by: Mike Seeklander and Brian Hill (helped with an alternate version)
General Description: This skills test will have multiple stages of fire. Each stage will normally be repeated more than once. Most allow as many hits as possible. If using a timer, time will be set on PAR time (start and stop beep), but we strongly recommend using a turning target. IF PAR time is used on a timer, time each shooter individually and mark down extra shots (later, in the scoring section).

- There are limitless points available, and theoretically no maximum score. The better and faster you shoot, the higher your score!
- The point of this test is to measure your skill at any given time, and then have a consistent way of re-testing that skill in the future. Keep track of the score you shoot, and all other details. Also, if you skill any stages such as the one-handed shooting and manipulation stage (requires higher level of skill), then make sure when you take the test the next time you only count the score for the stages you shot previously so you have a comparison. For consistent measurement, skills will be tested from concealment, duty gear (police officer or full-time security professional), or open carry for those who are legally allowed to carry this way. Whichever way you shoot the test, keep it consistent so you can track and compare scores to the last test.
- A Pact or similar type timer will be required for this skills test, but turning targets are recommended if available. PAR times for each stage are listed. The PAR time listed is the EXPERT time for those that have a higher level of skill. If this PAR time is too fast for your current skill, add .5 seconds to each PAR, and go through the test with the NOVICE PAR times. Keep track of which PAR times you are using.
- Start positions are documented in each stage of fire.
- All reloads will be emergency or tactical reloads (dictated reloads). You may perform tactical reloads during the course to keep gun hot. If you fail to keep it hot, and lose points because of it, that will not incur an alibi. The rule is to know the status of your weapon at all times.
- If a malfunction is experienced and you attempt to clear it, an alibi will be given. If no attempt to clear the malfunction is made, no alibi will be given. You are allowed one alibi for a malfunction per course, as more than that demonstrates that you have a firearm that is not reliable enough to carry.
- Scanning and general after-action tactics should be used for each string of fire.
- Each skill should be shot at a speed that is best described as: "as fast as you can execute the skill under control."

Required Gear:
- Rifle
- Handgun
- Magazines (4)
- Rifle sling; Handgun holster; Magazine Pouches
- Eye and Ear Protection
- 150+ rounds of ammunition (for consistency, use the same ammunition each time you shoot this course; it is recommended that you use your defensive ammunition)
- IDPA targets or West Metro Swat Photo targets (2) per shooter

Target Setup:

- IDPA targets (or the alternate target: http://www.letargets.com/estylez_item.aspx?item=WM-SWAT) set with the shoulder of the target the same height of the shoulder of the shooter. Scoring zones are 0/1/5 (IDPA) on IDPA target.

Scoring:

- General:
    - Each shooter will have 2 targets unless otherwise specified in the individual course of fire
    - Target one (1) will be used for the first half of the course, and target two (2) for the second half (for ease of scoring).
- Hits:
    - At course completion, count total 0, and 1 hits on all targets. The 3 scoring zone does not count for any points. Multiply the total 0 and 1 hits by the factors below and figure out what the raw score is. Now subtract total penalties and the final score will be assessed.
        - 0 = 2 Points
        - 1 = 1 Points
        - 3 = 0 Points
- Penalties:
    - **Late shots .30 or more over time (example 2.0 seconds is time, you can have up to 2.30 on the timer):** -2 points per late shot
    - **Failure to follow stage instructions.** -2 points per infraction, or course failure. If you are running this course for a group, failure to follow instructions will result in disqualification if the course proctor determines the failure was intentional (to increase score).
    - **Misses off the primary threat target (a clean backer will be used).** -5 points per miss.
- **Tactical Errors:** -2 points each (more than 5, earns an automatic failure)

Instructions: You are about to be tested on all of your rifle skills. You will prepare magazines and load in the beginning of the course, and after that you will be responsible for the condition of your firearm at all times. Certain stages require a specific set up before the stage, so ensure you pay attention to those instructions. This course consists of 10 stages of fire. During each stage of fire you should use your tactics such as post-event scanning. Employ all of the skills learned during your rifle training. Most stages allow you to fire as many rounds as you can, which will increase your score. Ensure you fire only at a pace where you control the impact of your shots, and are safe. After you have finished your scanning process on each stage, take the time you need to top off, or re-prep your magazines.

At this time go ahead and prepare all of your magazines but one to full capacity. Leave one empty. It is your responsibility to keep magazines fully prepped between stages. Now mount two targets with the shoulder of the target equal to your shoulder and centered on a white backer. Paper IDPA targets with a white background are also acceptable for this test. Move to the 7-yard line and ensure you have all of your gear accessible. Load your handgun.

1. <u>Skill:</u> mount/bilateral mount (from low ready below 45 degrees)
   - **Target:** IDPA set 5 feet high at the shoulder
   - **Time:** 1.0 second
   - **Distance:** 10 yards
   - **Start Position:** Looking over rifle, rifle depressed at least at 15-degree angle, safety on.
   - **Skill Details:** Mount and fire as many shots as possible in <u>**1.00 second**</u>.
   - This drill will be done twice from each shoulder, for a total of four repetitions.

2. <u>Skill:</u> 90-degree Turn and Mount/**Rifle**
   - **Target:** IDPA set 5 feet high at the shoulder
   - **Time:** 2.0 seconds
   - **Distance:** 10 yards
   - **Start Position:** Rifle at low ready, safety on.
   - **Skill Details:** Face left and right. Turn, mount and fire as many shots as possible in <u>**2.0 seconds**</u>. (1 right / 1 left.)

3. <u>Skill:</u> 180-degree Turn and Mount/**Rifle**
   - **Target:** IDPA set 5 feet high at the shoulder
   - **Time:** 2.0 seconds
   - **Distance:** 10 yards
   - **Start Position:** Rifle at low ready, safety on.
   - **Skill Details:** **Face up range,** Mount and fire as many shots as possible in <u>**2.0 seconds.**</u> (1 right / 1 left.)

Score and re-face / paste

4. **Skill:** Transition to Handgun
    - **Target:** IDPA set 5 feet high at the shoulder
    - **Time:** 4.0 seconds
    - **Distance:** 10 yards
    - **Start Position:** Rifle at low ready, safety on.
    - **Skill Details:** Mount and fire on <u>rifle target</u> until rifle goes to bolt lock (5 rounds) and then transition to handgun and fire as many rounds as possible in <u>**4.0 seconds**</u>
    - **Notes:** Load rifle with 5 rounds total. Handgun should be loaded to capacity

5. **Skill:** Firing rifle with only one hand
    - **Target:** IDPA set 5 feet high at the shoulder
    - **Time:** 2.0 seconds
    - **Distance:** 5 yards
    - **Start Position:** Rifle aimed in on target.
    - **Skill Details:** Fire as many rounds as possible in <u>**2.0 seconds.**</u>

6. **Skill:** Extreme Close Range
    - **Target:** IDPA set 5 feet high at the shoulder
    - **Time:** 1.0 second
    - **Distance:** 2 yards
    - **Start Position:** Rifle at low ready, with the muzzle touching the target, safety on.
        - Note: The shooter should start so close that they cannot raise the rifle into a shooting position.
        - Note 2: If your muzzle brake/comp rips the target apart at this range, perform this drill on a separate target so scoring the previous hits is still possible.
    - **Skill Details:** Tuck the rifle under the shoulder, mount and fire as many rounds as possible in <u>**1 second.**</u>

Notes: New or pasted target required. Load rifle with 5 rounds total.

7. **Skill:** Intermediate Range / **Unbraced**
   - **Target:** IDPA set 5 feet high at the shoulder
   - **Time:** 8.0 seconds
   - **Prop:** Set up a barricade or similar to be used as cover for this stage.
   - **Distance:** 25 yards
   - **Start Position:** Rifle at low ready, safety on.
   - **Skill Details:** Mount and fire 5 rounds to upper chest until rifle goes to bolt lock (5 rounds), reload, then fire as many rounds as possible, all in **8 seconds**. Cover must be used during the reload.
   - **Notes:** Load rifle with 5 rounds total.

8. **Skill:** Intermediate Range / **Braced**
   - **Target:** IDPA set 5 feet high at the shoulder
   - **Time:** 8.0 seconds
   - **Prop:** Set up a barricade or similar to be used as cover for this stage. Barricade must be suitable for use while bracing.
   - **Distance:** 50 yards
   - **Start Position:** Rifle at low ready, safety on.
   - **Skill Details:** Mount and fire 5 rounds to upper chest until rifle goes to bolt lock (5 rounds), reload, then fire as many rounds as possible, all in **8 seconds**. Cover must be used during the reload.
   - **Notes:** Load rifle with 5 rounds total. Depending on your skill level, you might not finish the reload and have the ability to fire more shots in the time allotted.

Final Verbal Instructions: This concludes your course of fire. At this time, unload and show clear, or reload for duty carry. If you reload, remember, you're carrying a loaded firearm.

CHAPTER 11

Manually Operated Rifles

This section addresses the manually operated rifle spectrum that might be used for self-defense. The lever action rifle was an incredibly effective fighting tool in the past, and can be used just as effectively today if that is what you possess or are limited to. This chapter contains the keys to training with and shooting your manually operated rifle to a high level of skill.

The topics I will cover in this chapter:

1. Manually-Operated Rifles
2. Pistol Caliber Carbines
3. Lever-Action Rifles
4. Pump-Action Rifles
5. M1 Garand

"Arm yourself with the best tool you can find, but once armed – preparation is the key."

Author Unknown

FOR THOSE WHO HAVE LIMITED OPTIONS

Thus far our discussions have centered on those people who have very few restrictions or limitations in the options available for selecting a home defense rifle. Unfortunately, there are states in our wonderful union who have decided to outright ban or severely restrict the types of firearms available to their citizens for lawful personal use. If you have the unfortunate distinction of residing in one of these states, the information in this book may turn out to have very limited benefit as ownership of the AR-15 rifle may be prohibited for you. For those of you who cannot own an AR-15 rifle, let's explore some other options for a home defense rifle.

The first and most important step when considering options other than AR-15 rifles is to research your local laws and determine exactly what, if any, types of semi-automatic rifles you can possess. It's beyond the scope of this book to examine every individual State and make recommendations based on each state's laws. That burden will fall to you, but do not be discouraged. Many state's laws are a patchwork of laws similar to the original 1994 Assault Weapons Ban that prohibited certain types of features such as flash suppressors, pistol grips, collapsible stocks, high capacity magazines, and the list goes on. The law also grandfathered firearms manufactured prior to September 13, 1994 as exempt from those regulations. Many state's adopted the concepts found in this Federal law and created similar state laws. The patchwork of ridiculous laws rarely makes any logical sense and many loopholes exist that allow the citizen to be in compliance with the letter of the law and still effectively own a semi-automatic rifle. The best advice is to check with your local gun store to learn exactly what you are permitted to own and what regulations apply to such ownership. In the event that you reside in a state that has completely banned possession of the AR-15 rifle, let's look at some out "out of the box" ideas that can still effectively serve as an adequate home defense rifle.

Pistol Caliber Carbines

While many laws on the books are written specifically with rifles and rifle calibers in mind, consider researching the laws of your state to identify if Pistol Caliber Carbines (PCC) are legal. Several manufactures offer AR15 style rifles chambered for pistol calibers with 9mm being the most popular. PCC's offer every performance and manipulation advantage of the rifle, but in a smaller caliber pistol chambering. Terminal performance of the PCC's are certainly lacking when compared to rifle calibers, but do not overlook their effectiveness. The increased velocity from the longer rifle length barrels give pistol calibers, magnum or +P terminal performance boosts without the increased case pressure and recoil associated with higher velocity performance ammunition. Most PPC's have a magazine capacity of 25 rounds or higher and will often use older and widely available, classic submachine gun magazines such as Uzi, Sten, and H&K MP-5 magazines. Many newer designs are built around pistol magazines such as Glock and Beretta magazines. Sig Sauer has recently introduced the new SIG MPX carbine chambered for 9mm, 40 S&W, and .357 Sig, with all of the ergonomics you would expect from a modern design. SIG's offering is sure to be a dominant success in the often-overlooked PCC market. A well-configured PCC is an excellent choice for a home defense carbine if you live in a state with restrictive laws, don't overlook this option simply because it's not chambered for a traditional rifle cartridge.

Lever-Action Rifle

Yes, we said it, a lever-action rifle – America's first assault rifle. Yes, the rifle that is in every John Wayne western can be a very effective home defense carbine. First of all, they are usually widely available and not subject to even the most restrictive rifle bans. They are chambered for both rifle and pistol calibers ranging from the extremely powerful 45-70 down to the mild 38 special. They have magazine capacities that range from 5-6 rifle rounds to 15 rounds or more in their pistol caliber models. They have the capacity to accept scopes and red dot sights in addition to excellent factory rifle sights. They are relatively lightweight, easy to use, and they can be pretty quick to reload with a moderate amount of practice. If you doubt these rifles are serious home defense options, take a few minutes and do a YouTube search for Cowboy Action Shooting. You will see what a properly configured lever-action rifle coupled with a practiced hand can accomplish. Consider a lever-action rifle chambered in 44 Magnum with 12 rounds in the magazine, equipped with a mini-red dot sight and a mounted weapon light. There are very few scenarios where such a setup would be insufficient for home defense. Although the technology may date back to the days of the old west, their effectiveness in a home defense role can still be as modern as ever.

Pump-Action Rifle

Along with the lever-action rifle, the pump-action rifle is another similar option. The pump-action rifle is usually not subject to any types of bans or restrictions and is widely available, even in the more restrictive states. The pump-action rifle works on the exact same principal as the pump-action shotgun. After a shot is fired, the forward handle is pumped aggressively to the rear until it reaches the limit of its travel and then it is aggressively pumped back forward until the action closes and locks. This motion will eject the spent cartridge and reload a fresh cartridge for use. The action is very fast and easy to operate. For many years Remington has dominated the pump-action rifle market with their model 760 and 7600. Chambered for various popular rifle calibers, the rifles offer four or five round magazine capacities depending upon the caliber chosen. Recently, Remington offered a patrol rifle model 7600, chambered in .223 that uses traditional AR15 style 30 round magazines, although 20 and 10 round AR magazines would also work. Configured with a red dot sight and a rifle mounted light, the pump-action rifle would offer a very effective home defense rifle to those with limited options.

M1 Garand

"The greatest battle implement ever devised." This often quoted remark from General George S. Patton regarding the value of the M1 Garand rifle to the WWII war effort, pretty much sums it up. Chambered for the powerful 30-06 rifle caliber, the M1 Garand is a man's rifle. Millions were made and the rifle operated around the World in every crappy environment that Mother Nature could create. It's a battle proven, semi-automatic design that was the basis for M-14/M1A series of rifles chambered in 308. If you're concerned about its recoil, don't be. It's without a doubt the softest shooting 30-06 rifle you will ever shoot. The M1 uses an en-bloc 8-round clip that is loaded through an opening in the top of the upper receiver. The user pushes the clip down into the receiver until it latches and then bumps the bolt handle forward, initiating the loading process. When all 8 rounds have been fired, the bolt locks to the rear and simultaneously ejects the empty clip with a distinctive pinging sound. A quick reload is just another clip away. While the rifle is large and long when compared to modern carbines, it balances well and with practice can be easily maneuvered and manipulated. Relegated to mostly competitive shooting circles, the M1 Garand is a hidden diamond in the rough to those looking for a home defense rifle. The M1 does not feed from a detachable magazine, is uses an en-bloc clip that is contained internally within the receiver. It also does not possess a pistol grip or a flash suppressor. The absence of these features means that this very powerful and capable semi-automatic rifle will most likely have slipped completely past any restrictive laws. While it is true that the rifle is not as adaptable as more modern designs when it comes to the additions of scopes and lights, there are some aftermarket companies offering accessories to fit the M1 Garand. A little Internet research should show you what options are available. The M1 Garand also ranks pretty high on the intimidation scale. Remember Clint Eastwood in the movie *Gran Torino?* "Get off my Lawn!" If you are not familiar with the scene, YouTube it – it's worth the look. Although its 80 years old, the M1 Garand is still an extremely effective home defense option for those living in restrictive states. Plenty of German, Japanese, and North Korean soldiers ended up on the wrong end of the M1 and quickly paid the ultimate price. This old soldier has plenty of fight left and should be on anyone's short list options.

Mechanical Operation Of Manually Operated Rifles

One thing to remember is that "manually" operating your rifle is a key detail you will want to pay attention to in your training drills. What this means is that no matter what you are armed with, the way you manipulate your rifle might make the difference between life and death. As discussed previously in this document, it is very important that you build proper skills while doing your training drills. The sequence you should follow with any manually operated rifle is as follows: shoot, operate the action, shoot, operate the action, etc. until the threat has ceased to be a threat. Note that the last step in the process is always to operate the action again so there is a loaded round in the chamber and you have the ability to shoot again if necessary. The next operation you should consider is loading the gun. I recommend some sort of side-saddle ammunition carrier or pouch that has ten or so additional rounds in it, that allows you to top the rifle off. We work this concept a bunch when operating a shotgun since most shotguns do not hold many rounds. The sequence might go like this:

1. Shoot and operate the action until the threat is down.
2. Perform a post-engagement scan process to verify you are safe.
3. Load the gun. If you needed to re-engage, follow the same process.

Shoot – Operate action – Shoot – Operate action…threat is down…scan and load.

Chapter Summary and Action steps:

1. Manually operated rifles are solid choices for defensive rifles if your options are limited.
2. A second choice would be a pistol caliber carbine.
3. The operation of any manual rifle requires the user to continually operate the action to ensure the gun stays loaded. Additionally, reloading the gun is a skill you must develop in your training.
4. When performing training drills, make sure you incorporate the above-mentioned processes in your actions to ingrain good habits.

Your Defensive Rifle Training Program Summary: You have finished the book, and hopefully are ready to begin to implement all of the steps I have outlined in it. Each of the components covered in the chapters is important, and should be addressed if you truly wish to train yourself to the highest levels. Anything less than that is an opening for possible failure, and I challenge you to train yourself not just to perform on demand, but to refuse to fail! This program is work, and will take time out of your day if you expect results. My challenge to you is to find ways to overcome the hurdles that life throws at you, and as Nike would say: "Just do it!" Strongly consider using the DVD's or downloadable Vimeo videos filmed specifically to show the drills and technique in this book to enhance your skill development. They can be found on the Shooting-Performance website (www.shooting-performance.com) and on my Vimeo page (Vimeo.com/ondemand/defensiverifle).

I am more than interested to hear about your progress, and extend an open invitation to email me if you ever use this material to defend yourself, or if you have questions or need guidance along the way. Instructors learn from students and their experiences almost as much as students learn from their instructors! I teach a variety of programs throughout the U.S. and would welcome you as a student in them. Those class listings can be found on my website, as well as a variety of other information that you might find useful.

You may be the person who stands between violence and criminal intent and the innocent. I applaud you for decision to train your rifle skills to a high level, and I hope to have helped you reach a skill level that will make you successful. You might be one of the members of the U.S. Military that is defending my freedom, a patrol officer that is tasked with saving my family members life, or simply a force multiplier that might save my life one a bad day. Remember:

I am counting on you….

An innocent person is counting on you….

YOU are counting on you…

Until Then, Train Hard!
Mike Seeklander

More about Shooting-Performance, (www.shooting-performance.com):

Founded in 2007, Shooting-Performance is a coaching, consulting, and research company that specializes in performance related firearm instruction and information for use in both combative and competitive environments. Mike Seeklander, owner/founder has extensive experience in and has been a full time instructor since December of 2001. For more information or to **get a Shooting-Performance class near you**, please visit www.shooting-performance.com.

Thanks for your interest in Shooting-Performance, and I know you will surpass your goals with the use of this program, the proper gear, and a lot of hard work. I know you can do it, now get to work!

Until Then, Train Hard!

Mike Seeklander

To order a copy of this book or other books and DVD's, please visit my website (www.shooting-performance.com)

Take the class! Host a class near you and train for free.

Course Name: *Your Defensive Rifle Training Program Level 1*
Course Length: Two Days
Course Cost: $395.00 (with class minimum of 10) **Note: all range fees for guest range are the responsibility of the student, not S-P.
Open to: Anyone. This class assumes a minimum skill level with the firearm is possessed. Brand new shooters should take a familiarization course prior to attending.

Course Description: This training program is a complete tactical rifle training program designed to teach you how to train for combative purposes with a rifle as your primary weapon. The program will take your rifle shooting to the next level. It is a medium range course designed for those who will employ a rifle a close to medium ranges (10-100 yards). The program is like nothing else available today, focusing in not only the execution of skills but in the process to properly train those skills and subsequently improve your results. It is the pre-requisite course for those wishing to take other Shooting-Performance advanced rifle courses.

Class Learning Objectives:

- Principles of Adult Learning
- Heart Rate Management /Combat Breathing
- Mental Preparation for the Fight
- Physical Preparation for the Fight
- Legal Preparation for the Fight
- Principles of an Effective Training Program
- Carry Gear and Firearm Setup
- Principles of Dry Fire Training (manipulation training)
- Principles of the Firing Cycle (high performance marksmanship)
- Live Fire Skill Developing Drills (firing cycle)
- Concepts of a Proper Live Fire Training Session

Required Gear/Support Items (** please read and bring all items):

- 1200 rounds rifle ammunition
- 300 rounds of handgun ammunition
- Rifle and all related equipment (including a sling) * Please bring 2-3 magazines minimum
- Handgun and all related equipment
- Notebook and pen
- Personal protective gear (eye and ear protection)
- Weapon Mounted light (for recommendations call or email) and handheld light
- Dummy rounds appropriate for your caliber/s (rifle and handgun) (10)
- Water, snacks, chair, sunscreen, or any other personal comfort items desired.

Your Notes:

ABOUT THE AUTHOR

Currently Mike Seeklander is owner of Shooting-Performance LLC (www.shooting-performance.com), a full service training company. Mike is also the co-host of The Best Defense, the Outdoor Channels leading self-defense and firearm instruction show.

From 1995-98, I was employed by the Knox County (TN) Sheriff's Department's Corrections division and was a member of its highly trained Special Operations Response Team. From 1998-2001, I worked as a police officer for the Knoxville (TN) Police Department where I was assigned as a patrol officer and also as an investigator for the Organized Crime section, investigating narcotics and vice-related crimes at the local, state and federal levels.

After that, as an employee of the federal government, Mike served as the Branch Chief and Lead Instructor for the Firearms division with the Federal Air Marshal Service as well as a Senior Instructor at the Federal Law Enforcement Training Center (F.L.E.T.C.), the premier federal training facility in the U.S. Mike has extensive formal training and experience in all phases of military and law enforcement training and is a highly sought after defensive and competitive trainer.

Following his federal career, Mike was Chief Operating Officer, Director of Training, and a Senior Instructor at the U.S. Shooting Academy in Tulsa, OK. He was directly responsible for the development of more than fifty firearm-training programs.

Currently a nationally ranked competitor on the practical handgun competition circuit, Seeklander has authored/produced instructional books, DVD's and has developed hundreds of lesson plans specifically related to both basic and advanced firearms training.

Mike is the recipient of numerous awards and honors in the law enforcement community, and as a semi-professional shooter. Mike is the 2013 and 2014 I.D.P.A. B.U.G. (Back up Gun) national champion, winner of the 2011 Steel Challenge World Speed Shooting Championships (production division title), and numerous state and area championships. The United States Practical Shooting Association currently ranks Mike as a Grandmaster. Having competed in the shooting sports nationally, Mike adds to this experience with more than 20 years of experience in various martial arts holding multiple ranks including a Black Belt in Okinawan Freestyle Karate.

Mike is a combat veteran of Desert Shield and Desert Storm, with five years of active duty and four years of reserve duty in the U.S. Marine Corps, as an intelligence specialist and primary marksmanship instructor, and combat engineer. Prior to receiving my honorable discharge in 2000, he was attached to a Federal multi-agency task force investigating large-scale international drug trafficking in Los Angeles, CA.

Made in the USA
Middletown, DE
11 May 2017